Spa Management: An Introduction

Mary S. Wisnom, Ph.D.
Florida Gulf Coast University

Lisa L. Capozio, M.A.

Boston Columbus Indianapolis New York San Francisco Upper Saddle River
Amsterdam Cape Town Dubai London Madrid Milan Munich Paris Montreal Toronto
Delhi Mexico City Sao Paulo Sydney Hong Kong Seoul Singapore Taipei Tokyo

Dedication

To family and friends who enrich my life every day and to my inspiration, my beautiful boy, Stuart—MSW

To Joe, my heart, my home, and my friend—LC

Editorial Director: Vernon Anthony
Senior Acquisitions Editor: William Lawrensen
Editorial Assistant: Lara Dimmick
Director of Marketing: David Gesell
Campaign Marketing Manager: Leigh Ann Sims
Senior Curriculum Marketing Manager: Thomas Hayward
Senior Marketing Coordinator: Alicia Wozniak
Marketing Assistant: Les Roberts
Associate Managing Editor: Alexandrina Benedicto Wolf

Production Editor: Kris Roach
Project Manager: Susan Hannahs
Senior Art Director: Jayne Conte
Cover Designer: Suzanne Behnke
Full-Service Project Management: Nitin Agarwal
Composition: Aptara®, Inc.
Text Printer/Bindery: Edwards Brothers
Cover Printer: Lehigh-Phoenix Color
Text Font: Perpetua

Credits and acknowledgments borrowed from other sources and reproduced, with permission, in this textbook appear on the appropriate page within the text.

Library of Congress Cataloging-in-Publication Data
Wisnom, Mary S.
  Spa management : an introduction / Mary S. Wisnom, Lisa L. Capozio.
    p. cm.
  ISBN-13: 978-0-13-503944-1
  ISBN-10: 0-13-503944-4
 1. Health resorts—Management. I. Capozio, Lisa L. II. Title.
RA794.W57 2012
613'.122068—dc22   2011001755

10 9 8 7 6 5 4 3 2 1

www.pearsonhighered.com

ISBN 10:   0-13-503944-4
ISBN 13: 978-0-13-503944-1

BRIEF CONTENTS

CONTENTS

CHAPTER 3 Spa Offerings   **19**

CHAPTER 4 Spa Facility Design and Construction   **45**

CHAPTER 10   Spa Financial Management   161

CHAPTER 11   Spa Marketing and Promotion   173

As the demand for spa and wellness professionals is exceeding the number of qualified candidates, we are faced with the challenge of providing information to enable new managers to succeed in meeting industry needs. Spa and wellness has, in the past, been represented as an amenity, fad, or niche market, but a major study conducted by SRO International (SRO), released at the 2010 Global Spa Summit (GSA) in Istanbul, Turkey, reveals that the yearly worldwide wellness industry is poised to cross the $2 trillion mark. In a report titled "Spas and the Global Wellness Market," we find one of the first analyses of the wellness industry and the consumer forces driving its growth. The study finds that there are currently 289 million active wellness consumers worldwide. The spa industry is perfectly aligned as a key provider of wellness services. Consumers associate spas with wellness, and increasingly, spa offerings are expanding far beyond the pampering treatments of the past. Today's services are integrating fitness, complementary and alternative medical practices, preventive practices, advanced beauty and anti-aging treatments along with lifestyle counseling, weight loss, and nutrition. In addition, spa offerings are quickly becoming a driving force in medical and wellness tourism. This rapid growth and definition of the qualifications necessary to evolve in our mission of providing effective wellness care and education in the prevention of illness requires a manual. This manual should contain the basics of our business, the best practices that have been distilled by our practice, and a vision for the potential we have to shift the paradigm. We hope we have made a substantial contribution to this effort.

TEXT ORGANIZATION

The fourteen chapters of *Spa Management: An Introduction* present foundational information to learn and grow as a spa manager. Chapter 1, which constitutes Part I, "Spa Industry Basics," sets the stage with industry information, provides the reader an overview of the spa industry, and describes the different types of spas. Part II, "Establishing the Business," includes three chapters devoted to helping the manager make key decisions when starting a spa business or moving a spa operation forward, including business basics, spa offerings, and spa design.

Part III, "Operations and Management," which includes Chapters 5 through 8, were developed as a unit. In the belief that the success of a spa operation is in the details, Chapter 5 provides an overview of how to develop the "details" of a spa operation and where these details are found in the business, the standard operating procedures (SOPs). Chapters 6, 7, and 8 represent the three key areas that, when combined, make up a spa operation: employees, clients, and the facility. Materials on managing both human and structural resources are included. In addition, SOP policy and procedure samples are provided at the end of each of the final three chapters in Part III.

Part IV, "Business Skills and Knowledge," includes information related to the business proficiencies needed to run a spa, including, law, financial management, marketing, and evaluation. The final part of the text, Part V, "Spa Professionals and the Future of the Industry," contains two chapters. Chapter 13, "The Spa

Management Professional" reveals ideas to increase your success as a spa manager. Chapter 14, "Trends and the Future of the Spa Industry," discusses current industry trends and what spa leaders predict as the future direction of the industry.

An Appendix and online resources provide supplemental materials for the text. The Appendix includes resources for the spa manager, with listings of written and online resources, spa company information, and a comprehensive list of professional associations that support spa industry workers.

Beyond the printed text, the reader also has access to an extensive amount of online resources developed specifically for *Spa Management: An Introduction*. Visit www.pearsonhighered.com/wisnom and search a wide variety of additional materials, some containing interactive elements to use for any spa operation. Whether you are a spa professional, a student, or a teacher, these invaluable resources are available at the click of a mouse. The following is a list of a few of the online resources:

▶ Sample Employee Handbook and Standard Operating Procedures Manual
▶ Sample Business Plan
▶ Interactive spreadsheets for Spa Operational Budgets and Financial Statements
▶ Interactive spreadsheets to assist in the calculation of performance data and ratios

Exclusively for faculty:

▶ PowerPoint slide presentations for each chapter
▶ Suggestions for in-class exercises, including case studies and group assignments
▶ Direct links to online resources

TEXT FEATURES

Spa Management: An Introduction is designed for student learning and teacher effectiveness. Each chapter contains a variety of elements to facilitate and inspire learning. Following is an overview of chapter organization, student learning tools, and faculty resources, each provided to enhance the overall learning experience.

▶ *Learning Objectives.* To identify learning outcomes for the chapter, each begins with a selection of learning objectives. Each objective highlights the primary elements of the chapter and prepares readers for the content that follows.
▶ *Photos, Tables, and Figures.* Photos, tables, and figures expand or enhance chapter contents.
▶ *Reality Checks.* These features, included in several chapters, share real-world stories of spa management. These vignettes allow reader to see some of the subtle nuances of spa management.
▶ *History Facts.* In selected chapters, mainly Chapters 1, 3, and 14, History Fact inserts share some of the rich and influential spa stories of the industry's past.
▶ *Key Terms.* Throughout each chapter, key terms are introduced and defined. Each key term is printed in boldface in the chapter text and listed at the end of the chapter. Readers should master these concepts to understand fully the chapter content.
▶ *Review Questions.* Subjective review questions at the end of each chapter allow students to describe what they have learned in the chapter. The key

goal of review questions is for students to discuss information, voice opinions, and share experiences.

▶ *References.* At the end of each chapter is a list of references recognizing the vast number of individuals who have contributed to the body of knowledge on the subject of spa management.

ACKNOWLEDGMENTS

We wish to acknowledge and express great appreciation for the efforts of many who helped bring *Spa Management: An Introduction* to life. Thank you for your abundant contributions:

▶ To our family and friends, who, throughout the development of the book, listened when we needed to talk, were a calming presence when we needed to scream, were always there for a laugh, and were the first to cheer our successes.
▶ To Ginna Beckett, our editor extraordinaire. Your countless hours of work were amazing and your support of this project truly remarkable.
▶ To our colleagues in the spa industry, who were quick to lend a hand.
▶ To those who reviewed the book and provided invaluable feedback at various stages of development. They are: Dr. Carl Boger, University of Houston; Dr. Donna D. Brown, Virginia College, Biloxi; Jeannie Faulkner, Hocking College; Shawn A. Hallum, Hallum Consulting; Dr. Soo K. Kang, Colorado State University; Dr. Ken W. Meyers, University of Minnesota, Crookston; and Larry R. Woodruff, Arizona State University.
▶ To the HRCP Stillwater Spa team, for years of practical education, trust, and support.
▶ To Dr. Sherie Brezina and Karen Royal, for your unwavering encouragement and support.
▶ To the Resort and Hospitality Management students at Florida Gulf Coast University, who are great teachers and motivators.
▶ To Bill Lawrensen, Lara Dimmick, Kris Roach, Lynne Lackenbach, Nitin Agarwal, Susan Hannahs, and the entire Pearson team, for keeping us on task and helping with the development of this important project.
▶ To Stephanie Kelly for your insight, assistance, and for inspiring our writing during the early stages.
▶ To James Beckett, for the creation of the flower logo used throughout the text.
▶ To Stuart Wisnom, for being patient during the countless times your mom was researching, writing, and editing, on weekends, evenings, and holidays when she should have been playing with you!

Mary Wisnom, Ph.D.

Dr. Mary Wisnom is an Associate Professor and coordinator of the Spa Management program in the Division of Resort and Hospitality Management at Florida Gulf Coast University (FGCU). Mary boasts thirty years of experience in the hospitality industry as a practitioner and educator. After completing a B.A. degree at Wittenberg University in Business and Psychology and a M.S. at Michigan State University (MSU) in Parks, Recreation and Tourism Resources (PRTR), she returned to the industry, working in a variety of resorts and private clubs, including destination resorts, yacht, athletic, golf, and country clubs in Michigan, Colorado, and Florida. Following her desire to direct recreation amenities, Mary circumvented traditional hospitality roles and focused her leadership efforts in the areas of fitness, wellness, aquatics, recreation, adult events, and children's activities. In the early 1990s, Mary left her position as Recreation Director of The Ritz-Carlton, Naples, to return to MSU and pursue her Ph.D. and passion for teaching. In 1996, she began teaching full time as a member of the Recreation, Parks and Leisure Services Administration faculty at Central Michigan University, and in 2006 she moved to Naples, Florida, and joined the FGCU faculty.

Lisa Capozio, MA, CNC, LMT

A nutritionist, licensed massage therapist, esthetician, and holistic lifestyle educator, Lisa has twenty years in the health, wellness, and spa industry. Lisa is the Director of Education for Sundari, LLC, an Ayurvedic Wellness and Skincare company. She completed her formal education at Emory University, University of Miami, and The University of Central Florida, and completed additional continuing education resulting in certifications in Herbology, Chronic Pain Management, Reflexology, Shiatsu, Trager I and II, Manual Lymphatic Drainage, Traditional Thai Massage, Ashiatsu, Qi Gong, Pediatric and Adolescent Nutrition and is a newly certified Yoga Alliance instructor. Truly dedicated to "health maintenance" as a preventative measure in our "disease care" culture, Lisa has incorporated her teaching, coaching, and strong nutritional background to provide her clients and patients a clear picture of health, balance, and well-being. Lisa is a member of the FGCU Spa Advisory Board, the American Massage Therapy Association, the Yoga Alliance, and the International Spa Association.

Introduction to the Spa Industry

LEARNING OBJECTIVES

At the end of this chapter, readers will be able to:

- Explain the origin of *spa* as a concept.
- Understand and appreciate the impact of the spa industry on the global economy.
- Describe and define modern spas.
- List the different types of spas.
- Identify the elements and apply them in differentiating types of spas.

Learning is the beginning of wealth. Learning is the beginning of health. Learning is the beginning of spirituality. Searching and learning is where the miracle process all begins.

—Jim Rohn

Consider the word *spa*. What images come to mind? Some may visualize water, others peaceful surroundings. Some may experience a feeling of well-being; others picture an intense workout. Throughout history, the word *spa* has invoked a variety of images with one common link: wellness.

ORIGINS OF THE WORD *SPA*

In today's society, the word *spa* has many meanings. A spa can be a mineral spring, a resort, a hot tub with air jets, or a business providing health, fitness, weight loss, beauty, and pampering services. Although *spa* has several interpretations, each is richly steeped in history, and all have water as their foundation. Since the beginning of time, water has been used for purification, cleansing, and healing; bodies of water have attracted visitors for reasons of health, recreation, relaxation, and to socialize.

HISTORY FACT

Archeologists have uncovered ancient artifacts and structures evidencing the use of water for a variety of purposes in early cultures. Archeologists indicate that hot springs in what is now Bath, Virginia, were inhabited in the Late Mesolithic period as early as 7000 B.C. (Pogue and Cullinane, 2008).

There are many theories as to the origin of the word *spa*. Some claim that the word derives from several Latin axioms, including *sanus per aqua*, meaning "health through water." According to Johnson and Redman (2008), many Latin renditions can be used to obtain the word *spa*. Each has "health, hygiene, or healing" in its interpretation and includes the Latin word for water, *aqua*.

The word *spa* may also originate from the Latin words *spargere*, *sparsi*, or *sparsa*, meaning to scatter or sprinkle, or the Walloon word *espa*, meaning fountain (Walloon is spoken today in many areas of Belgium.) In 1326, a small town in eastern Belgium acquired the name Spa. This town housed many mineral springs, known locally as *pouhons* (*Encyclopaedia Britannica*, 2008). In 1551, William Slingsby discovered mineral springs in England, compared them to those found in Spa, Belgium, and called the area the "English Spa." From then on, places frequented for health and healing have utilized the word (de Vierville, 2003; Leavy and Bergel, 2003).

SPAS TODAY

Spa began as a word to describe relaxing water experiences, healing towns with mineral springs, or the natural springs themselves. The word is now most often used to name businesses concerned with health and beauty. Over the years, there have been many attempts to define these places of health, relaxation, and revitalization. In North America today, the most common definition of a **spa** was developed in 2004 by the International Spa Association (ISPA, 2010a):

Spas are places devoted to enhancing overall well-being through a variety of professional services that encourage the renewal of mind, body, and spirit.

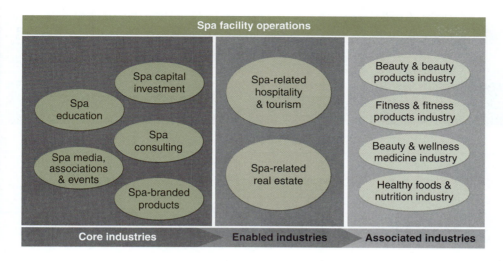

Figure 1.1   The Spa Industry Cluster
Source: The Global Spa Economy 2007, part of the Global Spa Summit summary or research for survey respondents. Distributed electronically by Global Spa Summit, May 2008.

With more and more people embracing a healthy lifestyle, spas have become an integral part of modern living. Once places visited by a select few, they are now enjoyed by many. Once places with limited offerings, they are now overflowing with wellness and relaxation options.

The spa industry is booming. It is estimated that over $250 billion a year is generated by the global spa economy; approximately $60 billion in core spa industries and another $194 billion in "spa-enabled" industries (Global Spa Summit, 2008). Figure 1.1 shows the breakdown of income generating categories in the spa industry.

The U.S. spa industry generated just over $12 billion in gross revenue in 2009 (ISPA, 2010b). There were more than 20,000 spas in the United States in 2009. There were approximately 143 million spa visits in North America. The growth of the spa industry over the last fifteen years has been staggering. As the industry has grown and matured, spas have begun to differentiate themselves, developing into new types of spas.

TYPES OF SPAS

Spas today strive to deliver services to enhance perceived feelings of health and wellness. All spas seek to embody the primary concepts expressed in the ISPA definition. All are places, mainly for-profit businesses, that promote well-being and provide services to enhance the mind, body, and spirit. However, as new spas have opened, a variety of distinguishing features have become apparent. Some spas provide accommodations, whereas others are available only for day use. The majority of spas are available to the general public; however, some are available only to members or guests lodging at the establishment. Revenue is generated in a variety of ways, depending on the type of spa. Spas commonly bring in revenue through user fees, but some earn income by other means, such as room fees, membership dues, or medical insurance reimbursement. Table 1.1 shows the different types of spas and what differentiates them from each other. Spas generally fall into one of the following nine categories. (*Note:* Definitions are adapted from the following sources: ISPA, 2007; Johnson and Redman, 2008; McCarthy and James, 2006.)

Day Spa

A **day spa** is a business that offers a variety of professionally administered spa services to day-use clients. Day spas are open to the public and offer a la carte spa services to customers who can enjoy one or two individual treatments or a full day of treatments.

TABLE 1.1

Differentiating Types of Spas

Spa Type	Primary Target Audience	Primary Funding Source(s)	Defining Element	Accommodations	Sample Spa
Day	Public	User fees	Convenience	Day use only	Red Door Salon
Medical	Public	User fees Medical reimbursement	Medical services	Day use only	Medspa on the Hudson
Day club	Members	Membership dues User fees	Exclusivity	Day use only	The Aspen Club and Spa
Mobile	Public	User fees	Spa services at home	Day use only	MobileSPA
Mineral spring	Public	User fees	Mineral waters	Lodging or day use	Solage Calistoga
Resort/hotel	Resort guests	User fees	Convenient vacation amenity	Lodging	Spa at Mandarin Oriental Resort, New York
Destination	Destination spa guests	User fees Room fees	Wellness retreat	Lodging	Miraval Spa
Cruise ship	Cruise ship guests	User fees	Convenient vacation amenity	Lodging	The Greenhouse Spa and Salon on Holland America Line
Residential club	Home/condominium owners	Membership dues User fees	Spa lifestyle	Homes or condominiums	Canyon Ranch Living, Miami Beach

Compared to other types of spas, day spas typically offer less costly spa experiences, and many focus on beauty treatments. They range from select service to multiservice offerings. The majority (79 percent; ISPA, 2010c) of spas are day spas, making them readily available to the spa customer. Day spas are convenient for regular spa goers, repeat customers, or for those seeking a service that requires multiple visits.

HISTORY FACT

In the 1970s, beauty salons looking to expand their services started offering spa treatments. In 1972, the first salon that offered more than the traditional salon services changed its name to a day spa. It was Noel De Caprio who first used the term in naming her Stamford, Connecticut, business, Noelle the Day Spa (Johnson and Redman, 2008).

Medical Spa

A **medical spa** is a business that offers a variety of professionally administered spa services, including medical and wellness care, to day-use clients, typically with on-site supervision by a licensed health-care professional. Medical spas are the fastest-growing segment of the spa industry. These spas offer a blend of conventional and alternative medicine therapies in a clinical setting. "Medi-spas" require a full-time, on-site, licensed health-care provider for all medical services and are generally located in a medical practice. Unlike day spas, medical spa services can include skin injections (Botox and fillers), cosmetic dental services, and laser-based skin care, some of which may allow for insurance reimbursement. Medical spas may offer fee-based a la carte beauty and wellness services. Similar to day spas, medical spas are convenient for regular spa goers or for those seeking a treatment that requires recurring visits.

Day Club Spa

A **day club spa** is a business that offers a variety of professionally administered spa and fitness services to its membership. Day club spas emerged from fitness clubs looking to provide more comprehensive wellness offerings to their customers. To receive services in a club spa, you are generally required to be a member. Membership dues are likely collected when individuals join the club and may be assessed on a monthly or annual basis. There are typically additional charges for personal spa offerings. Day club spas are day-use facilities that offer exclusivity to interested customers.

Mobile Spa

A **mobile spa** is a business that offers select professionally administered spa services that are brought to the client. These "spas on wheels" are gaining in popularity. For the ultimate in convenience, spa professionals bring the spa to the client. Mobile spas provide on-site spa services at special events, parties, or in the comfort of the client's home or hotel room.

Mineral Spring Spa

A **mineral spring spa** is a business that offers an on-site source of natural mineral, thermal, or seawater used in professionally administered hydrotherapy treatments. There is much variation among mineral spring spas. Some may offer only hydrotherapy treatments, whereas others may offer a wide range of spa services, lodgings, fitness, and other opportunities. The size of the spa may determine many of the business attributes, but it is the "spring" that makes it unique.

Hydrotherapy Pool

HISTORY FACT

The first lodgings for visitors to America's springs and "healing waters" were developed in Hot Springs, Virginia. In the 1700s, many famous people frequented mineral springs, and word spread of individuals being healed while "taking the waters." A frequent visitor to these early spas was George Washington, who later worked to establish the town of Bath, Virginia, as the country's first spa (Bullard, 2004; Mozier, 2008).

Resort/Hotel Spa

A **resort/hotel spa** is a business that operates as a division of and within a resort or hotel. It provides professionally administered spa, wellness, and, occasionally, medical services primarily to guests of the establishment.

Resort and hotel spas serve mainly their vacationing guests. Because they are part of a larger facility, these "stay spas" typically offer a variety of fitness, recreation, and healthy cuisine options. At the resort, the spa is considered an amenity available to guests. To even out the seasonal nature of many resort businesses, some spas may be open to the public or allow a limited number of local members to join the spa. Some resorts and hotels, rather than including a spa as part of their own offerings, elect to partner with a day spa near the facility to allow guests the benefits of a spa without having to manage the operation. These arrangements, however, are not technically considered to be resort/hotel spas.

Resort/hotel spas are the second largest segment of the spa industry, representing 9 percent of the total number of spas in the United States (ISPA, 2010c).

Cruise Ship Spa

A **cruise ship spa** is a spa that operates on board a cruise ship and provides professionally administered spa and wellness services to passengers. These unique spas serve exclusively those on a cruise vacation. As with a resort, cruise ship spas are one of many amenities available to passengers. In comparison to resort spas, cruise ships are small in number. However, because of the nature of a cruise ship vacation, the majority of cruise ships have spas.

Destination Spa

A **destination spa** is an extended-stay resort with the primary purpose of providing guests with healthy lifestyle services. Destination spas have health, wellness, and "spa-ing" as the focal point of the visit. Modern destination spas encourage stays of a week or longer but usually do allow shorter stays. Healthy lifestyle changes are accomplished by providing a comprehensive, personally guided program for guests that includes a blending of fitness activities, professionally administered spa treatments, wellness education, healthy cuisine, and medical testing and services.

HISTORY FACTS

Elisabeth Arden's pioneering spirit drove her to open the first American vacation spa, Maine Chance, in Maine in 1926. Maine Chance cost visitors from $250 to $500 per week, for which they received spa services of exercise, sports, yoga, facials, massage, beauty training, a healthy diet, and pampering (Williams, 2007).

Edmond and Deborah Szekely founded the first holistic destination spa in North America in 1940 in Baja California, Mexico. A visit to Rancho La Puerta, the 3000-acre "health and wellness center," cost $17.50 per week (Rancho La Puerta, 2008).

Residential Club Spa

A **residential club spa** is a residential lifestyle community with the primary purpose of providing owners with a healthy living environment. Similar to golf club communities, these spa communities allow residents to enjoy the spa lifestyle all year long.

Residential club spas are relatively new to the spa industry; the first opened in 2003. Residential club spas offer home and condominium owners fitness activities, professionally administered spa treatments, wellness education, and healthy cuisine right in their "own backyard."

Other wellness businesses have also integrated spa services into their practices. Recognizing the therapeutic effects of spa services, some hospitals, rehabilitation and wellness centers, and dentists' offices integrate spa treatments into their patient services. (See Figure 1.2 for a breakdown of the major types of U.S. spas.)

Although all spas focus on the well-being of their clients, many spa services also facilitate beauty and body maintenance. Day spas often integrate hair and nail services. Resort spas may offer body scrubs and makeup application. Medical spas may integrate hair removal, cosmetic dentistry, and permanent cosmetic procedures.

Most spas are for-profit businesses; occasionally, however, a club or residential spa may be a nonprofit (social) club. Most spas are independently owned and operated; however, it is common for some types of spas to be corporate-owned or franchised. Elizabeth Arden opened the first day spa in the United States in 1910, and today her Red Door Spa franchise operates thirty day spas in the United States and one in London.

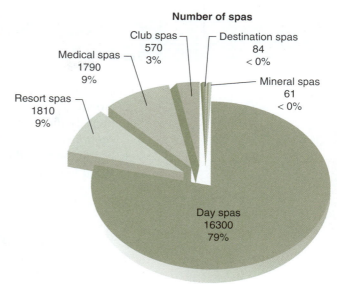

Figure 1.2 Types and Numbers of Spas in the United States *Source:* 2010 U.S. Spa Industry Study, International Spa Association.

REALITY CHECK

Are government-owned and -operated spas a new trend or a rare exception? In 2007, two public-sector "luxury" day spas in deprived and ethnically mixed areas of the United Kingdom opened their doors (Spa Business, 2007).

No matter what your spa interest, the industry has a growing need for knowledgeable managers. Today's spas are a vibrant combination of ancient traditions, modern innovations, and services focused on the customer's well-being. To be a successful spa manager, one must understand the foundations of the industry, general business operations, spa offerings and the human resources necessary to implement them, spa clientele, and the global and national issues affecting the industry. This book will provide the reader with the foundation of knowledge necessary to embark on a career in spa management.

KEY TERMS

Day club spa

Day spa

Cruise ship spa

Destination spa

Medical spa

Mineral spring spa

Mobile spa

Residential club spa

Resort/hotel spa

Spa

REVIEW QUESTIONS

1. What is the definition of a spa? What are the three key elements of the definition?
2. How much economic impact does the spa industry have on the global economy?
3. Identify the core, enabled, and associated industries that make up the global spa economy.
4. Name the nine different types of spas.
5. What key elements help differentiate the types of spas?

REFERENCES

Bullard, Loring (2004). *Healing Waters: Missouri's Historic Mineral Springs and Spas*. Columbia, MO: University of Missouri Press.

de Vierville, Jonathan Paul (2003). Taking the Waters: A Historical Look at Water Therapy and Spa Culture over the Ages. *Massage & Bodywork,* February/March.

Encyclopaedia Britannica (2008). Spa. Retrieved July 31, 2008, from Encyclopedia Britannica Online, www.britannica.com/EBchecked/topic/557285/spa.

Global Spa Summit (2008). The Global Spa Economy 2007. Unpublished report, part of the Global Spa Summit summary or research for survey respondents. Distributed electronically by Global Spa Summit.International Spa Association (2010a). History of ISPA. Retrieved November 29, 2010, from www.experienceispa.com/about-ispa/history-of-ispa.

International Spa Association (2010b). 2010 U.S. Spa Industry Update: The Big Five. Presented at ISPA Annual Conference, Washington, DC, November.

International Spa Association (2010c). ISPA 2010 U.S. Spa Industry Study. Retrieved November 29, 2010, from www.experienceispa.com/includes/media/docs/ISPA2010USSpaIndustryStudy.pdf.

Johnson, Elizabeth M., and Redman, Bridgette M. (2008). *Introduction to Spa*. Lansing, MI: American Hotel and Lodging Educational Institute and International Spa Association.

Leavy, Hannelore R., and Bergel, Reinhard R. (2003). *The Spa Encyclopedia: A Guide to Treatments and Their Benefits for Health and Healing*. Clifton Park, NY: Thomson Learning.

McCarthy, Jeremy, and James, Jennifer (2006). *FabJob Guide to Become a Spa Owner*. Calgary, Alberta, Canada: FabJob, Inc.

Mozier, Jeanne (2008). The Early Days of Bath. Retrieved July 28, 2008, from www.berkeleysprings.com/bath.htm.

Pogue, Melissa, and Cullinane, Kathleen (2008). The Homestead: A History of Hospitality in the Virginia Countryside. Retrieved July 28, 2008, from www.thehomestead.com.

Rancho La Puerta (2008). The Early Days. Retrieved July 28, 2008, from www.rancholapuerta.com/home/history-vision/early-days.html.

Rohn, Jim (1996). *7 Strategies for Wealth & Happiness: Power Ideas from America's Foremost Business Philosopher*, 2nd ed. New York: Three Rivers Press/Crown Publishing.

Spa Business (2007). Access for All. *Spa Business,* 3:64–68.

Williams, Anne (2007). *Spa Bodywork: A Guide for Massage Therapists*. Philadelphia: Lippincott Williams & Wilkins.

Spa Business Basics

➜ LEARNING OBJECTIVES

At the end of this chapter, readers will be able to:

- Understand the difference between vision and mission.
- Develop a concise vision, mission statement, and strategic plan.
- Understand the fundamentals of SWOT analysis.
- Comprehend the elements of a successful business plan.

Successful and unsuccessful people do not vary greatly in their abilities. They vary in their desires to reach their potential.

—John Maxwell

Organizations need to establish a strategic structure for significant success. This structure should consist of:

- ▶ A vision for the future
- ▶ A mission that defines the operation
- ▶ Values that shape your actions
- ▶ Strategies that define key success approaches
- ▶ Goals and action plans to guide tasks

The business of a spa is the same as that of any for-profit business: to provide a service or product and generate a profit. Whether you are opening a new spa or taking on a spa management position for a large corporation, the expectations are the same: to deliver an extraordinary product to every client and to create prosperity for all involved. At the most basic, this process begins with a *vision* (the dream), a *mission* (the purpose), and a *strategic plan* (the steps to realize the dream). As these elements take shape, a spa manager can better approach the financial elements of the spa, the current economic climate, and the development of strong leadership skills.

CREATING A MISSION STATEMENT AND A VISION STATEMENT

For any business to succeed, it must know its purpose. It must be keenly aware of why it is there, and what it is there to achieve. Developing a vision and mission statement is a way of projecting these ideas to customers, staff, and to the world.

- ■ A **mission statement** describes the fundamental purpose of the organization. It defines the customer and the critical processes. It identifies the desired level of performance.
- ■ A **vision statement** outlines what the organization wants to be. It concentrates on the future. It is a source of encouragement. It provides inspiration for operational decisions.

The mission statement and the vision statement do two distinctly different jobs (Yeoresources.org, 2010). A **mission statement** defines the organization's purpose and primary objectives. Its primary function is internal to the business, to define the key measure or measures of the organization's success. Its prime audience is the leadership team, employees, and stakeholders. A **vision statement** also defines the organization's purpose, but this time in terms of the organization's values rather than bottom-line measures. **Values** are guiding beliefs about how things should be done. The vision statement communicates both the purpose and the values of the organization. For employees, it gives direction about how they are expected to behave and inspires them to give their best. Shared with customers, it shapes the customers' understanding of why they should support the organization.

REALITY CHECK

Customer retention is highest when the spa team is consistent and committed to upholding the core values of the spa.

Vision Statements Inspire

There is value in knowing your destination. If you know where you are going, you can focus on the paths that will lead you there. Vision statements help identify that path. Vision statements can take many forms, but their main purpose is to articulate the ultimate destination of your spa business. In crafting a vision statement, answer the following questions (Tough, 2010):

▶ Why did I start this business?
▶ What do I hope to be my business legacy?
▶ What am I really providing for my customers beyond products and services?
▶ If my business could be everything I dreamed, what would it be?

Here are two examples of powerful vision statements from familiar businesses:

▶ **Google:** To organize the world's information and make it universally accessible and useful.
▶ **Amazon.com:** Our vision is to be earth's most customer centric company; to build a place where people can come to find and discover anything they might want to buy online.

Creating a Vision Statement

To create a vision statement:

1. First, identify what you, your customers, and other stakeholders value most. Refine these into values for your organization.
2. Combine your values with goals and aspirations for the future, and polish the words until you have a vision statement inspiring enough to energize and motivate people both inside and outside your organization.

SAMPLE VISION STATEMENT FOR A DESTINATION SPA

A holistic retreat offering opportunities to learn healthier behaviors for personal enrichment, professional growth, and lifestyle change.

Once you have created a vision statement for your business, it becomes the foundation for all other decisions. Your vision statement should inspire and challenge the operation, the industry, and you as a manager.

A Clear Mission

For any business to succeed, its leaders need to know and be able to describe what the business does. A mission statement is this description. It states why your organization is in business and what you hope to achieve. A well-crafted mission statement identifies the purpose, the business, and the value.

Creating a Mission Statement

To create a mission statement (Mindtools, 2006):

1. First, identify the elements of the spa that will make it stand out from your competitors or the reason that customers will return to you and not your competitors.

2. Identify the key measures of success, choosing the most important measures.
3. Combine the "stand-out" elements and success measures into a tangible and measurable goal.
4. Refine the words until you have a concise and precise statement of your mission, which expresses your ideas, measures, and desired result.
5. And remember, the mission statement needs to include the purpose, business, and values.

SAMPLE MISSION STATEMENT

Sylvan Spa is a place where minds, bodies, and spirits are nourished, where your well-being is our first priority and our reputation for the highest-quality professional spa services assures you the best treatment experience.

Purpose: Health, well-being, nourishment

Business: Professional spa services

Values: Quality, professionalism

THE PLANNING PROCESS

How will the vision and mission be realized? The details of implementation are incorporated in a document called a strategic plan. **Strategic planning** is the process of defining the direction of the business and making decisions about allocating both the people and the money necessary to pursue this strategy. Before you can make a strategic plan, you must thoroughly understand the business. A number of business analysis techniques can be used in strategic planning. One technique that is used often in the spa industry is called **SWOT analysis**. SWOT means the **S**trengths, **W**eaknesses, **O**pportunities, and **T**hreats of the business. SWOT analysis can be used to understand the spa's situation by specifying its internal resources and capabilities in terms of *strengths* and *weaknesses* and its external conditions in terms of *opportunities* and *threats*.

What makes SWOT particularly powerful is that, with a little thought, it can help uncover opportunities that the spa is well placed to exploit. By understanding the weaknesses of the business, the threats can be managed and sometimes eliminated before they become actual issues. SWOT analysis can help uncover the elements that are shaping, or will shape, your business and provide direction for the future of your spa. In using SWOT analysis, the following questions will be helpful (Yeoresources.org, 2010):

Strengths

▶ What advantages does your company have?
▶ What do you do better than anyone else?
▶ What unique or lowest-cost resources do you have access to?
▶ What do people in your market see as your strengths?
▶ What factors help you "make the sale"?

Consider strengths in relation to your competitors. For example, if all your competitors provide high-quality treatments, then a high-quality treatment process is not a strength in the market—it is a necessity.

Weaknesses

▶ What could you improve?
▶ What should you avoid?
▶ What are people in your market likely to see as weaknesses?
▶ What factors cause you to lose sales?

Consider your weaknesses from an internal viewpoint and an external viewpoint. Do others perceive weaknesses that you do not see? Are your competitors doing better than you are? It is best to be realistic and face any unpleasant truths now, because it is impossible to change what is not acknowledged.

Opportunities

▶ What are the opportunities available to you?
▶ What are the interesting trends you are aware of that may be advantageous to the business?

Useful opportunities can come from such things as:

▶ Changes in technology and markets on both a broad and narrow scale
▶ Changes in government policy related to your field
▶ Changes in social patterns, population profiles, lifestyle changes
▶ Local events

Threats

▶ What obstacles do you face?
▶ What is your competition doing that you should be worried about?
▶ Are the required specifications for your job, products, or services changing?
▶ Is changing technology threatening your position?
▶ Do you have bad debt or cash flow problems?
▶ Could any of your weaknesses seriously threaten your business?

Completing a SWOT analysis will provide a solid foundation on which to build your strategic plan.

A small spa business might create the following SWOT matrix:

Strengths
■ Because of its size and relatively small number of managers, the business is flexible and can adjust quickly to changing needs of the business.
■ We are known for personalized, excellent customer care.
■ Our lead esthetician has a strong reputation in the spa market.
■ As a small business, there is little overhead, so can offer good value to customers.

(continued)

Weaknesses

- Our company has little to no market presence.
- We have only a small staff with a shallow skills base in the area of massage and body work.
- We are vulnerable to vital staff being sick or leaving.
- Our cash flow has been unreliable over the last year.

Opportunities

- Our customer base is expanding, providing many future opportunities for success.
- Our local government wants or has begun efforts to market local businesses.
- Our competitors seem slow to adopt new technologies.

Threats

- Developments in technology could change the market beyond our ability to adapt.
- A small change in focus by our primary competitor might wipe out any market position we have achieved.
- A shifting economy may create a financially unstable situation.

The spa may therefore decide to specialize in rapid response and good-value services to local customers. The business should keep up to date with changes in technology where possible and be conservative when making decisions to change the operation.

Strategic planning is the formal consideration of an organization's future course. In many organizations, this is viewed as a process for determining the business's future from one to five years out. Some even extend their plan to twenty years in the future. To determine where it is going, the organization needs to know exactly where it stands, then determine where it wants to go and how it will get there. The resulting document is its strategic plan. Strategic planning can incorporate many tools to plot the direction of a company; however, strategic planning itself cannot foretell exactly how the market will evolve and what issues will arise in the future. Therefore, revisiting and revising the strategic plan must be a cornerstone strategy for an organization to survive in a turbulent business climate. Key elements of a strategic plan are the goals, objectives, and actions plans for the operation.

→ GOALS, OBJECTIVES, AND ACTION PLANS

The mission statement can stimulate individuals to achieve a spa operation's goals and objectives. **Goals** are overarching statements that define a future achievement. Goals need to reflect the direction set by the vision and mission of the organization, and they typically don't exceed a time dimension of one to two years. As an example, the spa may have a goal to improve customer service scores. **Objectives** are statements developed to reflect precise activities needed to help the spa reach its goals. To be effective, they should be **S**pecific, **M**easurable, **A**chievable, **R**elevant, and **T**ime-bound (**SMART**) (Doran, 1981):

▶ **Specific.** Objectives must be specific. In other words, they should describe specifically the result that is desired. Instead of "better customer service score," the objective should be "improve the customer service score by 12 points using the customer service survey."

▶ **Measurable.** Objectives must also be measurable. To be able to use the objectives as part of a review process, it should be very clear whether the person met the objective or not.

▶ **Achievable.** The next important consideration in setting objectives is that they be achievable. For instance, an objective that states "100 percent customer satisfaction" is not realistically achievable. It is not possible to expect that everyone must be 100 percent satisfied with the service. A goal of "12 percent improvement in customer satisfaction" is better—but may still not be achievable if it is assigned to, say, the database developers. They are not likely to have enough influence over the customer interaction process to improve satisfaction by 12 percent.

▶ **Realistic.** Realistic objectives recognize factors that cannot be controlled. Said another way, realistic goals are potentially challenging but not so challenging that the chance of success is small. They can be accomplished with the tools that the person has at their disposal.

▶ **Time-based.** The final element of a well-written objective is that it is time-based. In other words, it is not enough to say, "Improve customer service by 12 percent"; the objective should say, "Improve customer service by 12 percent within the next 12 months." Time is the final anchor in making the objective real and tangible. The implied date is the date of the next review, when employees will be held accountable for the commitments they have made in their objectives.

An **action plan** lists strategies that, when implemented, are intended to achieve the established objectives and goals. The action plan is where "the rubber meets the road." It should be tactical, allocating the human, financial, and material resources necessary to carry out the organization's strategies for achieving its goals, mission, and vision. It should identify the individuals (or job roles) who should undertake specific tasks within specified time frames. These individuals will be held accountable by the organization for producing results on time. Results are evaluated against predetermined benchmarks. If they are successful, the collective actions of those involved in designing and implementing an organization's strategic plan will help that organization achieve success.

SAMPLE ACTION PLANS

- To increase business: Medical spa advertising on a local radio channel for four weeks for $3000. Effectiveness measured by patient load, tracked weekly by the medical spa's executive assistant.
- To increase number of members: Health club marketing director writing six feature articles annually for trade journals. Effectiveness measured by linked new membership and membership renewals over the next 12 months.
- To increase number of treatment hours scheduled: Destination spa reception team will offer each customer the option of extending the treatment currently scheduled, adding a complimentary back exfoliation or foot treatment. Effectiveness measured by total treatment hours booked each month. Tracked by spa manager over a 12-month period.

A focus on strategic planning has become more important to business managers of late, a result of fluctuating economic conditions, constantly changing technology options, and increasing competition. These circumstances have made the business environment less stable and less predictable. To survive and prosper, a spa manager must take the time to identify the areas where there is the greatest likelihood of success, and to identify and pursue the resource demands that must be met. The foundation and process of identifying the chances of success are formulated in a quality business plan.

THE BUSINESS PLAN

A **business plan** accurately defines the business, identifies goals, and serves as the spa's résumé. It guides the allocation of resources, helps with unforeseen complications, and assists in making the right decisions. The plan provides specific and organized information about the company and how borrowed money will be repaid. It can also tell a sales/marketing team, vendors, and others about the operations and goals of the business. A business plan is essential for a new spa manager entering an existing organization as well as starting a new operation. It is important to have a clear understanding of past operations and goals for the business. The strategy at this point is assessment, possible changes, and a plan for future growth.

All successful businesses maintain an up-to-date business plan. A business plan is a work in progress. It is great to have the opportunity to create the plan, but there are times when the task will be implementing or continuing a plan that already has been established. Being able to assess the goals and create an outline for the evolution of the growth of the company is the challenge at hand.

To create a good business plan, you must be willing to roll up your sleeves and dig through information. Not all the information you can gather will be relevant to the development of the business plan, so it will help to know what you are looking for before you start. According to the U.S. Small Business Administration (SBA, 2010), every successful business plan should cover each of the following topics:

- ▶ Executive Summary
- ▶ Market Analysis
- ▶ Company Description
- ▶ Organization and Management
- ▶ Marketing and Sales Management
- ▶ Services and Product Lines
- ▶ Funding Request
- ▶ Financials
- ▶ Supporting Documents

The body of a business plan can be divided into four sections:

- ▶ Description of the Business
- ▶ Market Analysis
- ▶ Organization
- ▶ Management and Financial Data.

Most business plans start with an executive summary and include supporting documents and financial projections. Although there is no single formula for developing a business plan, some elements are common. Those elements are summarized in the following outline. The financial elements will be discussed in detail in Chapter 10.

ELEMENTS OF A BUSINESS PLAN

Cover Sheet, Statement of Purpose, Table of Contents
I. Executive Summary
    A. Description of the Business (including Vision, Mission, and Goals)
    B. Market Analysis
    C. Organization and Management
II. Financial Data
    A. Loan Applications
    B. Capital Equipment and Supply List
    C. Balance Sheet
    D. Break-Even Analysis
    E. Income Projections (Profit and Loss Statements)
    F. Three-Year Summary
    G. Detail by Month, First Year
    H. Detail by Quarters, Second and Third Years
    I. Assumptions on Which Projections Are Based
    J. Cash Flow Statement
III. Supporting Documents
    A. Tax Returns of Principals for Last Three Years
    B. For Franchised Businesses, Copy of Franchise Contract and All Supporting
        Documents Provided by the Franchisor
    C. Copy of Proposed Lease or Purchase Agreement for Building Space
    D. Copies of Licenses and Other Legal Documents
    E. Copies of Résumés of All Principals
    F. Copies of Letters of Intent from Suppliers, etc.
    G. Business Insurance

Compiling the information necessary to complete a business plan requires a number of decisions. These decisions are not limited to selecting a location, deciding on a business structure, and obtaining the necessary licenses, permits, and insurance. In addition, determining which financing options will meet the short-term needs and long-term goals of the business is crucial.

START-UP COSTS

Every business is different and has its own specific cash needs, so there is no one method for estimating start-up costs. Some businesses can be started on a minimal budget, whereas others may require considerable investment in real estate, construction, inventory, and/or equipment. It is vital to determine if enough start-up money is available to launch the business venture.

To determine start-up costs, all the expenses the business will incur during this phase must be assessed. Some of these expenses will be one-time costs, such as the fee for incorporating and the price of a store-front sign. Some expenses will be ongoing, such as the cost of utilities, inventory, and insurance. While identifying these costs, decide whether they are essential or optional. A realistic start-up budget should include only those elements that are necessary to start the business. Then these essential expenses can be divided into two separate categories: **fixed expenses** (overhead) and **variable expenses** (related to business sales). Fixed expenses include amounts such as the monthly rent/mortgage payment as well as administrative and insurance costs. Variable expenses include inventory, commissions, utilities and other costs associated with the delivery of a retail product or service. Variable costs will be discussed in detail in Chapter 7.

FORMS OF OWNERSHIP

One of the first decisions that must be made when starting a spa business is how the company will be structured. This decision will have long-term implications, so consultation with an accountant and an attorney are highly advised to help select the appropriate form of ownership. In making a choice, consider the following: your vision regarding the size and nature of the business, the level of control for each position, the business's vulnerability to lawsuits, tax implications of the different ownership structures, expected profit (or loss) of the business, and whether earnings will be reinvested into the business. Details on the various forms of ownership can be found in Chapter 9.

With the critical decisions of ownership structure and start-up costs made, the creation of the remainder of the business plan details is much easier. Developing the business plan helps ensure that everything that can be done has been done before opening. It expresses why you are proposing this business, how it will operate, and the expected results. The next phase of the project is to implement the plan. (See the online resources for a full sample business plan.)

KEY TERMS

Action plan	SMART
Business plan	Strategic planning
Fixed expenses	SWOT analysis
Goals	Values
Mission statement	Variable expenses
Objectives	Vision statement

REVIEW QUESTIONS

1. What is the difference between a vision statement and a mission statement?
2. How is SWOT beneficial as an analytical tool?
3. Create a SWOT matrix for your career objectives.
4. What is the purpose of a business plan?

REFERENCES

Doran, George T. (1981). There's a S.M.A.R.T. Way to Write Management's Goals and Objectives. *Management Review*, 70(11).

Maxwell, John (n.d.) Retrieved June 22, 2010, from johnmaxwell.com.

Mindtools (2006). Unleashing the Power of Purpose. Retrieved November 20, 2006, from www.mindtools.com/pages/article/newLDR_90.htm.

SBA (2010). Making Decisions. U.S. Small Business Administration, www.sba.gov/smallbusinessplanner/manage/makedecisions/SERV_GOODDEC.html.

Tough, Megan (2010). Creating a Mission and Vision Statement. Retrieved December 10, 2007, from www.sideroad.com/business_communication/mission-and-vision-statement.htm.

Yeoresources.org (2010). SWOT Analysis. Retrieved June 7, 2009, from http://yeo-resources.org.

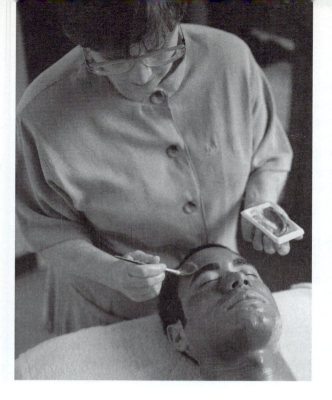

Spa Offerings

⟶ LEARNING OBJECTIVES

At the end of this chapter, readers will be able to:

- Identify the forms of medical practice and those to which spa offerings correspond.
- Classify spa services and treatments by technique, origin, provider, and facility.
- Explain the influences of various cultures on modern-day spa treatments and services.
- Understand the fundamental elements of a variety of spa offerings.
- Develop a sample spa menu based on distinct elements of a spa.

There are many paths to wellness.
—Anonymous

Modern-day spas pledge to "renew your mind, body, and spirit." Whether stand-alone or part of larger businesses, all spas strive to be places of wellness and healing that promise to "leave you better than they found you." At their inception, spa owners and managers should define a vision, focus, or concept for their business, answering the question: "What do we hope to provide for our clientele?" Then, through their selection of staff and development of the spa setting, managers begin to define what treatments and services the spa will offer.

WELLNESS AND BEAUTY

Spas are not alone in the wellness industry. **Conventional medicine** is the term used to describe wellness practiced by licensed medical doctors, doctors of osteopathic medicine, psychiatrists, physical therapists, and the like. This "Western" medical system is the traditional form of medical practice in North America. The term **alternative medicine** is used when nontraditional treatments are used in place of conventional practices. Alternative practices can be implemented within a doctor's practice, but they also can be carried out by nutritionists, massage therapists, cosmetologists, estheticians, reflexologists, and others. The terms **complementary medicine** and **integrative or integrated medicine** are used interchangeably to describe when alternative and conventional practices are combined to maintain health, prevent illness, or cure disease. Spas have different wellness missions and so they follow different paths to health and healing. Most spa businesses provide alternative medical practices and commonly beauty services as well. Medical spas are the exception: Having a health-care practitioner on staff often leads to an integrated approach.

Wellness and beauty offerings come in many varieties, and the possibilities can seem endless. Reading a spa menu can be daunting, even for a seasoned spa visitor. Similar spa services often have different names or may utilize a variety of products or techniques to achieve similar results. Some treatments have a long history; others are quite new. Some are provided by skin-care professionals, some by massage therapists. A few treatments require a special facility or equipment, whereas others can be provided just about anywhere. Many treatments require movement of the body, but others depend on stillness.

To list and describe all spa services in one chapter would be impossible and beyond the scope of this book. However, as spa managers, a good understanding of common spa services is essential. By understanding spa offerings according to their origin, technique, provider, setting, and tools used, individuals interested in managing a spa can acquire the knowledge necessary to manage, implement, and even develop their own blend of spa offerings.

This chapter assumes a general familiarity with common spa offerings. For a detailed description of the treatments mentioned, readers can refer to the Spa Offering Glossary at the end of the chapter. All *italicized* terms in this chapter, are explained in the Spa Offering Glossary. Some resources for better understanding the preparation, methods and protocols, supplies, equipment, and contraindications associated with each spa offering are provided in the Appendix at the end of the book.

TREATMENTS BY TECHNIQUE

Spa offerings are commonly divided into categories based on distinct and similar elements in the various services or treatments. *Hydrotherapy* is defined as the therapeutic use of water and often refers to spa offerings that primarily utilize water in the treatments. Knowing that the word "spa" has water as its foundation, one might guess that many spa offerings can be categorized as hydrotherapy. Hydrotherapy treatments are further classified by the type of water used. *Balneotherapy* refers to hydrotherapy services that utilize mineral water, whereas *thalassotherapy* refers to treatments that use seawater and other products from the sea.

Hydrotherapy treatments can be self-administered, as in a *steam room* or *chamber,* or therapist-administered, as in a *Vichy shower.* Water therapies can be motionless, as in still tubs, swimming or immersion pools, steam rooms and *saunas,* or moving, as in *Swiss showers, whirlpools,* or bubbling *mineral springs.* Hydrotherapy is typically a full-body treatment but can be used to spot treat specific areas of the body—for example, *Kneipp* protocols of hot or cold immersion or *Scotch hose* treatment focused on a specific area of the body. No matter what type of water or which technique is used, the common element of water places these treatments into the category of hydrotherapy.

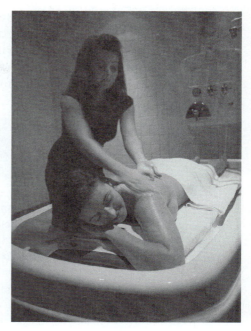

Hydrotherapy Treatment

HISTORY FACT

Archeologists have uncovered sweat houses dating back 1200 years and surmise their use in ancient Maya. When the Spaniards arrived in the New World in the sixteenth century, they found extensive use of sweat houses by Mayan and Aztec tribes (Aaland, 1997).

REALITY CHECK

Sauna is a form of traditional sweat bathing aimed at cleansing the body through perspiration. This treatment creates an artificial fever, the same intent as a hot bath, hot spring, steam, or whirlpool treatment. Although no external source of water is used, sauna is often categorized as hydrotherapy.

Body therapy describes services in which the whole body, or a large area of the body, is treated. The focus of body therapy is to enhance health and well-being. Body therapies are further divided into biologically based treatments, manipulative practices, movement, and body energy therapies. **Biologically based** treatments, sometimes referred to as diet, are treatments that are literally consumed or inhaled by the participant. Prescribed healthy eating practices, *herbal and dietary supplements,* breathing exercises, and *aromatherapy* are considered biologically based body treatments. **Manipulative practices** in conventional medicine include chiropractic and osteopathic manipulation. A common alternative, typically less invasive, manipulation practice is massage. **Massage** is the manual manipulation of soft body tissues to enhance health and well-being (University of Minnesota, 2010). According to the International Spa Association (2007), massage is the most popular service in every type of spa in North America and around the globe. Massage comes in many varieties. In the United States the most common massages are *deep tissue (therapeutic) massage* and *Swedish massage,* followed by *hot stone massage* (ISPA, 2007).

REALITY CHECK

What Is Deep Tissue Massage?

There is no actual protocol or technique for deep tissue massage, but the term is commonly used in the spa industry. Like all forms of massage, a deep tissue massage works the soft body tissues. Although some associate pain with deep tissue massage, this style of treatment does not need to be a muscle-pounding, hurt-inducing experience. In most spas, deep tissue is a Swedish massage with deep work in specific areas. When performing a deep tissue massage, the therapist uses core body strength and intent to make a deep impact without inducing pain. At present, the industry seems to be moving away from the term "deep tissue" and toward the term "therapeutic massage."

In contrast to body therapy, **beauty therapy** provides services aimed at improving the attractiveness of the client and often enhancing the client's perceived sense of well-being. Although the most popular beauty therapies focus on the face, hands, and feet, any area of the body can receive beauty therapy. Common spa beauty therapies include nail treatments, hair removal, tanning, and skin care, including *facials* and *body scrubs.* Medical spas include many beauty therapies in their business practices. The most common are *microdermabrasion, chemical peels,* and *Botox* (ISPA, 2007). Although beauty therapies are commonly offered in spas, wellness is not the primary purpose of beauty therapies, so these services are not categorized as alternative medical practices.

Exercise, fitness, or **movement practices** are common wellness offerings at most types of spas. These practices can be completed one-on-one but usually are offered in a group class format. They are considered body therapies because of the strength, movement, and/or aerobic benefits they provide. Common movement practices include personal training, cardio fitness, muscular fitness using resistance machines and free weights, *Pilates,* and group fitness programs. Movement practices also can include activities such as yoga, dance, hiking, tennis, golf, and aquatic fitness. *Tai Chi* and *Qi (or Chi) Gong* are movement meditation practices that are also considered mind therapies.

When a service is focused on educating clients, improving brainpower, or calming the mind, offerings are categorized as **mind therapy**. Commonly available at destination, cruise, and resort spas, mind therapies are occasionally offered at special-service day spa facilities. Examples of mind therapies include nutritional counseling, stress management, sound therapy, and self-healing classes. Wellness practitioners have long recognized the healing connection between the mind and body. Improving one's mind and body through cognitive therapy or patient support groups are common conventional medicine practices, whereas *meditation, prayer,* mental healing, and *creative therapy* treatments are alternative forms of mind therapy.

Therapies that work with the natural energies of the body to heal and bring vigor to the mind and body are commonly called **energy therapies**. During an energy therapy treatment, specially trained practitioners work with the body's vibration or biofields using hands or instruments to create energy and heal the body. For example, in a *Reiki* treatment, a therapist hovers both hands over a specific area of the body or lightly touches it for the desired effect; in *therapeutic or Healing Touch,* a light touch is used; in *acupuncture,* small needles are used. Bioelectromagnetic equipment may also be used, such as magnets or mild electric currents.

TREATMENTS BY ORIGIN

Most spa offerings are steeped in history and tradition and have been practiced for centuries, if not for thousands of years. We can pinpoint the original source of many of today's spa treatments; consequently, spa offerings are often identified and categorized by their place of origin. Some wellness treatments, however, were used in numerous early civilizations, so it is difficult to pinpoint their origin. For example, bathing, massage, steam lodges, and many beauty treatments were chronicled in several ancient societies, so identifying these offerings with any one culture would be difficult. Other spa offerings have distinct foundations that are easily identified by their country of origin.

India

The system of medicine in India, called *Ayurvedic medicine* or **Ayurveda,** dates back more than 4000 years. With "ayur" meaning life and "veda" meaning knowledge, this medical practice is a philosophy of life and living well. Ayurvedic doctors take a preventative and curative approach to healing. It is believed that health exists only when there is balance in an individual's mind, body, and spirit. The life energy in Ayurveda is called prana, which animates the body and activates the mind. In Ayurveda, energy centers in the body are called chakras. There are seven chakras generally believed to be located in the body along the spinal column. Chakras support and bolster the physical body and are associated with the connections of the mind, body, and spirit. There are also approximately 108 major marma points (energy sites) in the body that are used during Indian massage and Ayurvedic healing.

A foundational principle of traditional Ayurvedic medicine is that everything is composed of five elements: space/ether, air, fire, earth, and water. These five elements comprise three doshas (tridosha). The doshas, known individually as vata, pitta, and kapha, govern the functions of the body. Every individual has elements of all three doshas; however, one or more is typically predominant in an individual, and this predominance contributes to the individual's overall health and well-being. An individual's principal dosha assists a treatment provider in selecting a suitable treatment.

Ayurvedic medicine is a complex system of medicine, and to say that modern-day spa treatments are Ayurveda is naive, but many of today's spa offerings are inspired by Indian practices. Ancient Ayurvedic practices incorporated breathing exercises, essential oils, herbs, chants, cleansing, meditation, nutrition, and yoga body postures. As a result, these techniques are the foundation of a variety of contemporary spa offerings.

Ayurveda-inspired body treatments today include *Abhyanga,* a massage using a dosha-specific oil performed by one or more therapists working in synchronicity to balance the recipient's doshas and increase circulation; *Shirodhara,* bringing calm to the customer through a threadlike drizzle of warm refined sesame oil poured in the area of the "third-eye" or brow chakra; *Pinda,* a relaxation massage by one or more therapists who hold and use muslin bags of herbs, rice, and milk; and *Udvartana,* a stimulating massage incorporating the application of an herbal paste.

Movement therapy with *yoga* postures at their foundation can be considered to be of Indian origin. *Thai massage* actually originated in

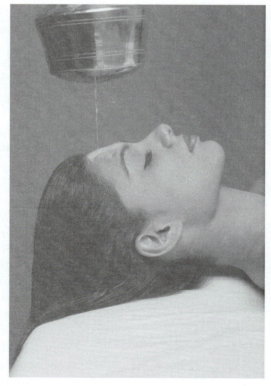

Shirodhara Treatment

India and was later brought to Thailand, where it was further developed around 2500 years ago (Busch, 2008). Although it is commonly considered an Asian treatment, traditional Thai massage is a deep, full-body treatment that incorporates provider-assisted yoga-like stretches and *acupressure.*

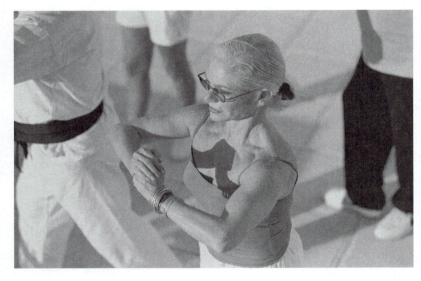

Thai Chi Class

East Asia

Traditional Chinese medicine (TCM) or **Asian medicine** also relies on a model of the human body as an energy system. TCM has its foundation in Ayurveda and incorporates similar principles. In TCM, this system involves the circulation of qi (chi) energy, the assimilation of 365 acupuncture points, and 12 meridian (energy) channels. TCM began in China and found its way to Korea and Japan. As with Ayurveda, the focus of TCM is on wellness and prevention of illness.

A primary principle in TCM is yin and yang. Yin and yang are opposing forces that are contained in all elements of life: Yin is dark, tranquil, cold, and, generally, feminine; yang is its opposite—light, aggressive, hot, and, generally, masculine. They occur together in nature, and their balance is believed to affect everything in the universe. Yin and yang are further refined into the system of the five elements, fire, wood, earth, metal, and water. These elements form a cycle that explains the workings of the human body. When they are out of balance, illness and instability occur.

These concepts are the foundation of TCM wellness practices and are followed today in spas that incorporate any of the ancient wisdom of traditional Chinese medicine in their offerings. The ancient Chinese practices of *reflexology, acupressure (shiatsu* in Japan), and *Tui Na* massage all have at their core the stimulation of various points on the body to facilitate the flow of energy to create a healing response in the body. *Reiki,* developed by a Japanese businessman, is also based on TCM meridian lines. *Tai Chi* and *Qi Gong* movement and mind therapy originated in China, and both are practiced to bring greater balance, healing energy, and mental focus to one's life.

Europe

Several modern spa services originated in Europe. We know that massage was practiced in many ancient societies, including Greece and Rome; however, one of today's most popular forms of massage is best known as *Swedish massage.* This relaxing form of massage is also known as *a relaxation* or *classic massage.* Named for Swede Peter Henrik Ling, it was actually Dutch Johan Georg Mezger who named the four movements of Swedish massage (Calvert, 2002). The first modern *sauna,* originally called sweat baths and used in several early cultures, was developed in Finland.

Several hydrotherapy treatments also arose first in Europe. A *Vichy shower* is a horizontal shower of five to eight jets named for its town of origin in France. *Scotch hose* treatments originated in Germany. In 1855, Father Sebastian Kneipp, a Bavarian priest, published "My Water Cure," detailing his system of healing involving the application of water through various methods, temperatures, and pressures. Today this is the basis of a popular treatment called *Kneipp* treatment.

America

There are traces of ancient traditions in many contemporary spa offerings. Contributions from India, Asia, Europe, and Africa are distinct yet familiar. Some spa offerings, however, are truly American developments. Some were new ideas and others were adaptations from other cultures. Americans have been inclined to develop wellness services that work directly with muscles, joints, fascia, bones, and the lymphatic system. These American-made spa offerings include craniosacral therapy, Rolfing, Watsu, Trager, Hellerwork, Lomi Lomi, and modern hot stone treatments; many of these are described in Table 3.1. Americans invented the Jacuzzi and were the first to use the descriptive term "aerobic."

TABLE 3.1

History of American Spa Offerings

1824	As recounted in John Harvey Kellogg's book, *The Art of Massage* (1895), in Hawaii, *lomi-lomi* massage is said to have been performed on the king and queen after they had eaten, to allow them to eat more.
1886	Harriett Hubbard Ayer of Chicago introduces face creams and anti-aging products through her cosmetics business, Recamier Manufacturing Company.
1895	Dr. John Harvey Kellogg publishes what is to become a classic textbook on massage, *The Art of Massage*.
1899	William Sutherland, D.O., develops a system of examination and treatment for the bones of the skull, launching what we know today as craniosacral therapy (Upledger, 2006).
1913	Dr. William Fitzgerald rediscovers reflexology and calls it *zone therapy*.
1914	Elizabeth Arden introduces eye makeup to America, and then a nongreasy skin cream in 1915.
1940s	Dr. Ida P. Rolf of New York develops her body work practice known as Structural Integration. In 1977, she wrote Rolfing: *The Integration of Human Structures* (Rolf Guild, 2008).
1940s	The term "myofascial" is used by Janet G. Travell to refer to musculoskeletal pain syndromes. In 1983, Drs. Travell and David Simons published a book detailing *myofascial/trigger point* methods of spa therapy.
1947	Dr. Randolf Stone publishes his first book on *Polarity Therapy* (Osborne, 2008).
1949	Milton Trager opens a clinic to instruct and implement his psychosocial integration technique, now called the *Trager method*. He began teaching at the Esalen Institute in California in 1975 and established the Trager Institute in 1980.
1968	Dr. Kenneth H. Cooper, from San Antonio, Texas, coins the term *aerobics* and publishes a book of the same name, helping to start the fitness movement in the United States (Jowers, 2008).
1968	Roy Jacuzzi invents the first self-contained whirlpool tub, from an idea developed in 1956.
1978	Joseph Heller, trained by Ida Rolf, develops *Hellerwork*, a variation of rolfing. (Heller, 2010).
1980	*Watsu* is developed by Harold Dull in Harbin, California.
1993	Although using warm stones for body therapy had been practiced since ancient times, Mary Hannigan, a massage therapist from Arizona, publishes a modern version of the treatment called LeStone Therapy, which propels the popularity of hot stone treatments in America (Turley, 2008).
1998	Deborah Szekely brings the first meditation *labyrinth* to America. Housed at the Golden Door in Escondido, California, this is a replica of the famous floor labyrinth laid in the Cathedral of Chartres sometime between 1194 and 1220.

↪ TREATMENTS BY PROVIDER

It is essential for a spa manager to know who is permitted to provide spa treatments. Many spa services require rigorous, specialized training and some kind of license to practice. Although the process is not as rigorous as for doctors of conventional medicine, obtaining a license for alternative spa and beauty services will likely consist of completing an education program, passing an exam, and completing a set number of training hours. The requirements vary greatly in North America and are set by a state, province, or a national regulatory agency. More detail about this process is provided in Chapter 6. Categorizing spa offerings according to the service provider allows the spa manager to select providers based on business needs.

In general, the most common licensed spa professional positions include estheticians, massage therapists, nail technicians, cosmetologists, fitness instructors, and personal trainers. **Estheticians** are licensed to treat the epidermal layer of the human skin. Hence, esthetic practice may include, but is not limited to, *facials,* skin exfoliation using abrasion or chemicals, makeup application, body wraps and scrubs, and most hair-removal processes. Additional licensure may allow a wider set of treatments, including *electrolysis* and *micropigmentation,* also called permanent makeup.

Massage therapists may specialize in a variety of styles of massage and body work. Massage involves manipulating the client's body with pressure, tension, motion, or vibration, done manually or with mechanical aids. Upon completing most training programs, a licensed massage therapist will be proficient in *classic / Swedish* massage. As with estheticians, additional certifications and training allow a wider set of treatments, such as *reflexology, Reiki, hot stone,* or *shiatsu.*

HISTORY FACT

The New York State Society of Medical Massage Therapists was established in 1927 to support massage therapy professionals, making it the first association of its kind in the United States.

Licensed **nail technicians** can provide *manicures, pedicures, polishing, nail extensions, nail art,* and perform hand and foot treatments, including basic hand and foot massage. **Cosmetologists** are certified to work with the skin, nails, scalp, and hair. In addition to skin and nail services, cosmetologists also provide haircuts, styling, and *chemical hair services.* Cosmetologists can provide therapeutic hair and scalp treatments, temporary hair removal, and limited nail services.

Certified **fitness instructors** and **personal trainers** are trained to assist clients with exercise and movement practices. Personal trainers tend to work with clients one-on-one, whereas fitness instructors likely teach group fitness classes. Specialized training allows the fitness professional to specialize in many areas, such as *yoga, Pilates,* or *water aerobics.* Depending on the focus of the spa, licensed counselors, dieticians, and wellness professionals may also provide services. Some medical spas also employ licensed psychologists, dentists, dermatologists, medical doctors, and the like.

When a spa integrates services into its menu that do not require a treatment provider, **spa attendants** may assist in preparing for these offerings. Spa attendants are generally not licensed or certified, but can (in many states) still assist with some client services. Spa attendants may assist with self-administered steam, sauna, pool, and tub treatments. They can also assist with client purchases of nutritional supplements or skin products.

TREATMENTS BY FACILITY AND EQUIPMENT

Some spa services require a special facility or equipment to be provided; others do not. Spa offerings can be categorized based on the space and equipment needed to perform the service. An example might be the equipment needed to perform *electrolysis* (permanent hair removal) or the special room design needed to create the traditional *hammam* (Turkish bath). Generally, in a spa, the guest areas can be separated into revenue-producing spaces and non–revenue-producing spaces. Non–revenue-producing areas generally include the registration area, relaxation areas, self-administered treatment areas (i.e., *steam, sauna*), and preparation areas, such as changing rooms or locker facilities. Revenue-producing spaces include treatment rooms, salon, retail space, and fitness areas.

Treatment rooms can be dry or wet spaces. **Dry treatment rooms** are generally more comfortable and plush and are used for table and floor massage services and facials. **Wet treatment rooms** are developed to be easy to clean and commonly accommodate exfoliation, mask, wrap, tanning, and nail treatments. Some wet treatment areas house hydrotherapy equipment such as *still* and *whirlpool tubs* or *Vichy* and *Swiss* showers. Some treatments can be performed in either a dry or a wet room. Wet treatment rooms can accommodate dry room treatments, and some wet treatments can be performed in dry rooms. For example, a self-contained body mask, such as paraffin, or a tanning session using lotion instead of spray can generally be performed in a dry room.

Although spa spaces tend to be places of peace and quiet, clients expect a more energetic and social atmosphere in the retail, salon, and fitness areas. A salon is traditionally a space used for hair and nail beauty services. Spas with a fitness studio are able to host group and individual fitness exercise classes. Those with exercise equipment rooms can have drop-in clients or provide greater selection with their personal fitness training. A multipurpose room allows for group educational offerings. Small one-on-one counseling spaces permit the spa to integrate more personalized sessions with clients.

Select therapies require areas and equipment specifically designed for their execution. For example, spas offering *Watsu* require a pool of a specific size and depth. Larger pools are necessary for water fitness classes. Kneipp treatments require hot, warm, and cold plunge facilities or equipment. Steam and sauna facilities are self-contained and distinctive.

Music/sound therapy, light/color therapy, aromatherapy/inhalation treatments, and cooking demonstrations need special equipment and most likely a designated room for implementation. Outdoor areas may be developed for services such as labyrinth meditations, walking paths, challenge activities, sports, and recreation.

Table 3.2 classifies twenty of the most popular spa treatments (ISPA, 2007) using the categories just covered.

Although the ISPA (2007) identified the spa services in Table 3.2 as being most popular, there are variations in offerings based on the type of spa. Differentiating among the four most common types of spas— day, resort/hotel, medical, and club—the types of services available generally differ. Whereas it is very common (over 96 percent) for day,

Sauna

TABLE 3.2

Top Spa Services by Category

Category	Top Spa Treatments	Technique	Origin	Provider	Facility
Hydrotherapy	Steam	Hydrotherapy	Prehistory	Self-administered or spa attendant	Unique
	Sauna	Hydrotherapy	Europe	Self-administered or spa attendant	Unique
	Vichy shower	Hydrotherapy	Europe	Esthetician or massage therapist	Wet treatment room
	Baths	Hydrotherapy	Prehistory	Self-administered or massage therapist	Wet treatment room
Massage	Therapeutic/ sports	Manipulative body therapy	Prehistory	Massage therapist	Dry treatment room
	Swedish	Manipulative body therapy	Europe	Massage therapist	Dry treatment room
	Hot stone	Manipulative body therapy	Prehistory, revived in America	Specially trained massage therapist	Dry treatment room
Beauty/salon	Pedicure	Beauty therapy	Prehistory	Nail technician	Salon
	Manicure	Beauty therapy	Prehistory	Nail technician	Salon
	Makeup services	Beauty therapy	Prehistory	Esthetician or cosmetologist	Salon
Alternative	Reiki	Energy therapy	China and East Asia	Specially trained massage therapist	Dry treatment room
	Ayurvedic abhyanga	Manipulative body therapy	India	Specially trained massage therapist	Dry or wet treatment room
	Acupuncture	Energy therapy	China and East Asia	Acupuncturist	Dry treatment room
Mind therapies	Meditation	Mind therapy	India	Fitness/wellness instructor	Multipurpose room
	Yoga	Movement practice	India	Fitness/wellness instructor	Fitness studio
	Relaxation classes	NA	NA	Fitness/wellness instructor	Fitness studio
Educational programs	Nutrition counseling	Mind therapy	NA	Dietician	Multipurpose room
	Stress management	Mind therapy	NA	Counselor	Multipurpose room or one-on-one counseling space
Fitness	Personal training	Movement practice	NA	Personal trainer	Exercise equipment room or fitness studio
	Cardio fitness	Movement practice	NA	Fitness/wellness instructor	Fitness studio
	Free weights	Movement practice	NA	Self-administered or spa attendant	Exercise equipment room

Labyrinth

resort, and club spas to have massage services, only 78 percent of medical spas offer massage. Facials and body treatments are offered more often in day and resort spas (in the 90th percentile), and less often in medical and club spas (in the 80th percentile). Resort spas are most likely to offer hydrotherapy (68 percent), compared to only half of all day, medical, and club spas.

SPA MENU DEVELOPMENT

There are many ways to examine spa treatments and services. If a spa manager has the ability to categorize spa offerings as described, he or she will have the basic knowledge necessary to develop a menu of services for the spa. In developing a spa menu, the goal is to create selection and variety that is attractive to the target market, matches the spa's vision and concept, utilizes the staff effectively, and fits the space available at the spa.

In considering your spa menu, it is important to know that there are some flexible elements of your business and some not-so-flexible elements. The spa facility is inflexible, meaning it would be difficult (and costly) to change the facility, so work with it. Your primary competition is out of your control, thus also inflexible. It will be your job as a spa manager to know the competition and position your business to stand out. Probably the most inflexible element of your business is the need to be financially profitable. In developing your spa menu, you must create a blend of spa offerings to ensure that you will meet the projected bottom line.

The rest is flexible, and with moderate effort, changeable. The equipment and products used in the spa can be exchanged. The hours of operation, spa concept, and types of services all can be modified. And with a little more effort, the treatment provider staff can be changed. Once you are aware of these elements, you should consider the following questions and start the menu-development process:

1. What is your spa vision and concept (as covered in Chapters 2 and 3). What services and products do you select from to fit this vision? For example, if you decide to have an Asian concept in your spa, your treatments should offer a focus on balance, enhancing clients' flow of qi through the body's meridians. Massage treatments may focus on shiatsu, acupressure, and Reiki healing. It

may be wise to minimize focus on the more Western-based massages such as Swedish, deep tissue, or myofascial.

2. Who is your target market, and what are their wants, needs, and expectations? Wellness or beauty? Social or serene? Luxury or efficiency? What will you do to meet your customers' needs? For example, a medical spa, with beauty as its primary focus, would be well inclined to select treatments directed toward this focus. Facials, hair removal, and other beauty offerings such as Botox and dermal fillers would be typical, whereas relaxing Swedish-type massage might not.

3. Who is your primary competition, and how will you differentiate your spa from theirs?

4. There are many ways to make your spa stand out: selecting a unique concept or theme, offering a service unlike those of your competition, enhancing your refreshment offerings, or offering a small giveaway. What are your primary business goals, financial and otherwise?

   First and foremost, a spa is a business, and therefore, it must be profitable. Each spa menu item will need to be analyzed to determine costs and pricing structure of your services, to ensure the prosperity of the business. Spa menu items must be selected to ensure financial rewards for the business. See Chapter 10 for more information about spa financial operations. Other primary business goals may include an admirable customer retention rate. Developing the customer experience to increase his or her chances of returning. See Chapter 8 for more information about spa client management.

5. What type of space and equipment are available? Larger spaces, usually available at resorts and destination spas, allow for more pretreatment hydrotherapy offerings and treatments needing unique spaces such as Watsu or Vichy. The most common element of a spa is a dry treatment room, because it allows for many wellness and beauty offerings.

6. What type of employees do you anticipate needing to hire? Whereas estheticians and massage therapists are limited to skin care and hands-on massage services, respectively, cosmetologists may offer a wider range of services and acupuncturists a smaller and more specialized offering.

Once you have answered these questions and while you are developing the spa menu, keep the suggestions in Table 3.3 in mind.

TABLE 3.3

Simple Suggestions for Spa Menu Development

- Keep it simple; too many selections is confusing.
- Select treatments that match the spa concept.
- Select techniques that support rather than compete with each other.
- Be creative; offer a small number of signature services.
- Offer services in a range of prices.
- Consider publishing separate price sheets for easier modification.
- Present spa services in an organized fashion and on quality material.
- Design the menu and write descriptions with the spa concept in mind.
- Select offering based on the treatment provider staff, spaces available, and financial goals.
- Consider the length of the treatment and overall scheduling of treatment spaces.
- Create a format that will allow you to be flexible, because the majority of spas change their menus every year.

REALITY CHECK

A recent Cornell research project compared three different options for showing prices on restaurant menus: (1) prices displayed using a numerical dollar-and-cents format with a dollar sign, (2) prices displayed in numerical format without a dollar sign, and (3) prices written out. The results indicated that the numerical format without the dollar sign yielded the highest dollar sale.

Selecting appropriate treatments for your spa is where it all comes together. Developing a spa menu for a special-service day spa requires a very different approach than developing a full-service resort spa menu. Table 3.4 provides a potential selection of menu offerings based on the size, type, and vision of the spa.

Consider the sample spa menu in Figure 3.1. This is not a typical day spa menu, but for educational purposes it is a good use of the suggestions in Table 3.3 and a good exercise for review of the preceding menu development questions. Looking at Figure 3.1, let's consider the menu development process in reverse.

1. Can you identify the concept? Do the services fit the concept?
2. What type of customers will you attract with this spa menu?
3. Does the menu differentiate this spa from others?
4. What are your space and equipment needs?
5. What providers would need to be hired?

Figure 3.1 Sample Spa Menu

SPAcifically for Teens

If you are between the ages of 13 and 17 you can join your parent in the spa for one of these healthy and relaxing treatments. You will be escorted to your own personal treatment room for your service.

Meltdown Hand and Foot Paraffin: Wrap your hands and feet in warm wax to smooth and soften the skin.
25 minutes $40

Skin Glow Mini Facial: Choose a deep cleansing or moisturizing treatment to give your skin a fresh look.
25 minutes $70

The Professional Shave: Let us show you a shave that will keep your skin clear, smooth and conditioned, includes shaving kit with brush, pre-shave oil, shave cream and aftershave cream.
25 minutes $70

Brain Teaser Scalp Massage: Close your eyes and let us stimulate your brain with warm oil being massaged into your scalp.
25 minutes $70

Even if you're Ticklish Foot Reflexology: We can relax your entire body just using the pressure points on your feet. You won't believe how it's all connected.
25 minutes $70

Rolling Stone Hand and Foot Massage: Warm and cold river stones are used on the Zen points on your hands and feet to chill you out.
25 minutes $70

On the go manicure or pedicure:
Choose your polish and let us do the rest. Add your choice of nail art and dress up your fingers and toes.
Pedicure - 25 minutes $35
Manicure - 25 minutes $30
Nail art $5 per nail

TABLE 3.4

Sample Spa Selections by Size, Type and Vision

Spa Treatments	Massage						Alternative					Hydrotherapy					
Spa Type	Swedish	Therapeutic	Hot Stone	Maternity	Sports	Other*	Reiki	Aromatherapy	Acupuncture	Acupressure/ Shiatsu	Other**	Steam/ Sauna	Vichy	Whirlpool	Baths	Swiss/ Experience Shower	Other***
Small Day Spa (beauty-focus)	X						X										
Small Day Spa (wellness-focus)	X	X	X	X	X		X										
Large Full-Service Day Spa	X	X	X	X	X	X	X	X				X				X	
Small Medical Spa (beauty-focus)																	
Small Medical Spa (wellness-focus)	X	X	X	X	X	X	X	X	X								
Small Hotel or Fitness Spa	X	X	X		X							X		X			
Small Resort, Cruise Ship, Residential, or Club Spa	X	X	X	X	X			X		X		X		X	X	X	
Large Resort, Cruise Ship, Residential, Club or Destination Spa	X	X	X	X	X	X	X	X	X	X	X	X	X	X	X	X	X

Spa Treatments	Beauty									Fitness††			Education		
Spa Type	Nail Services	Hair Services	Makeup	Facials	Paramedical Facials†	Hair Removal (Waxing)	Hair Removal (other)	Body Wraps & Mud	Body Scrubs	Other††	Group Fitness	Personal Training	Nutrition	Creative Therapy	Other†††
Small Day Spa (beauty-focus)	X	X	X	X		X									
Small Day Spa (wellness-focus)				X	X										
Large Full-Service Day Spa	X	X	X	X	X	X		X	X						
Small Medical Spa (beauty-focus)				X	X	X	X			X					
Small Medical Spa (wellness-focus)													X	X	X
Small Hotel or Fitness Spa				X							X	X			
Small Resort, Cruise Ship, Residential, or Club Spa	X	X	X	X	X	X		X	X		X	X			
Large Resort, Cruise Ship, Residential, Club or Destination Spa	X	X	X	X		X	X	X	X	X	X	X	X	X	X

*Thai, reflexology, couples, craniosacral, lomi lomi, shirodhara, cold stone, etc.
**Herbal supplements, breating therapy, chiropractic, etc.
***Scotch hose, mineral baths, Kneipp, foot baths, etc
†Microdermabrasion, laser skin resurfacing, Botox®, high concentration glycolic peels, etc.
††Cosmetic dentistry, surgery, permanent makeup, tattoo removal, etc.
††Cardio/aerobic training, yoga, tai chi, qigong, pilates, hiking/walking, aqua aerobics, strength training, sports, recreation, etc.
†††Stress management, healing therapy, life skills, meditation, feng shui, etc.

KEY TERMS

Alternative medicine

Asian medicine

Ayurveda

Balneotherapy

Beauty therapy

Biologically based treatments

Body therapy

Complementary medicine

Conventional medicine

Cosmetologists

Dry treatment rooms

Energy therapy

Estheticians

Fitness/wellness instructors

Hydrotherapy

Integrative or integrated medicine

Manipulative practices

Massage

Massage therapists

Mind therapy

Movement practices

Nail technicians

Personal trainers

Spa attendants

Thalassotherapy

Traditional Chinese medicine

Wet treatment rooms

REVIEW QUESTIONS

1. How do spa operations fit into the wellness industry?
2. Describe the five different categories of spa treatment based on the service technique.
3. What are the foundational contributions of Ayurveda and Asian medicine to the modern spa industry?
4. List several American spa treatment inventions.
5. What types of treatments do licensed estheticians, massage therapists, nail technicians, cosmetologists, fitness personnel, and spa attendants perform?
6. What are several services that would be offered in each of a dry and wet treatment room?
7. What are the six foundational questions that must be addressed when developing a spa menu?

↳ REFERENCES

Aaland, Mikkel (1997). Native American Sweat Lodge. Retrieved July 27, 2006, from www.cyberbohemia.com/originofthetemescal.

Busch, Kristi (2008). A Cultural Abbreviation of Spa Methods Around the World. Unpublished transcript. Distributed by the University of Houston's Hilton School of Hospitality.

Calvert, Robert Noah. (2002). History of Massage. Rochester, VT: Healing Arts Press.

Heller, Joseph (2010). Joseph Heller's Biography. Retrieved November 29, 2010, from www.josephheller.com/bio.html.

International Spa Association (2007). 2007 Spa Industry Study. Lexington, KY: ISPA.

Jowers, Angie (2008). Spastory. *LiveSpa* (International Spa Association), 1:80–81.

Kellogg, John Harvey (1895). *The Art of Massage*. Whitefish, MT: Kessinger Publishing.

Osborne, Karrie (2008). The Bodywork Tree: Exploring the Bounty of Bodywork. *Body Sense,* Spring/Summer, pp. 8–12.

Rolf Guild (2008). The History of Ida Rolf. Retrieved December 21, 2008, from www.rolfguild.org/idarolf.html.

Turley, Chris (2008). The History Behind the Hot Stone Massage. Ezine Articles, September 30. Retrieved December 21, 2008, from http://ezinearticles.com/?The-History-Behind-the-Hot-Stone-Massage & id=1542879.

University of Minnesota (2010). Taking Charge of Your Health Glossary. Retrieved November 29, 2010, from www.takingcharge.csh.umn.edu/glossary/3#letterm.

Upledger, John (2006). Exploring the Therapeutic Value of CranioSacral Therapy. *Massage Today,* 6(2). Retrieved November 29, 2010, from www. massagetoday.com/mpacms/mt/article.php?id=13372.

SPA OFFERING GLOSSARY

Abhyanga (oil massage)   Ayurvedic external treatment in which one, two, or more therapists use massage and aromatic herbal oils to bring balance to the body.

Acupressure   Ancient healing art that uses the fingers to press key points on the surface of the skin to stimulate the body's natural self-curative abilities; when these points are pressed, they release muscular tension and promote the circulation of blood and the body's life force (sometimes known as qi or chi) to aid healing.

Acupuncture   Ancient Oriental healing technique based on the Taoist philosophy of balancing energy meridians within the body, thus allowing the body to heal itself; fine needles are painlessly inserted at key points corresponding to body organs to relieve pain and cure disease and dysfunction.

Aerobics   A system of physical conditioning involving exercises (such as running, walking, swimming, or calisthenics) performed strenuously, so as to cause a marked temporary increase in respiration and heart rate.

Alexander technique   An energy method used to reeducate the mind and body to improve posture and balance and to reduce stress.

Anaerobic   Meaning "working without oxygen"; nonaerobic exercises, such as weight lifting, involve working muscles in such a way that more oxygen is expended than is taken in.

Aqua aerobics   Aerobic exercise performed in a pool or body of water and using the water to support and resist during movement.

Aromatherapy   The use of essential oils (extracted from herbs, flowers, resin, woods, and roots) in body and skin care treatments; used as a healing technique for thousands of years by the Egyptians, Greeks, and Romans, essential oils aid in relaxation, improve circulation, and help the healing of wounds.

Ayurvedic medicine   A form of holistic alternative medicine that is the traditional system of medicine of India.

Balneotherapy   Ancient use of waters to restore and revitalize the body; has been used to improve circulation, fortify the immune system, relieve pain, and treat stress.

Body mask (masque) or wrap   A body treatment using the application of algae, seaweed, mud, clay, lotion, or cream. Treatments typically begin with exfoliation; if called body wrap, is followed by wrapping the body with sheets, towels, blankets, or bandages.

Body scrub (polish)   Skin treatment in which the upper layer of dead skin cells is sloughed off; a variety of techniques can be used, and the treatment is called, accordingly, loofah rub, salt scrub, body glow, brush and tone, etc.

Botox   A trademark for a preparation of botulinum toxin, a protein that relaxes muscle contractions; it is sometimes injected under the skin to erase facial wrinkles.

Caldarium   Steaming Roman bath used for sweating and detoxification.

Chemical (enzyme) peels   A general classification for a number of chemical treatments used to exfoliate and rejuvenate the skin; a chemical solution is applied to the skin and works by dissolving the upper layers of the skin; as the tissue is dissolved, a wound is created on the skin that stimulates the body's healing response, causing new tissue to emerge.

Chemical hair services   Treatments performed to color, wave, or straighten hair.

Chiropractic   A medical system based on the theory that disease and disorders are caused by a misalignment of the bones, especially in the spine, which obstructs proper nerve function.

Cold plunge   Immersion in a pool of cold water, intended to stimulate circulation.

Color therapy   The use of color and its vibration to balance energies in the body; dates back to ancient Egypt and other premodern societies.

Craniosacral therapy   A method of evaluating and enhancing the function of a physiological body arrangement called the craniosacral system, which consists of the membranes and cerebrospinal fluid that surround and protect the brain and spinal cord. The craniosacral system extends from the bones of the skull, face, and mouth—which make up the cranium—down to the sacrum or tailbone. The craniosacral therapy practitioner uses a light touch to assist the natural movement of fluid within the craniosacral system.

Creative therapy   Therapies that integrate art, dance, music, crafts, etc., to enhance an experience.

Cryotherapy   The therapeutic use of cold in treatments; involves cooling the body using ice, cold towels, and compresses to reduce the temperature of the tissues on or below the surface of the skin.

Deep tissue (therapeutic) massage   Massage techniques administered to affect the sublayer of musculature and fascia. These techniques require advanced training and a thorough understanding of anatomy and physiology. The techniques help with chronic muscular pain and injury rehabilitation and reduce inflammation-related pain caused by arthritis and tendinitis. They are generally integrated with other massage techniques.

Drumming   Rhythmic drumming and percussion sounds used to promote emotional healing and spiritual release.

Dry brush   Treatment using a natural bristle brush to exfoliate skin and stimulate circulation.

Ear candling (coning)   Using a specially designed hollow candle, the administrator places the candle at the entry of the ear canal and lights the opposite end to encourage the elimination of wax.

Electrolysis   Hair removal using destruction of hair roots by passage of an electric current through an electrolyte.

Facial   The integration of services for the skin, including massaging the face (back or body), cleansing, toning, steaming, exfoliating, and moisturizing.

Fangotherapy   The use of fine-grained natural materials such as clay, mud, or peat for body treatments.

Feldenkrais   Developed by Russian-born Dr. Moshe Feldenkrais, this method consists of verbal and touch therapy combined to reorganize the body's fundamental movements and relationship with the central nervous system.

Fridigarium   A room having a bath of unheated water.

Hammam (hamam in Turkey)   Originally the word for bathhouse, now used to describe a spa treatment; the treatment generally includes body cleansing, exfoliation, massage, and wrapping and takes place in a heated steam-room–like chamber.

Healing Touch   Developed by Janet Mentgen, RN, this energy-based therapeutic approach to healing uses touch to influence the energy system, thus affecting physical, emotional, mental, and spiritual health, as well as healing, the goal being to restore harmony and balance in the energy system to help the person self-heal.

Hellerwork   Named after its founder, Joseph Heller, a series of eleven 90-minute sessions of deep-tissue bodywork and movement designed to realign the body and release chronic tension and stress; verbal dialogue is used to assist the client in becoming aware of emotional stress that may be related to physical tension; regarded as preventive rather than curative and reflects a holistic approach to health; designed to produce permanent physical change.

Herbal and dietary supplements   Products proposed to supplement the diet, containing herbs, botanicals, minerals, vitamins, or amino acids; intended to be ingested in capsule, tablet, gelcap/softgel, or liquid form.

Hot stone therapy   Stones of all shapes and sizes and varying temperatures, ranging from 0 to 140°F, are used to elicit physical healing, mental relaxation, and a spiritual connection to earth energy; warm stones encourage the exchange of blood and lymph and provide soothing heat for deep-tissue work; cold stones aid with inflammation, moving blood out of the area, and balancing male/female energies; stones are placed in varying positions on the body for energy balancing or may be used by the therapist for specific trigger-point work; the alternating heat and cold of thermotherapy brings the entire body into the healing process, with a rapid exchange of blood and oxygen and alternating rise and fall of respiration rate as the body seeks homeostasis (balance).

Hydrotherapy   The therapeutic use of water; common methods include underwater massage, herbal baths, thalassotherapy, Kneipp therapy, steam, sauna, Vichy treatments, Scotch hoses, and Swiss showers.

Inhalation therapy   Steam vapor treatment used to improve respiratory function; the vapor is often mixed with herbal and aromatic elements.

Injectables   Term used to categorize wrinkle fillers that are injected into the skin, such as trademarked Botox, Dysport, Restylane, Juvederm, Perlane, and Radiesse.

Jin shin jyutsu   Traditional Chinese medicine technique used to restore balance and reduce stress; intended to balance the flow of energy through the body.

Kneipp (contrast bath)   Treatments combining hydrotherapy, herbology, and a diet of natural foods, developed in Germany in the mid-1800s by Pastor Sebastian Kneipp; these highly regarded European therapies are particularly popular in Austria, Switzerland, and Germany; Kneipp combines the practice of physical exercise with a healthy diet and hydrotherapy to achieve physical and emotional well-being.

Labyrinth A place constructed of intricate passageways; used in a spa as a form of meditation or contemplative walk.

Laser hair removal Use of concentrated beams of light to permanently removed unwanted hair.

Light therapy Exposure to daylight or to specific wavelengths of light using lasers or lamps to treat skin conditions, eye disorders, and seasonal effective disorder (SAD).

Lomi lomi Hawaiian for "rub rub"; a system of massage that utilizes very large, broad movements; two-handed, forearm, and elbow application of strokes, which cover a broad area, are characteristic of lomi lomi.

Lymph drainage A type of massage in which hands and fingers apply gentle, wavelike movements meant to stimulate circulation in the lymphatic system.

Makeup application The art of applying or teaching cosmetic application, based on the individual's skin type, style, and age.

Manicure A cosmetic treatment for the care of the hands and fingernails that includes shaping and polishing.

Massage Manipulation of soft and connective tissue (usually by hand) to relax muscles, relieve tension, improve circulation, and hasten elimination of wastes; also stretches connective tissue and improves circulation; various forms include accupressure, athletic massage, polarity massage, reflexology, Rolfing, shiatsu, sports massage, Swedish massage, Traeger massage, Watsu.

Meditation The act or process of engaging in mental exercise (such as concentration on one's breathing or repetition of a mantra) for the purpose of reaching a heightened level of spiritual awareness.

Microdermabrasion A procedure in which the dead outermost surface of the skin is partially or completely removed by light abrasion; used to remove sun-damaged skin and to remove or lessen scars and dark spots on the skin.

Micropigmentation Also known as permanent makeup; a cosmetic procedure in which metabolically inert pigment granules are implanted below the dermis; the technique used is similar to a tattooing process.

Mineral springs Water from natural springs and wells, which contains a minimum of 1000 mgr/liter solid components of rare, biologically active elements or compounds; may be cold or hot.

Myofacial (trigger-point) therapy Based on the discoveries of Drs. Janet Travell and David Simons, who found the causal relationship between chronic pain and its source; used to relieve muscular pain and dysfunction through applied pressure to trigger points of referred pain and through stretching exercises; trigger points are defined as localized areas in which the muscle and connective tissue are highly sensitive to pain when compressed; pressure on these points can send referred pain to other specific parts of the body.

Nail art Using polishing, nail painting, applications, and nail creation to decorate finger or toe nails.

Nail extensions Applications of acrylic or gel substances to lengthen and beautify nails.

Naturopathy Integration of a range of natural therapeutics emphasizing the healing power of nature to treat the causes of disease, rather than suppressing the symptoms; as part of a holistic medical health-care system with an emphasis on education and prevention, the naturopathic physician seeks to motivate the individual toward a healthy and balanced diet, lifestyle, and mental attitude; treatments such as homeopathic medicines, clinical nutrition, traditional Asian medicine, and acupuncture are used to enhance the body's natural healing processes.

Oxygen therapy   Use of humidified oxygen infused with aromas for therapeutic purposes.

Parafango   A mixture of ash and paraffin, heated and molded to portions of the body in need of increased circulation and rehydration; parafango may be infused with essential oils for added aromatherapy benefits.

Paraffin treatment   Heated paraffin wax is either applied on the body or the body part is dipped into the wax to cleanse, exfoliate, and hydrate the skin.

Pedicure   A treatment of the feet, toes, and toe nails that includes massage, exfoliation, and cleaning of the feet as well as buffing or polishing the nails.

Photo rejuvenation   Using laser light to smooth wrinkles and diminish the appearance of age spots, broken capillaries, and rosacea (redness).

Pilates   A series of movements, done from a sitting, reclining, kneeling, or standing position, designed to increase strength and flexibility, release tension, and relieve chronic neck and back pain; developed by German-born Joseph Pilates in the 1920s; uses a specially designed apparatus for stretching and strengthening exercises and can be calibrated to the client's needs.

Pinda   A relaxation massage by one or more therapists who hold and use muslin bags of herbs, rice, and milk.

Polarity therapy   Based on universal principles of energy—attraction, repulsion, and neutrality; interrelation of these principles forms the basis for every aspect of life, including our experience of health, wellness, and disease; founded by Austrian-born naturopath Dr. Randolph Stone in the mid-1950s; a clothes-on, noninvasive system complementing existing modalities with an integrated, holistic model; based on the belief that positive and negative poles exist in every cell; the body is gently manipulated to balance the positive and negative energies as well as eliminate blockages and toxins through a cleansing diet and simple exercises; treatments are suggested in a series of four.

Prayer   The act or practice of praying to God or a god.

Pre/post-natal massage   A massage treatment designed specifically to address the physical challenges and changes in a woman's body during and after pregnancy.

Qi (chi) gong (chi gung or chi kung)   Traditional Chinese treatment that combines hands-on and hands-off techniques to balance the flow of qi (energy) through the body, move and relieve qi blockages, and improve circulation; a combination of timed breathing and gentle flowing movement, meditation, visualization, and conscious intent all working together to achieve an integrated adjustment of mind and body to better cultivate, circulate, and balance qi or life force.

Reflexology   Manipulation of specific reflex areas in the foot, hands, and ears that correspond to other parts of the body; sometimes referred to as zone therapy; based on an ancient Chinese therapy, it involves application of pressure to these reflex zones to stimulate body organs and relieve areas of congestion; similar to acupressure principles, reflexology works with the body's energy flow to stimulate self-healing and maintain balance in physical function; the technique is used to reduce pain, foster relaxation, and stimulate circulation of blood and lymphatic fluids.

Reiki healing system   Hands-on energy healing art; originated in Japan in the early twentieth century by Mikao Usui, who developed a system of practices that enabled others to become effective healers; the practitioner, trained to access and serve as a channel for the life force (chi), places his or her hands on or just above the client's body to activate healing energy within receptive points on the body; the practitioner's hands move progressively with a passive touch through twelve positions on the body, remaining in each position for 3 to 5 minutes; as a harmonic flow of energy is strengthened within the client and the practitioner, healing occurs through the return of physical, mental, and spiritual balance.

Rolfing/structural integration   A method for reordering the major body segments; founded by American biochemist Dr. Ida Rolf in the 1940s; utilizes physical manipulation and movement awareness to bring the head, shoulders, thorax, pelvis, and legs into vertical alignment; allows more efficient use of muscles with less expended energy by lifting the head and chest and lengthening the body's trunk; a sense of lightness and greater mobility often results; treatments are offered in a ten-session series, as well as advanced sessions.

Salt glow   An exfoliation and skin circulation treatment in which the skin is rubbed with coarse salt.

Sauna   A form of traditional sweat bathing aimed at cleansing the body through perspiration; a pile of stones covering a stove is heated using wood until it turns red hot; then water is thrown over the heated stones to generate steam.

Scotch hose   Standing body massage delivered by the therapist with high-pressure hoses; this invigorating shower tones circulation by contracting and then dilating capillaries as water from sixteen needle-spray shower heads and two high-pressure hoses (operated by an attendant), ranging in temperature from 45 to 105°F, is turned quickly from hot to cold and back to hot for several seconds at a time; this massage aids circulation and helps relieve the pain of arthritis and rheumatism.

Shiatsu   A finger-pressure technique developed in Japan that utilizes traditional acupuncture points; similar to acupressure, shiatsu concentrates on unblocking the flow of life energy and restoring balance in the meridians and organs to promote self-healing; with the client reclining, the practitioner applies pressure with the finger, thumb, palm, elbow, or knee to specific zones on the skin located along the energy meridians; treatment brings about a sense of relaxation while stimulating blood and lymphatic flow; benefits may include pain relief and a strengthening of the body's resistance to disease and disorder.

Shirodhara   An Ayurveda treatment which brings calm to the client through a threadlike drizzle of warm refined sesame oil being poured in the area of the "third eye" or brow chakra.

Sports massage   Designed to enhance athletic performance and recovery; useful to an athlete in three contexts: pre-event, post-event, and injury treatment. Pre-event massage is delivered at the performance site, usually with the athlete fully clothed. Fast-paced and stimulating, it helps to establish blood flow and to warm up muscles. During the massage, the athlete generally focuses on visualizing the upcoming event. Post-event massage is also delivered on site, through the clothes. The intent here is to calm the nervous system and begin the process of flushing toxins and waste products out of the body. Post-event massage can reduce recovery time, enabling an athlete to resume training much sooner than rest alone would allow.

Steam room   A ceramic-tiled room with wet heat generated by temperatures of 110 to 130°F; designed to soften the skin, cleanse the pores, calm the nervous system, and relieve tension.

Sugaring   A hair removal (depilation) process that involves applying to the skin and then quickly removing a sugar-based paste on a cloth or paper strip.

Sweat lodge   Traditional Native American enclosed sauna-like environment used for ceremonial purification and meditation.

Swedish Massage   One of the most commonly taught and well-known massage techniques; a vigorous system of treatment designed to energize the body by stimulating circulation; five basic strokes (kneading, rolling, vibration, percussive, and tapping movements), all flowing toward the heart, are used to manipulate the soft tissues of the body; oil is applied to reduce friction on the skin; benefits may include generalized relaxation, dissolution of scar tissue adhesions, and improved circulation, which may speed healing and reduce swelling resulting from injury.

Swiss (experience) shower   A shower that provides a unique shower experience, combining an overhead deluge shower with multiple showerheads surrounding the recipient.

T'ai chi chih (t'ai chi)   A series of simple, nonstrenuous movements to relax the body and refresh the mind; moves can be performed by anyone, regardless of age or physical condition; can help individuals feel calm and helps relieve daily tensions and stress; based on principles of relaxed breathing, rhythmic movements, and equilibrium of weight.

Temazcal   Domelike sweat lodge structure originating from Central and North America, meant to relax and detoxify the body and promote meditation.

Thai massage (naud bo rarn)   Practiced in Thailand for approximately 2500 years; although the origins are somewhat vague, credit for Thai massage is given to a famous Indian doctor, Shivago Komarpaj, who was the personal physician of the Buddha and Magadha king. Historically, manipulation was one of four major branches comprising traditional Thai ceremonies or magical practices; based on the theory that the body is made up of 72,000 sen, or energy lines, of which ten have top priority; also involves peripheral stimulating, meaning that it acts as an external stimulant to produce specific internal effects; this point serves as the main division between Thai and Western massage. Thai massage is practiced on a firm mat on the floor instead of on a table, a fact that is instrumental in the effective use of the practitioner's body weight. Except for the feet, the client remains fully clothed, so draping is not necessary.

Thalassotherapy   Uses the therapeutic benefits of the sea and seawater products—vitamins and minerals—to restore health and vitality to the skin and hair; may include a seaweed and algae paste spread on the body and being insulated with sheets or blankets; seawater baths may include massage with strong, underwater jets or manual hose massage by the therapist.

Therapeutic massage   Massage techniques administered to affect the sublayer of musculature and fascia. These techniques require advanced training and a thorough understanding of anatomy and physiology. Therapeutic massage helps with chronic muscular pain and injury rehabilitation and reduces inflammation-related pain caused by arthritis and tendinitis. It is generally integrated with other massage techniques.

Therapeutic Touch   Developed through the collaboration of a nursing professor and a spiritual healer; based on ancient energy healing methods; practitioners, primarily nurses, are trained to feel or sense energy imbalances in the client and to use the movement of hands away from the body to disperse blocks and channel healing forces to the client's body; the therapist uses a light touch or holds the hand above the body, with the client generally seated.

Threading   Ancient method of hair removal developed in the Middle East and Asia; uses a cotton thread to pull out unwanted hair.

Trager approach   An approach to body work developed in the 1920s by American medical practitioner Dr. Milton Trager; makes extensive use of touch/contact and encourages the client to experience the freeing up of different parts of the body; the approach consists of simple exercises called Mentastics and deep, nonintrusive hands-on work, including fluid, gentle, rocking movements; the idea is to use motion in the muscles and joints to produce positive sensory feelings that then are fed back into the central nervous system; a session takes from 60 to 90 minutes; no oils or lotions are used; the client wears a swimsuit or underwear and lies on a well-padded table in a warm, comfortable environment; after getting up from the table, the client is given instruction in the use of Mentastics, or "mental gymnastics," a system of simple, effortless movement sequences, to maintain and enhance the sense of lightness, freedom, and flexibility instilled by the table work; because it is this feeling state that triggered positive tissue response in the first place, every time the feeling is clearly recalled, the changes deepen, become more permanent, and are more receptive to further positive change; changes described have included the disappearance of specific symptoms, discomforts, or pains; heightened levels of energy and vitality; more effortless posture and carriage; greater joint mobility; deeper states of relaxation than were previously possible; and a new ease in daily activities.

Tui na   Ancient Chinese system of manual therapeutics with a range of techniques and indications; while traditional Chinese medical precepts form its theoretical basis, clinical experience governs its application; techniques range from light and soothing to strong and invigorating. Refined over the centuries, tui na facilitates healing by regulating the circulation of blood and qi (vital energy), which controls body function and enhances resistance to disease; the term *tui na* (pronounced t-weigh na) combines the names of two of the hand techniques, *tui* meaning to push and *na* meaning to lift and squeeze, which are used to represent the system; the term *tui na* first appeared in the Ming Dynasty text, *Pediatric Tui Na Classic,* in 1601.

Udvartana   A stimulating massage incorporated with the application of an herbal paste.

Vichy shower   Invigorating shower treatment from several water jets of varying temperatures and pressures applied while lying on a waterproof cushioned mat or table; treatment is often integrated with exfoliating treatments such as Dulse scrub, loofah, or salt glow.

Vinotherapy   Body treatment that incorporates grapes and wine, including grape syrups, juices, pips, pulp, and grapeseed oil.

Water aerobics (aqua aerobics)   Aerobic workouts performed in a swimming pool; water resistance is utilized to stretch, strengthen, and increase stamina.

Watsu (aquatic shiatsu)   Incorporates stretches that release blockages along the meridians—the channels through which chi or life force flows. Watsu began at Harbin Hot Springs, where Harold Dull brought his knowledge of Zen shiatsu into a warm pool; Dull found the effects of Zen shiatsu could be amplified and made more profound by stretching someone while having him or her float in warm water; by supporting, rocking, and moving the whole body while stretching a leg or arm, Watsu lessens the resistance when a limb is worked in isolation; when the whole body is in continual movement, each move flowing gracefully into the next, it is difficult to anticipate and resist what's coming next

Waxing   Hair removal (depilation) method that involves application and quick removal of a warm wax (sometimes followed by a strip of cloth).

Weight training   Use of free weights or weight machines in a series of repetitive exercises meant to tone the body, build lean muscle mass, and increase metabolism.

Whirlpool/Jacuzzi   A patented design of a whirlpool bath or a mechanism that swirls water in a bath with underwater jets.

Yoga   A variety of Hindu practices developed in ancient India to unify body and mind with universal spirit, thereby encouraging physical and mental well-being; most commonly involves a series of stretching postures (called asanas), breathing exercises, and meditative practices; increases flexibility, improves muscle tone, and is helpful in the reduction of stress.

Note: Some glossary definitions come directly or are adaptations from the following sources: www.curezone.com; http://encarta.msn.com/dictionary; www.experiencefestival.com; www.experienceispa.com; www.healthandwellness.com; www.merriam-webster.com; www.righthealth.com; www.spafinder.com.

Spa Facility Design and Construction

4

LEARNING OBJECTIVES

At the end of this chapter, readers will be able to:

* Describe and understand the spa design process, including site selection, spa construction, and the members and roles of the spa development team.
* Explain general considerations for the design and layout of a new or expanded spa facility.
* Disclose the legal requirements for spa design and construction.
* Understand the development of spa themes and concepts and explain their influence on design.
* Describe various interior design and decoration ideas for a spa.
* Identify various spa design trends.

Design allows a more direct and pleasurable route.

—Charles Eames

With the continuing growth of the spa industry, it is likely that spa managers will encounter several spa design and development projects during their career. Whether the project is as simple as room decoration or as elaborate as the construction of a new full-service spa, some common techniques are required for success. This chapter explores the fundamentals of spa development, design, and construction in the three main sections. First, we define the fundamental elements of spa development, including the vision, concept, and goals. Then we provide an overview of the design process and take the reader from dream to reality. We also address such construction essentials as layout, flow, interior design, spa trends, and common spa requisites. The chapter concludes with a detailed overview of design considerations for each spa area.

➜ SPA DEVELOPMENT

Spa Vision and Goals

All successful plans begin with clear and thoughtful goals, and spa development is no exception. A spa developer usually starts with a vision—a "dream." However, that dream can easily become a nightmare if suitable goals are not established before starting. The vision provides the focus, and the goals are the guiding pathways.

Spa developers should begin by asking a few basic questions: What is the purpose of the spa? Why will guests visit the spa? What type of experience do you hope to provide? And what expectations will the customer have upon entering the spa? Addressing these fundamentals will allow better definition of the spa's operational goals. Moving ahead with a design project requires clarity in the following areas:

▶ **Type of spa:** What category of spa best fits your vision?
▶ **Target market:** What audience will be targeted?
▶ **Spa offerings:** What offerings will be necessary to meet the customer expectations?
▶ **Space:** What guest and operational areas will be needed to provide the desired offerings? How large a facility is necessary to house these areas?
▶ **Staffing:** What staff will be needed to offer the spa services? What types of areas will be needed to sustain staff needs?
▶ **Location:** What location will best fit the vision, the market, and the type of spa proposed?
▶ **Finances:** Based on these decisions, what are budget projections for construction and operation of the spa?

Developing a realistic and conservative budget for your space is likely the most essential step in the first stage of spa development. This budget will help you decide two fundamental questions: (1) How large a space can you afford? (2) Taking account of your projected space requirements, what design will allow you to reach your financial goals? It is common at this stage to find that your original dream may not equate to financial success; you may have to revise some of your earlier decisions and adjust the plan to better ensure long-term realization of your goals.

Spa Concept Development

The most important design considerations for a spa are concept, flow, function, and esthetic. A **spa concept** is a reflection of the vision of the spa—a theme or idea that is incorporated throughout the physical, sensual, and operational elements of the spa. Most sensory elements are integrated in later interior design stages of spa development, but if the physical structure of the spa needs to be altered to incorporate the spa concept, these details need to be clearly defined at the beginning of the project.

The purpose of a spa concept (like a spa "brand," as discussed in Chapter 11), is to differentiate the spa from its competition. A spa concept helps provide focus for the operations and marketing strategy of the spa. A spa concept is often incorporated into the mission and marketing statements of the spa and integrated into all elements of the spa business. Integrating the concept into the physical design of the spa can help the spa stand out and can help establish the spa as a place for an exclusive experience. Once the concept is clear, the spa developer must work to reinforce the idea throughout the design of the space.

The spa concept should be natural, not something the customers will have difficulty understanding. The concept should bring focus, but it should not be too restrictive. Every concept should incorporate something unique yet familiar to spa customers. The spa developer must then use every opportunity to creatively reinforce the concept throughout the design. As a manager, you want your customers to know that they will receive the benefits they seek, and a unique concept can help reinforce that the experience they receive will be unlike any other.

Most spa concepts derive from a few common ideas. Probably the most common is to incorporate natural features into the concept of the spa. For example, managers often use the physical setting of the spa in developing a concept. A spa located seaside or in a desert may have a concept based on its geography. The unique history or culture of an area can also be great fodder for a spa concept. Consider the area's Native American roots or a famous historical figure. Some spas choose to adopt an alternative culture for an exotic impression. Familiar choices, because of their historic influence on the industry, are concepts that integrate an Asian or Indian flavor. Area agriculture or flora might drive a concept; think pineapples in Hawaii, redwoods in

Japanese Garden

California, or cherries in Michigan. Man-made elements can also inspire a distinctive spa concept. The Kohler Corporation has developed two Kohler Water Spas in Wisconsin and St. Andrews, Scotland, which utilize existing and newly created plumbing products to develop a spa with a flowing water theme.

Some spa developers choose a concept based on operational elements of the company. Spa concepts can be based on common business practices, such as being eco-friendly or inexpensive; on a core customer benefit, such as detoxification or weight loss; or just the feeling they hope to impress on their guests.

EXAMPLE SPA CONCEPT IDEAS AND THEIR MARKETING STATEMENTS

Area Elements
- Geography
  - The Spa at Mohonk Mountain House, New Paltz, New York

    "Set in a spectacular natural landscape, The Spa at Mohonk Mountain House is perched atop legendary cliffs above a pristine mountain lake. Since 1869, generations of guests have found a place for recreation and renewal of body, mind, and spirit in our unique mountaintop setting. The Spa at Mohonk Mountain House brings a new dimension to your own remarkable journey. Welcome to our House. Welcome home" (Mohonk Mountain House, 2009).
- History/Culture
  - Skaná, The Spa at Turning Stone Resort, Verona, New York

    "Skaná, where soothing treatments and modern amenities combine with American Indian cultural themes to create the world's most luxuriously unique spa experience. Immerse yourself in the deep, restorative power of true spa therapy, an interpretive sweat lodge and stunning architecture. Skaná is designed to help you bring lifestyle, nutrition and fitness into perfect harmony" (Skaná Spa, 2009).
- Agriculture/Flora
  - GrapeSeed Spa, Southcoast Winery Resort and Spa, Temecula, California

    "Our . . . spa, soothes and re-energizes body, mind and soul with a blend of innovative vine based treatments, state-of-the-art fitness center, private movement studio and secluded places to simply unwind. Stroll tranquil paths among the vines. Soak in an alfresco whirlpool. Reflect on views of Mount Palomar from the veranda . . . paired with a complimentary glass of wine" (Grapeseed Spa, 2009).
- Man-Made Elements
  - The Spa at the Hotel Hershey, Hershey, Pennsylvania

    "Experience total luxury at The Spa at the Hotel Hershey, where chocolate inspires innovative treatments like the Whipped Cocoa Bath, Chocolate Bean Polish, and the Chocolate Fondue Wrap. Leave it to Hershey to make chocolate good for your skin!" (Hotel Hershey Spa, 2009).

Business Elements
- Belief
  - Aveda Spa, nearly 7000 locations in 24 countries

    "Aveda™, The Art and Science of Pure Flower and Plant Essences™, was founded in 1978 with the goal of providing beauty industry professionals with high performance, botanically based products that would be better for service providers and their guests, as well as for the planet" (Aveda, 2009).

- Core Benefit
  - Elizabeth Arden Red Door Spas, 30 locations in the United States and London

    "A leader in the industry, Red Door Spas is committed to enhancing the lives of our guests through beauty, harmony and well-being . . . and is the ongoing vision of day spa pioneer Elizabeth Arden. Her fundamental belief that beauty should be an intelligent union of nature and science to develop one's finest natural assets is carried out through our innovative treatments and quality services, with scientifically-proven and advanced ingredients" (Red Door, 2009).
- Impression
  - The Spa at the Bellagio, Las Vegas, Nevada

    "Step inside our ever so inviting Spa and breathe. Within, a bliss-inspiring, comprehensive selection of therapeutic facial and body care treatments, and an invigorating exercise facility will elate your senses. Soothe the mind and awaken the spirit in Las Vegas" (Bellagio Spa, 2009).

The spa concept can provide focus for spa operations such as selection of menu items, a company logo, treatment protocols, or music selections. A clear spa concept will lead naturally to a focus for any marketing campaign. Decisions made about the interior and exterior design of the spa can draw from the spa concept in many ways. A spa concept can be continuously integrated into many elements of design or can be focused on one or two signature elements to identify the business. Materials selected for construction, such as flooring, wall surfaces, and light fixtures, can all reflect the spa concept. Building colors, scents, and sounds can also support the selected concept. Space signage and clever wording can communicate the essence of the spa concept. Staffing, training, and even uniforms can help provide the customer with a one-of-a-kind themed experience.

THE GOLDEN DOOR CONCEPT

Known for her innovative and sometimes controversial business decisions, Deborah Szekley decided shortly after the end of World War II to design her first Golden Door spa in Escondido, California, with a Japanese theme. Although many spa owners would not have taken the risk, for Deborah it was only natural. Walking through this well-known spa, a guest will encounter koi ponds, Zen gardens, Japanese gardens, and a million-dollar Japanese art collection, all with the intent of immersing the guest in a place that is truly out of this world. During the period of spa development, Deborah Szekley was reading and learning about Zen philosophy and the simple structure and forms of the Japanese culture. Designing and building a Japanese inn in southern California helped her provide the guest a unique experience, which has welcomed and served the "weary traveler" for over 50 years (Caldwell, 2010).

SPA DESIGN

The Spa Design Process

Once the preliminary development tasks of defining the vision and concept and setting the goals are complete, it is time to start putting the ideas into action. All design projects follow the same general progression: focusing in on space needs and defining a preliminary layout; assembling a professional team; finding a location; and refining the plan. Once the site is identified, the spa development team enters the construction phase, which includes further modification of the floor plan, planning and implementation of construction, preparation for opening, and, finally, opening day.

Whether the dream is to develop and open a small day spa or to develop a destination resort, it all starts with a **schematic design**—a rough draft of the layout you anticipate for your spa. At this stage the drawings do not have to be perfect, just an estimated rendering of how you envision the space. Sometimes called block planning, this stage of the design process often includes a hand-drawn or rough sketch that simply shows the relationships among blocks of space such as reception, waiting, and retail; social and serene; dry and wet; guest and nonguest; mechanical, electrical, and plumbing. If the facility is spread over multiple floors, this may mean stacking various elements to ensure intelligent use of mechanics, electrical, and plumbing. This initial stage of design allows the developer to get a sense of the overall size and type of spa to be built, which allows for smarter decisions when selecting a site for the spa.

Site Selection

Choosing the right location for a spa can be the difference between spa success and failure. Some locations will obviously be more advantageous than others, but there may be many worthy options in selecting a new spa site. For example, one location may be of ample size and reasonable cost, but accessibility may be difficult for the anticipated target audience. Another may be in a visible location with impressive traffic flow, but the cost of acquisition and property taxes may put undue strain on the budget. In the end, selecting a suitable spa location requires considering a number of variables. Each variable can be integrated into either a regional analysis or a site analysis (Sawyer, 2005). **Regional analysis** includes gathering data about the off-site surroundings, both man-made and natural, to test the compatibility between the business and its environment. **Site analysis** focuses on characteristics of the location itself. Completing both types of analysis will ensure that the spa development team has the information it needs to make a suitable site selection.

A regional analysis should include each of the following:

1. **Population composition**—Is the site convenient to the defined target audience?
2. **Competition**—Who is the primary competition in the region? Will your spa attract an adequate number of guests to secure profitability?
3. **Regional accessibility**—Is the location easily approachable?
4. **Land uses**—What kind of development surrounds the site? Could there be off-site flooding, erosion, or pollution at the location?
5. **Regional influences**—Are there historic or aesthetic characteristics in the area that can be used to enhance or potentially cause problems for the project?

A site analysis should include:

1. **Availability**—Is the site obtainable? Does the type of agreement, such as lease, rental, or ownership, fit your needs?
2. **Zoning and easements**—Is the location zoned for commercial use and not restrictive to services to be offered at the spa?
3. **Size of the site or space**—Is there adequate space for construction or development of the facility, parking, etc.?

4. **Site accessibility**—Is the site physically easy to access, considering the entrance to the location and/or facility?
5. **Utilities availability**—Are adequate utilities available to run the operation? Consider water supply, sewage, electrical, telephone, and other utilities.
6. **Land characteristics**—Are they compatible with your plan, or will the land need to be adjusted?
7. **Adjacent land uses**—Do any properties next to the proposed site have the potential for noise, pollution, or other nuisances?
8. **Support services**—How close are local police, fire, emergency medical personnel, and hospitals?
9. **Economic impact of the site**—What economic conditions associated with the location may directly affect your bottom line, such as available workforce, property taxes, utility costs, labor costs, etc?
10. **Price**—What will it cost to acquire and prepare the site for construction or development?

Refining the Plan

Once a site is acquired and a site plan developed to fit the characteristics of the location, the original schematic drawings should be adjusted to fit the location. Moving from the schematic or block planning to a detailed design will advance the project by fitting the various elements of the facility toward the final floor plan. This stage takes into account fixed building constraints, such as the footprint of the building, structural columns, fire paths, stairs, and elevators.

Further refinements of the plan, incorporating the unique operational qualities of the spa, are integrated at this stage to arrive at the final drawings for the project. These final drawings (once called blueprints), when approved by the facility design team, spawn more detailed drawings that define the exact work to be completed. These subsequent drawings likely include site work, concrete and masonry, electrical, air circulation (HVAC), and water circulation (plumbing). If construction of the facility will enter a bidding process, this is the stage at which this practice will take place.

FACILITY DESIGN TEAM

There are often a number of individuals involved in the design and construction of a business space. The size and scope of the project will determine the level of assistance. For a small project, the team may include only a few; for a large project, a variety and greater number of professionals will be helpful. Following is a list of possible members of the facility design team and their responsibilities (Cohen and Bodeker, 2008).

- ▶ **Architects**—Prepare and review all plans for construction.
- ▶ **Interior designers**—Responsible for interior materials, finishes, colors, space planning, and layout.
- ▶ **Electrical engineers**—Responsible for electrical planning and permits.
- ▶ **Mechanical engineers**—Responsible for air and water circulation.
- ▶ **Contractors or builders**—Responsible for turning the architects' plans into reality.
- ▶ **Specialty contractors**—Tradespeople, including painters, roofers, plumbers, etc.
- ▶ **Acoustical engineers**—Sound and noise specialists.

> ▶ **Information technology and audio-visual specialists**—Responsible for communication and presentation elements.
> ▶ **Landscapers**—Select and place outdoor plants and design topography.
> ▶ **Interior plantscapers**—Select and position indoor plants.
> ▶ **Kitchen designers**—Develop plans and drawings for commercial kitchens.
> ▶ **Health inspector**—Reviews and approves new and remodel plans and spaces.
> ▶ **Owner or owner**'s representative—Coordinates the design team and manages the project.
> ▶ **Spa manager and/or spa consultant**—Additional manager of the project and occasionally liaison between owner and design team.

Because of the unique nature of a spa space and tremendous growth in the industry, there has been an increase in the number of spa design consultants. Spa consultants can be involved in various stages of spa development, including concept development, architecture and design, site acquisition, market analysis, supply and equipment acquisition, and project management for the spa development project. Whether or not a consultant is hired, a spa manager must have an understanding of the basic principles of spa design and be diligent about enforcing these principles throughout the project. Selecting an architect who has past success in spa design is essential to the overall success of the project.

A typical procedure for construction includes selecting or publicly broadcasting a detailed design document to qualified bidders. These documents may be for the entire project or for specific elements of the project. Typically, developers are hoping for three to five bids for comparison and successful selection. "Three allows a 'good, bad and ugly' comparison of quotations, and five begins to get unmanageable from a review and decision-making basis" (Cohen and Bodeker, 2008). Awarding of contracts follows the decisions, which should be based not just on cost, but also on qualifications, reputation, timeliness, and understanding of the project.

Once the development team has been selected, management issues begin to move into cost and budget control, program expansion and/or contraction, design review, schedule oversight, quality assurance, code compliance, and communication with the facility building team (Sawyer, 2005). Because construction is a multilayered process, meaning that many tasks depend on the completion of others, most developers lay out the assorted tasks in a detailed schedule to map the progression of the project and help ensure timely completion.

Once the project is complete, a formal "handover" of some sort occurs, at which the construction team carefully reviews the project with the owner or the owner's representative, who then accepts the work so that the owner can move forward with the operation of the business. Contractors will train management on any technical elements of the facility. Once the project is accepted, any outstanding payments are generally released.

SPA LAYOUT AND CONSTRUCTION

A spa developer must consider many elements in working out a detailed floor plan for a spa. Some of these considerations include legal requirements as well as general guidelines to enhance the flow, esthetics, and effectiveness of the space. The remainder of this chapter will highlight common laws associated with design and construction, provide written descriptions of the most important general considerations for the development of a spa, mention some current design trends, and conclude with a discussion of interior design and decoration. A list of detailed design considerations, organized by spa area, is provided at the end of the chapter.

⟶ LAWS GOVERNING SPA DESIGN AND CONSTRUCTION

There are laws that govern the operation of a spa, some of which will be described in Chapter 9, but there are also some legal aspects that must be considered during spa design and construction. These laws and regulations are found at various levels of government.

Local Regulations

In planning and building a spa, it is necessary to check into local regulations and requirements for building permits and inspections for construction, plumbing, and electrical installations. Other local regulations that may need to be considered are zoning restrictions as well as fire and emergency codes.

Spas can be situated in land zoned for commercial, industrial, or, sometimes, other uses by way of a conditional use permit. A **conditional use** is one that is not usually permitted for that type of zoning. For example, a residential spa to be located in a residential zone might require a conditional use permit (sometimes called a variance) in order to operate. Some cities also have specific zoning ordinances for businesses that perform massage services (Griffin, 2005).

A number of common local construction permits usually need to be acquired from a city hall office of zoning and building inspector (Tezak, 2002). These include a general building permit and plumbing, electrical, and sign permits. Pools (including whirlpools and hot tubs) are generally regulated and require use permits issued by a local or regional health department.

City, county, and state building codes dictate exit door placement; a minimum of two exits is always needed. Fire alarm systems and facility capacity policies must meet all state and local fire laws and regulations.

State Regulations

State Boards of Cosmetology and Departments of Health help regulate the majority of spas across the country, but other state agencies may also be in regulating spas. These regulations vary by state. Some design elements may even be dictated, such as flooring (Tezak, 2002, p. 67).

Federal Regulations

The Occupational Safety and Health Administration (**OSHA**), part of the U.S. Department of Labor, and the **Americans with Disabilities Act (ADA)**, enforced by the U.S. Department of Justice, have significant influence over how a spa is designed and constructed. OSHA was established to ensure a comfortable and safe working environment for workers. For example, OSHA regulates ventilation of chemicals in nail and hair areas of a spa to protect workers and guests from the fumes and particles emitted during these services. Sanitation, disinfection, and storage of equipment and supplies are also regulated by OSHA. For example, if you perform extractions or waxing and, consequently, have exposure to blood-borne pathogens, you are required to follow specified procedures and have special disposal cabinets for the lancets and other instruments. Further, treatment products and clean supplies, including linen, are required to be stored in closed containers. The numbers of toilets needed in a building are identified based on structure and capacity. The procedures for using hazardous chemicals are also specified (Griffin, 2005).

The Americans with Disabilities Act was enacted to extend civil rights protection to people with disabilities. When defining the structure of a public space, careful consideration must be taken to ensure that both spa guests and employees have equal access to all relevant areas of the facility. For guests this means "front of the house" areas; for employees, "back of the house" areas as well. It's all a matter of equal access, opportunity, and safety. As part of this landmark legislation, an ADA Accessibility Guidelines document was developed to detail rules for construction. Building contractors are generally familiar with these guidelines; however, your knowledge of the extent of these rules is also important.

ADA requirements are comprehensive and address items such as the required size and number of parking spaces for the handicapped, heights of drinking fountains and telephones, sizes and numbers of toilets for bathroom facilities, sizes of entrances, exits, corridors, and doors throughout the facility, dimensions for dressing areas, and signage requirements. Because spas typically have hydrotherapy and specialty offerings, be aware that ADA dictates that all guests are required to have full and equal access to all services and facilities. The law states that "reasonable accommodation must be made for the disabled person, unless such an accommodation would impose undue hardship on the employer." To review details of the ADA requirements, the federal government has available a great selection of online resources that can be examined at www.ada.gov.

➜ GENERAL SPA DESIGN CONSIDERATIONS

A Guest's Spa Experience

Spa design affects everything you experience through all the senses while visiting a spa. "A spa experience is the most sensual of all, as you are in a state of heightened awareness, very in touch with your body and how it reacts to everything around it—the sight of the room, the taste of the water, the sound of music, the smell of lotion. Design can orchestrate this experience in every detail—from beginning to end," Says Robert D. Henry, Spa Designer (Taylor, 2009). First and foremost, the spa design must have a logical flow that follows the sequential elements of a spa experience.

Each spa experience can be described as occurring in three primary phases. Phase one includes the guest entering the facility, being greeted, being checked in, and preparing for the experience. In phase two the guest may enter into a self-guided experience or, if receiving a treatment, is once again greeted, this time by the service provider, is escorted to the treatment location, and experiences the treatment and posttreatment. (Phase two will repeat if the guest has chosen more than one treatment.) Phase three is the guest preparing for departure, retail exposure, checking out, and a fond farewell. Each phase of the guest and employer experience can be influenced by design.

So, when developing the structure of the spa, consider the guest's path through all three phases of the experience. Consider that, depending on the guest's selected service, the experience will be different. Those entering the spa for a nail or hair treatment, for example, will likely have a different waiting space than those visiting for a treatment for which changing one's clothes or relaxing in a pretreatment hydrotherapy space may be desired. Those choosing a self-guided experience, such as working out on a piece of exercise equipment or enjoying a steam, may never stop to use a waiting area or be required to check out.

Bear in mind that if single-gender spaces are anticipated, the experience may be different for men and women. In all of the guest or **front of the house** areas, the design team must work to minimize duplicate passageways into the same area or location. This redundancy is a waste of space, and wasted space in a spa corresponds directly to lost revenue. As an example, place the locker rooms near the pretreatment and hydrotherapy areas for easy transition.

Guest areas need to be spacious and open, yet small enough or augmented to have a cozy, comfortable feel. Another key element to consider when designing a spa is privacy. Like a doctor's office, spas must be designed to protect the privacy of the visitors. There are several areas of a spa where guests may be wearing sparse clothing, such as robes or bathing attire. Guests will change clothing in treatment and locker rooms, and there may be some hydrotherapy areas where nudity is the norm. Each of these spaces must be designed to allow all guests to feel comfortable in whatever stage of undress they find themselves.

To protect a guest's physical privacy, treatment waiting and pretreatment areas should be shielded from public traffic areas. Improper line-of-sight issues can lead to guest privacy concerns. Like the doctor's office, doors to treatment and locker rooms typically open into the center of the room, so that providers can crack the doors and talk with guests without having them exposed to the provider or other passers-by. Many fitness centers have designed their fitness and movement studios to offer unrestricted viewing, and some viewing is necessary for safety and security purposes. However, the current trend in design is to be more protective of the privacy of the guests in these areas, and not allow for public viewing. Often medical conditions are discussed between the treatment provider or spa counselor and the guest. The areas where these topics are discussed must also be designed for privacy.

The Social and the Serene

All spa areas should be grouped by sound levels. There are two distinct areas in a spa, the social and the serene. The *social area* is where chatter, conversation, and lively music are common. In these areas the energy is high, lighting is bright, and individuals should feel comfortable speaking in an everyday voice. Social guest areas

Relaxation Lounge

consisting of reception, retail, exercise and fitness studios, and the salon and are commonly found near the front of the spa. Social staff areas include lounge and changing areas, storage and dispensary areas, and, because of the additional sound generation, laundry, elevator, and hydrotherapy equipment spaces.

A variety of spa offerings, however, lend themselves to a quieter setting. These *serene areas* include treatment rooms, pretreatment areas, lounge/waiting areas, client consultation rooms, and locker/changing areas. Grouping the serene areas helps protect this tranquil environment. Physical barriers and alcoves can be placed between social and serene areas to help maintain their unique atmospheres. Less foot traffic equals less chance for congestion and less noise in the facility, so it is important to orchestrate the guest experience to minimize the amount of foot traffic in the spa, especially in the serene areas. Surface and acoustic materials selected for the serene areas should help to mute sounds generated in the space. Sounds and music can be generated to help maintain the ambiance. Lights are typically muted to project a feeling of relaxation.

The Employee's Spa Experience

Employee traffic patterns must also be considered. Areas that are used only by the spa staff are often called the **back of the house** (BOH). The importance of the size and flow of these areas grows in direct proportion to the size of the spa. A small day spa may need very limited nonguest areas to function properly, but for large spas the staff areas can be more important than the guest areas for operational effectiveness. If the BOH areas are not laid out properly, the logistics of exchanging laundry, products, and therapists can be very difficult. The elements are the same no matter the size of the spa, yet the capacities and frequency of use will vary.

The size and number of staff areas varies, depending on the number and variety of spa offerings. In general, for a self-contained spa, 10 percent of the spa's floor space should be dedicated to BOH. At least 4 percent of the BOH area should comprise administrative and reservation offices and audio room (Lumley and Glover, 2008). Depending on the setup, resort and destination spas may require less BOH space, because the required areas for laundry, a staff lounge, and housekeeping may be located off-site.

It is suggested that a spa developer mentally walk through each possible guest and employee experience, test a variety of scenarios, and lay out the facility to ensure a smooth flowing experience for all. When testing the flow of the space, issues of safety for all individuals in the spa, as well as security of the facility and its property, should be examined. Although pathways may be dictated to some extent by fire codes, they must be checked for ease of exit in the case of any emergency.

Operational Efficiencies

In addition to separating areas into social and serene, it is also common to group areas by temperature and moisture. Heating, air, and plumbing systems can be more effective and efficient if they are concentrated in certain areas of a facility. Careful arrangement of these areas during the design process will not only simplify construction, it will also save on utility bills. Consider what areas of the spa may need to be maintained at a cooler temperature and, if possible, locate them together in the layout. Do the same for warmer areas. Cooler areas include those areas where equipment and/or the numbers and movement of people may make it difficult to maintain a consistent temperature, or areas where the comfort of the guest dictates a cooler temperature. Common cooler areas will likely include laundry, fitness and exercise studios, salon, and locker rooms. Warmer areas may include wet and dry treatment rooms, reception and waiting areas, and hydrotherapy rooms, where the local health department often dictates a temperature of 82°F to prevent condensation.

Similarly, wet and dry areas are typically segmented. Because of the temperature, flooring, plumbing, drainage, and the need to slope floors for drainage, wet areas are commonly located near one another. Ease of plumbing alone should not dictate the design of any space, but when possible, segmenting the space so that areas that use water are placed logically will reduce the cost of construction and facilitate the operation of the spa. Water sources in a salon area may include a hand-washing sink for therapists and acrylic nail clients, hair-washing stations, and pedicure baths, which are most often built-in sinks. In locker facilities there will be sinks, showers, and toilets. Pretreatment hydrotherapy areas where water and draining is needed include steam, sauna, whirlpools, and rinsing showers. All treatment rooms require sinks, and wet rooms need central drains and possibly a drain at the door threshold to prevent water leaking outside and into hallways. (Dry treatment rooms, if used only for select massage treatments, do not require a water source.) The dispensary room will need at minimum a utility sink and possibly a dish washer. The laundry requires proper draining for washing machines.

Consider guest supervision when designing the space. There are a variety of areas that require constant supervision—reception, retail, pools, cafes/kitchens, and fitness areas, to name a few. Depending on the size and offerings in the spa, the size of the staff may be anywhere from three to over a hundred. Supervising areas is one way to ensure the safety and quality of the guest experience. However, the spa manager must also consider the cost associated with these positions. It may be wise to review the types of spaces and the flow of guests and take measures to ensure that supervision stations are adequate, yet not too costly, for the maintenance of the operation.

Revenue-Generating Spaces

When it comes to design, the primary focus must be the return on investment (ROI). One of the most discussed concerns in the design of a spa is the ratio of revenue-generating to non–revenue-generating spaces. There needs to be a delicate balance of the two spaces, those that relate directly to revenue production and those that constitute "amenity space." **Revenue-generating spaces** include treatment rooms, retail spaces, salon, cafés, or any spaces where a guest must pay to participate. Common **non–revenue-generating spaces** include all back-of-the-house areas, waiting/lounge areas, consulting spaces, corridors, locker/changing rooms, and any spaces considered pretreatment, such as plunge pools, whirlpools, steam, sauna, and inhalation rooms.

Amenity space is certainly necessary to enhance the spa experience, but how much is too much? In a site with limited space, these spaces equate to less revenue for the spa and more overhead expense. Some say that, on average, 60 percent of the space must be revenue-generating. Of course, this figure will vary based on the type and size of spa. For example, day and medical spas are typically smaller and more limited in their offerings, therefore need less back-of-the-house and amenity space. Resort spas tend to be larger, offer a wider range of services, and although sometimes the back-of-the-house areas may be off-site, it is common for there to be more pretreatment options and therefore a need for more non–revenue-producing space. Here are some guidelines. Spas with less than 1000 square feet should use 70–80 percent of the space for revenue. Spas of sizes ranging from 1000 to 3000 square feet should use about 55–60 percent. Spas 3000 to 7000 square feet should use 45–50 percent, and spas larger than 7000 square feet should use about 40 percent as their guideline for revenue-producing space.

Plunge Pool

Unique and Single-Use Spa Service Spaces

All spa managers want to develop a spa that stands out from the competition. Design is one way to make a spa unique. Designing a signature area of the spa or using a unique design for a signature treatment area is an effective technique. Several spas in North America can provide examples of this technique. Consider a private napping space in New York City's YeloSpa, a Native American–inspired sound therapy room at Sanibel Harbour Resort and Spa in Ft. Myers, Florida, or a meditation labyrinth at Golden Door spas.

Outdoor Spaces

To expand an indoor spa facility or to enhance a spa treatment, some spas are moving outside, if the location and weather lends itself to this practice. In rural resort settings, it is common to find massages, exercise classes, and other offerings on resort grounds. Think about a massage on the beach or a Tai Chi class on a mountain.

While indoor facilities lend themselves better to privacy, intimacy, and security, the outdoors can bring benefits of its own. If developers select to design an outside space for use, the following elements must also be considered. There are climate and moisture concerns to consider. Exposure to sun, high levels of humidity, or salt air will accelerate the aging of spa equipment. Measures must be taken, and possibly additional space designated, for maintaining outdoor equipment. For example, storing tables in a clean, dry area when they are not in use is an option, or using a drape or cover on a table surface to protect the upholstery from sun, moisture, and oils. Additional maintenance may be needed, such as spraying metal equipment parts with with a light oil or lubricant as an extra layer of protection (Gemmill, 2006). Also consider that access to electricity may be limited or unavailable.

Whether the spaces are indoors or outdoors, as a spa manager it will be your responsibility to encourage the entire creative team, throughout the design process, to understand that if it comes down to a choice between operational flow and beauty, function must always win out. Understanding the operation will provide a spa manager with key insight into the design process. Only you can understand why squeezing one more treatment room into the plan can be the difference between profitability and failure, why you would not locate a treatment waiting area next to the café kitchen, or why the dispensary and laundry need to be easily accessible to the staff, yet unnoticeable to the guests.

For more detail on designing each area of a spa, refer to the special section at the end of the chapter, "Design Considerations by Spa Area." This section provides comprehensive information on the activities occurring and space considerations for each of the most common guest areas in a spa, including the public reception and welcome area, retail/spa boutique, men's and women's locker/changing/vanity areas, pretreatment hydrotherapy area, treatment waiting area, salon area, treatment spaces, including dry and wet treatment rooms, exercise/movement studio, and fitness equipment studio. In addition to these spaces, a spa developer may also consider private relaxation/meditation areas, swimming pools and other aquatics, multipurpose rooms for education, demonstrations, and group consultations, a spa café or juice bar, a library, and recreation and sports facilities. Back-of-the-house areas are also detailed, including, administrative offices, staff lounge and changing area, storage/dispensary areas, laundry/housekeeping, and equipment storage and utility spaces.

DESIGN TRENDS

Feng Shui

Feng Shui (pronounced "fung shway") is an ancient art of placement to bring balance and harmony to a physical space. Practicing Feng Shui brings balance to a space, increasing the likelihood of better health, wealth, and relationships (Kelly, 2000). Because the purpose of a spa is to assist in enhancing the well-being of the client, Feng Shui principles are commonly incorporated into the design and placement of items in a spa to assist in creating "good energy." Energy, also known as chi (or qi), is the life force of the universe and the focus of Feng Shui. A loose translation of Feng Shui is "wind and water." Feng represents the wind that carries the chi throughout the space. Shui is the water that meanders underneath the earth transporting chi.

The first principle of Feng Shui is harmonizing the flow of chi in the environment to support the goals of the spa. Those trained in Feng Shui design first identify where there may be restricted energy. Then they will rearrange or add elements to redirect and enhance the energy. Feng Shui designers traditionally use a **ba gua** (also known as ba-gua or pa kua) map to assist with this process.

One use of the ba gua map is to align the career area of the map with the entrance to the space (a room or the entire space). Some people who practice Feng Shui line up the map with a southwest compass direction. Once this is done, the eight primary areas of the space can be identified. Upon identification, the spa manager can enhance the areas of the spa based on operational goals. For example, if a spa manager hopes to improve the reputation of the spa, he or she may place enhancing

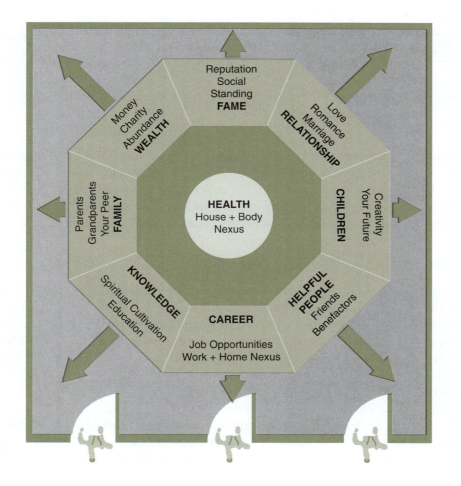

Figure 4.1 Feng Shui Ba Gua Map

Source: Feng Shui by Peter Reiss (2010). Retrieved on March 17, 2010 from http://www.feng-shuiconsults.com/2009/07/06/seeing-with-the-s-d-b-method-or-what%e2%80%99s-been-hiding-in-your-chi-closet/

Figure 4.2 Feng Shui Elements Chart

Source: Dr. Roger J. West (2010). Retrieved on March 17, 2010 from http://www.westfengshui.com/about fengshui.htm

Eight Trigram Attribute Chart

Name	Image	Family Member	Body Part	Illness Injury	Element	Compass Direction	Star Number
Chien	Heaven	Father (CEO, Owner)	Head Lungs	Head, Pulmonary	Metal	Northwest	6
Kun	Earth	Mother, Matriach	Abdomen, Womb	Digestive, abdominal	Earth	Southwest	2
Chen	Thunder	Eldest Son	Legs, Feet, Throat	Legs, Throat, Hysteria	Wood	East	3
Kan	Deep Abyss	Middle Son, Middle Aged Man	Ears, Kidney	Vertigo, Kidney, Bladder, Blood	Water	North	1
Ken	Mountain	Youth, Youngest son	Hands, Arms, Back	Hand, arms, small bones	Earth	Northeast	8
Sun	Penetrating Wind	Eldest Daughter	Buttocks	Hips, thighs, buttocks	Wood	Southeast	4
Li	Illuminating Fire	Middle Daughter, Middle Aged Woman	Eyes, Heart	Eye disease or injury, Heart problems	Fire	South	9
Tui	Joyous Marsh	Youngest Daughter, Women	Mouth, Chest	Injury illness to mouth or chest	Metal	West	7

elements such as water, plants, wind chimes, mirrors, or red items in the space directly opposite the front door to bring about greater fame to the business. Each point on the ba gua map is represented by a life aspiration, and also by a physical element, planet, color, shape, direction, and even an area of the human body. These corresponding elements can be used creatively to augment and energize the space.

Environmentally Friendly Design

Over the last 10 years, the spa industry has learned a lot about reducing its carbon footprint. Because of the nature of the business, spas are ideally suited to support the integration of environmentally friendly practices. Spas tend to generate a large amount of carbon output, so this step was not only reasonable but necessary. Terms such as *sustainability, eco-friendly, organic,* and *natural* are all used to describe this effort to become more environmentally friendly. As these efforts have increased, the industry has learned that incorporating "green" practices not only promotes a healthier work environment, it can also lower operating costs.

In terms of protecting the environment, spa managers should consider creating a space that functions in harmony with the earth and its inhabitants. Techniques such as using natural light and power, as well as organic and indigenous products, are a beginning. There are three areas of focus to make a spa eco-friendly: (1) space planning, (2) materials and finishes, and (3) energy efficiency. Ufland and Sternfeld (2009) provide several examples of things that spa managers can do to reduce their carbon footprint. When developing the floor plan for the spa, it is important to pay special attention to the flow of the space and effective use of space. A well-designed layout that minimizes unused spaces and maximizes revenue-producing spaces means greater efficiency of movement, less expenditure of energy, and a better bottom-line return for the spa. When it comes to design and construction materials, concentrate on recycled, reused, and re-sorted materials. To prolong the life of the space, select materials that are durable and timeless. Purchase paints and finishes with low or no volatile organic compounds (VOCs), non–petroleum-based fabrics, and formaldehyde-free materials, as these compounds are known to have harmful health effects. Whenever possible, use natural materials and buy locally. Consider integrating cultural and artistic traditions into design.

Energy efficiency has come a long way in recent years. Alternative energy sources, such solar and wind, are much more common and affordable than in the past. In addition, the federal Energy Policy Act of 2005 expanded the federal business energy tax credit for solar and geothermal energy property to include fuel cells and microturbines as well as hybrid solar lighting systems (Singer, 2009b). Installing larger windows and skylights in spas have helped lessen the need for artificial lighting and provide another avenue to let nature into the spa. On the other hand, strategic placement of trees, curtains, and using reflective film on windows can help decrease the heat entering the spa on a sunny day.

Using compact flourescent lamps (CFLs) and LED lighting can lower electricity bills. Energy Star ratings on large electric equipment, such as laundry machines, ceiling fans, and water heaters, have provided spa managers with the information necessary to be smarter and more energy-efficient consumers. Operating equipment more efficiently can also save on energy bills, such as using automatic timers on lights and on heating and cooling equipment.

REALITY CHECK

What is LEED?

If you are entering a spa construction project, you need to be familiar with LEED. **LEED** stands for Leadership in Energy and Environmental Design and is an internationally recognized green building certification system, providing third-party verification that a building or community was designed and built using strategies aimed at improving performance across all the metrics that matter most: energy savings, water efficiency, CO_2 emissions reduction, improved indoor environmental quality, and stewardship of resources and sensitivity to their impacts. The LEED program provides facility owners and operators with a framework for identifying and implementing practical and measurable green building design and construction solutions (U.S. Green Building Council, 2010).

Knowing the origin of the word *spa* to be water, it is no surprise that there are many areas of the spa that utilize water. Thus there are many options available to help conserve water. A few of these include: purchasing low-flow options for washers, toilets, and showers; reclaiming and reusing on-site waste water; and using nonpotable water for landscape irrigation, toilet flushing, and custodial needs.

↪ INTERIOR DESIGN AND DECORATION

The design of a spa space should enhance the treatments and services offered by the business. The design ultimately affects the overall guest experience. Good planning and attention to detail are fundamental to success. A tranquil décor is essential for instilling the appropriate sense of place for a spa. Interior design should provide a residential, not institutional, feeling.

A well-designed spa provides good flow and is functional, but it is also comfortable and pleasing to the senses. Subdued lighting, rich fabrics and carpeting, luxurious furniture, sophisticated art, and plants and fresh flowers are all avenues to this end. Interior designers commonly work with furniture, cabinetry, shelving, wall and window coverings, lighting, paint, and other elements to create the ambiance of the space.

Lighting

Lighting can be both esthetic and functional. Bright and ample lighting can help improve safety outside the spa walls and in parking areas. Inside the spa, lighting can be used to accent prominent facility features such as sculpture, artwork, or particular spa products. Light fixtures should be selected to harmonize with the concept of the spa and can be used to light pathways throughout the space. In treatment areas, lighting should support the task at hand. Soft lighting, such as accent lights or candles, are all that are typically needed for a massage treatment. For treatments that require detailed work, such as facials and hair removal, task lighting or brighter overhead lighting is needed.

There are a variety of ways to light a space, and each has a particular purpose. The basics include ceiling lights, spotlights, tube lights, chandeliers, wall lighting, and lamps (Tezak, 2002). Ceiling lights are standard. However, they will not give off much light unless many are used. Spot lights (free-standing, recessed in the ceiling or on tracks) can be directed to various areas of the spa. Be cautious with recessed spot lights, as once they are in place they cannot be moved, creating limits on movement of furniture and fixtures. Fluorescent tube lighting produces the most light and is the cheapest to operate, but it does little for the décor of the room (Tezak, 2002). If fluorescent lighting is used in the spa, be sure to use bulbs of warm tones in dressing areas and in the salon, as these are more flattering to the complexion. Chandeliers visually enhance a space. Chandeliers come in many shapes and sizes and should be selected based on the décor and concept of the spa and on ease of cleaning. Indirect lighting and wall sconces are used to provide soft lighting and ambiance. To add additional lighting to a dark space, table and floor lamps can be used.

Color

Color has an emotional affect on people and can prompt a wide range of reactions. While broad assortments of colors are being used in design today, it is important to be aware of the possible outcomes of a color selection. When selecting colors, consider the following guidelines (Minton, 2002; D'Angelo, 2006):

- ▶ Soft, muted color tones tend to be soothing; bright colors are more stimulating.
- ▶ Less is more: Select only four or five colors to use throughout the space.
- ▶ Select colors that complement or at least do not contrast with one another.
- ▶ When working with bold colors, use natural lighting and textures to balance the space.
- ▶ Select colors that will still look new after a little wear.
- ▶ In making color selections, consider the common color associations listed in Table 4.1.

TABLE 4.1

Colors and Their Associated Attributes

Warm colors	Red	Stimulation, power, strength
	Orange	Social, cheerful, bold, cheerful
	Yellow	Soothing, enlightenment, inspiration
Neutral colors	White	Purity, clean, safe, refreshing
	Brown	Natural, safe, casual, earthy
	Black	Dramatic, mysterious, sophisticated
Cool colors	Blue	Tranquil, conservative, refreshing
	Green	Relaxing, calming, balancing
	Purple/pink	Peaceful, spiritual, creative

The trend in spa color selection today is to focus on what are being called "Colorado colors" (Hill, 2009). These are muted tones of mushroom, beige, warm and soft tones based on browns and peaches to soft bronzes/rusts, or environmental colors of the sky, sand, and flowers. There is no perfect palette in spa color selection; it is best to consider the concept and the ambiance of the space to select colors that best fit the vision of the spa.

Materials and Surfaces

In selecting materials and surfaces for the spa, the focus should be on function. Select materials that are durable, lasting, and appropriate to the space. Stain-resistant, attractive, easily washable, and easy to repair (or match) are also important characteristics. Some areas of the spa can get moist, so materials selected for flooring need to also not be slippery.

As discussed earlier in the chapter, going "green" is in. So, understandably, the use of natural materials and surfaces may also be preferred. A wide range of ecologically sound, nontoxic, nonhazardous materials are available today that can be just as resilient as their synthetic counterparts. The "green" movement has also led to surfaces made from naturally textured woods, such as bamboo and cork, which are harvested without harm to the environment. Stone, tile, rock, clay, and recycled products are also being used (D'Angelo, 2006). Plants and flowers can also add ambiance to a spa, and with the variety of flora available can fit any concept.

KEY TERMS

Americans with Disabilities Act (ADA)

Ba gua

Back of the house

Conditional use

Feng Shui

Front of the house

LEED

Non–revenue-generating spaces

OSHA

Regional analysis

Revenue-generating spaces

Schematic design

Site analysis

Spa concept

REVIEW QUESTIONS

1. What are the primary steps in the spa design process?
2. Who are the key individuals on a design and construction team, and what are their roles?
3. What is a business concept? List the seven common foundational elements of a concept and provide examples of each.
4. When investigating a site for construction, what are the two common types of analysis?
5. Name ten key considerations for designing a spa.
6. Describe a current spa design trend.
7. What is interior design, and how does it affect spa spaces?

→ REFERENCES

Aveda (2009). Retrieved August 12, 2009, from http://aveda.aveda.com/aboutaveda/index.asp.

Bellagio Spa (2009). Retrieved August 12, 2009, from www.bellagio.com/spasalon.

Caldwell, Rachel (2010). Spa Director, The Golden Door Spa, Escondido, CA. Personal communication, June 17, 2010.

Cohen, Mark, and Bodeker, Gerard (Eds.) (2008). *Understand the Global Spa Industry.* Oxford, UK: Elsevier.

D'Angelo, Janet M. (2006). *Spa Business Strategies: A Plan for Success.* Clifton Park, NY: Thomson Delmar Learning.

Eames, Charles (n.d.). BrainyQuote.com. Retrieved June 16, 2010, from www.brainyquote.com/quotes/quotes/c/charleseam398429.html.

Gemmill, Ellen (2006). "C" to It That Your Spa Equipment Is the Best. *Resort + Recreation,* Summer, p. 30.

Grapeseed Spa (2009). Retrieved August 12, 2009, from http://wineresort.com/spa.

Griffin, Nancy (2005). Legally Bound. *American Spa,* April 2005, pp. 50, 52.

Hill, Richard (2009). Hospitality Design Trend Forecast for 2009. Retrieved February 2, 2009, from www.hotelsmag.com/blog/380000638/post/1920039992.html.

Hotel Hershey Spa (2009). Retrieved August 12, 2009, from www.thehotelhershey.com/spa/index.php.

Kelly, David Daniel (2000). *Feng Shui for Dummies.* New York: Hungry Minds.

Lumley, Sarah, and Glover, Leslie (2008). Back of House. *Spa Business,* 2, pp. 78–80.

Miller, Erica (1996). *Day Spa Operations.* Albany, NY: Delmar Thomson Learning.

Minton, Melinda (2002). *Opening a Spa.* Fort Collins, CO: Minton Business Solutions.Mohonk Mountain House (2009). Retrieved August 12, 2009, from www.mohonk.com/the_spa/spa_overview.cfm.

Red Door (2009). Retrieved August 12, 2009, from www.reddoorspas.com/AboutUs.aspx.

Sawyer, Thomas H. (Ed.) (2005). *Facility Design and Management for Health, Fitness, Physical Activity, Recreation, and Sports Facility Development,* 11th ed. Champaign, IL: Sagamore.

Singer, Judith (2009a). The "Anywhere & Everywhere Spa" Concept. Retrieved August 12, 2009, from www.ishc.com/uploadedFiles/PublicSite/Resources/Library/Articles/Anywhere_Everywhere_Spa_Concept.pdf.

Singer, Judith (2009b). Spa Sustainability Strategies for the Environment, The Guests and Your Business. Retrieved December 22, 2009, from www.hfdspa.com/pr_spa_sust_strat-111908.html.

Skaná Spa (2009). Retrieved August 12, 2009, from www.turningstone.com/spa/skana.php. Taylor, Julie (2009). Resorting to Retail: Spa Design Expert Robert D. Henry Talks About the Retail Advantage. Retrieved August 12, 2009, from www.resort-recreation.com/departments-SPA-resortingtoretail0404.html.

Tezak, Edward J. (2002). *Successful Salon Management for Cosmetology Students.* Albany, NY: Milady Thomson Learning.

Ufland, Alexis, and Sternfeld, Lisa (2009). Eco Design. *Spa Management,* 19(3), pp. 86–94.

U.S. Green Building Council (2010). LEED. Retrieved June 15, 2010, from www.usgbc.org/DisplayPage.aspx?CategoryID=19.

Wynne Business (2010). The Non-Revenue Producing Space Odyssey. Retrieved June 15, 2010, from www.wynnebusiness.com/Presentations/NonRevenueSpaceOdyssey.pdf.

DESIGN CONSIDERATIONS BY SPA AREA

Each spa sets out to be unique to the market. There are, however, many common planning and design requirements that each facility must consider to meet federal, state, and local regulations, as well as current customer demands.

General Observations for Overall Spa Design

- A clear system of signage should be installed for easy traffic flow and to ensure that guests know what areas are designated as back of the house. This system does not need to be very elaborate if guests are escorted during their spa experience.
- Music piped throughout the facility should, at a minimum, have individual controls in the salon, fitness areas, and treatment rooms. Other social areas, including public lounge areas and retail space, can be on one control. Serene areas, such as reception, waiting lounges, locker rooms, and pretreatment spaces, may be on one control, although most spa managers prefer individual controls. Fitness studios need their own separate sound system for group and individual classes.
- Individual temperature controls are necessary for each of the treatment rooms, the salon, wet area, fitness areas, laundry, and each locker room. Reception, office space, retail, and waiting areas can be on one control in most spas.
- Select windows carefully. Exterior windows are great for letting nature and natural light into the spa. Interior windows need to be selected with careful consideration of safety, security, privacy, and lighting needs. Use shatterproof glass in high-risk areas and use etched or decaled glass, instead of clear, on doors to prevent individuals from walking into them.
- Locate bathrooms in an area where all guests entering the spa have access. To lessen traffic, locate primary or additional bathrooms near the front of the spa. Include separate bathroom areas for employees.
- A simple yet effective zone keying system should be installed. This will provide all workers access to back-of-the-house areas (storage, dispensary, laundry, etc.), treatment providers access to their assigned areas, and housekeeping and the spa manager access to all rooms (including offices).
- Noncorrosive, easy-to-clean materials should be used in all high-moisture areas (vents, ducts, drains, ceiling, and wall coverings). Commercial-grade finishes should be used on walls and floors, maintaining the appearance of a clean, sanitary facility.
- Carpets should be used only in reception, consultation spaces, and possibly multipurpose spaces. Hard floors are preferred in most treatment spaces because of their durability and easy clean-up. Hardwood, ceramic tile, epoxy, polished concrete, marble, and vinyl are all possibilities.
- Where possible, integrate soft curves into the overall design of the space. Curves, unlike their 90-degree or square counterparts, tend to project a feeling of comfort and natural flow.

Front-of-the-House Guest Areas

Public Reception and Welcome Area

Activities
- Greeting guests, checking guests in and out, checking coats, guest lounging, and waiting for appointments, where pretreatment or changing clothes is unnecessary, are conducted here.
- Reception employees are generally responsible for opening and closing the reception spaces, taking guest reservations, scheduling spa areas, answering telephones, and orienting the guest to the spa spaces.

Space Considerations
- The public reception and welcome area sets the tone for the entire spa experience, as guests entering the spa encounter this space first.
- The space needs to be inviting yet functional. This space, at minimum, should include a reception desk and a guest lounge/waiting area.
- Private guest consultation spaces, separate from the administrative offices, may be included in this area.
- For large spas, check-in and check-out spaces may be located in different areas.
- The reception desk is supported by a telephone, a computer, register and/or appointment book, and files that contain paper supplies such as marketing materials, guest forms, and operations materials.
- Lounge chairs should be easy to clean, long-wearing, and comfortable. A selection of different seating options is typical.
- Consider a water feature in the reception area for sound and esthetics.
- Plan a presentation area for refreshments.
- Provide a display area for reading materials.

Retail/Spa Boutique

In smaller spas, the retail area will likely be located in the guest welcome area. In combined spaces, consider the following along with the reception area information above.

Activities
- Guest browsing, shopping, product testing, guest fitting, and purchasing items.
- Employees responsible for opening and closing area, displaying items for purchase, ordering and inventory of retail products, maintaining order and cleanliness of space, providing product information to guests, and assisting guests with purchases.

Space Considerations
- May be as large as 15 percent of the space or a very small boutique, perhaps 5 of the space (Taylor, 2009).
- Create countertop reception desk with storage cabinetry below for supplies and with space for a register and a phone on the desk.
- Provide ample in-store storage and wall shelving for retail products.
- Displays and retail racks need to be accessible for clients to pick up, touch, read, smell, and even use products.
- Install electrical outlets on each of the four walls, including an ample number for the point-of-sale area.
- Provide some seating for retail guests and/or others accompanying them.
- Provide a receiving and storage area for retail products.

Men's and Women's Locker/Changing/Vanity Areas

Activities

- Guest area for changing into treatment attire, storage of clothing and other personal items, washing hands, using restroom, bathing/rinsing, and vanity areas.
- Employees responsible for opening and closing area, maintaining order and cleanliness of the space, replenishing and displaying items for use in the vanity area.

Space Considerations

- Provide an appropriate number of half-size or full-size lockers, depending on client needs. Consider the number of spa clients, spa members, and the ratio of men and women to select the correct number of lockers.
- Locking systems vary; select from keyed, carded, or personal code (i.e., digilock) systems.
- Lockers may include towels, robes, hangers, shoes, and a range of other items. Select appropriate sizes depending on guest and spa needs.
- Utilize movable benches or ottomans on casters near lockers, for seating while changing.
- Place sinks in an easily accessible area. Sink areas typically include hair dryers, disinfecting units, electric shavers, electric rollers, etc. For security purposes, consider wall-mounted hair dryer units.
- Install an adequate number of electrical outlets for vanity equipment. Select adequate electrical amperage, as typically several pieces of equipment are working at the same time.
- Offer soap, shampoo, and conditioner for bathing, often provided in wall-mounted dispensers.
- Increase lighting around vanity mirrors and wall-mounted magnified mirrors for shaving and makeup application.
- Flooring in locker and changing areas should be covered with an easy-to-clean carpet or attractive easy-to-clean hard flooring. Use water-resistant flooring in the bathroom and shower areas.
- Provide clean linen storage and towel display.
- Plan for a covered soiled linen depository. To help with laundry sorting, consider separate guest depositories for towels, shoes, and robes.
- Provide trash receptacles.
- Install lockable staff storage for room amenities and cleaning supplies.

Pretreatment Hydrotherapy Area

Activities

- Guest self-guided treatments or pretreatment hydrotherapy space. Common to include steam, sauna, hot tubs, lounge area, and/or whirlpools for guest use. May include plunge pools of various temperatures, experience showers, full-size pools for individual or group exercise and relaxation, lounge area, mineral or thalassotherapy pools.

Space Considerations

- May separate genders, mix genders, or provide some facilities as single-gender and others mixed.
- Plan for towel display space, two to ten towels per visitor.
  - Consider locating near laundry.
- Include a guest rinsing shower in the space.*

- As guests tend to drip while using and moving from one hydrotherapy space to another, pay close attention to pathway flooring and select nonslip, easily maintained, waterproof flooring.
- Provide drains throughout wet area, with floors sloped to assist with draining.
- Private wet treatment spaces may be located in a section of the wet area.
- To improve the experience in rinsing showers, select models with water-conserving heads and quick drains.
- Include waterproof seating in the lounge area.
- Place clothing hooks throughout the area.
- Provide for noncorrosive ventilation ducts throughout the wet area.
- Outflow of HVAC should be provided for 25 air changes per hour.*
- Consider ozone water purification system for whirlpools to eliminate chlorine smell.
- Consider providing a self-service beverage station with sink, counter, storage cabinet, minifridge, and/or ice machine.
- Provide covered soiled towel depository.*
- Doors to hydrotherapy areas, including steam and sauna rooms, need to have windows.*
- Ceilings of steam rooms need to be sloped for controlled condensation dripping.
- For safety, do not place locks on the inside of any hydrotherapy spaces.*
- If select hydrotherapy areas will be unavailable to guests at any time while the wet area is open, consider placing locks on the outside of doors to these rooms.

*Check local health department regulations to confirm these requirements.

Treatment Waiting Area

Activities
Guest relaxation area. Treatment waiting area for those selecting treatments for which pretreatment or changing clothes is necessary. It is typical to include reading materials, refreshments, and product displays in this area.

Space Considerations
- Consider that treatments are typically offered on a common rotating schedule, so it is likely that any guests scheduled for one treatment time will be using the space.
- Plan for ample and comfortable seating for guests.
- Provide tables for guest use.
- Lighting is typically subdued, perhaps with lamps in select areas for guest reading.
- Plan a presentation area for refreshments.
- Provide display area for reading materials.

Salon Area

Activities
Beauty services, including nail, hair, and makeup offered. Each beauty area is unique and requires distinct equipment and supplies.

Space Considerations
- May include a separate check-in area; if so, may include retail display and guest check-out options.

- Floors should be of a material that is easy to clean: tile, wood, vinyl, epoxy, etc.
- Lighting should be flattering to hair and skin, but ample enough for services.
- Hair cutting/styling stations to include movable or permanent adjustable chairs, product and equipment display and storage, multiple electrical outlets, and mirrors.
  - Mirrors at styling stations must be tall enough for clients of different heights.
  - Electrical outlets at each styling stations need to support at least two irons and a dryer.
  - Hair styling chairs need to be hydraulic (either manual or electric). If electric, a floor outlet should be placed beneath the chair so the cord is not a hazard.
  - Include dryer chairs in the area.
- Hair washing stations include hair sinks and reclining chairs, product and linen storage and display.
- Manicure stations include chairs for the nail technician and guests, table, tool and supply storage. May include spot lighting and/or magnifying lamp and drying equipment.
  - To be able to vary the room layout, consider making manicure stations portable.
  - If planning to offer acrylic nails, include a sink for washing hands.
  - Manicure tables are generally 2½ feet high or such that the guest's arm and hand placement is comfortable.
  - Table surface need to be durable and stain-resistant.
  - Because of the odor and dust emitted, consider a separate area for acrylic nail work.
  - Consider multiguest manicure tables to save space.
  - The number of pieces of electric equipment will dictate outlet needs.
  - May designate a separate drying station from manicure station.
- Pedicure stations include guest chair, nail technician chair or stool, foot sink (portable or permanent) with foot rest, and tool and supply storage and may include spot lighting and/or magnifying lamp.
  - May designate a separate drying station from pedicure station.
  - If massage chairs are selected for pedicure clients, ensure that the outlet is away from any water source.
- Plan for adequate electrical amperage, as typically several pieces of equipment are working at the same time.
- For extra security, the spa can be configured to have electrical features turned off in the evening to help prevent fire that might be caused by these pieces of equipment.
- Because of chemical and acrylic odors in the space, a top-notch ventilation system is needed; air turnover in the room is an OSHA regulation. Refer to the latest requirements.

Treatment Spaces

Activities

Treatment rooms are generally divided into two categories, dry and wet rooms. Dry rooms house treatments that are "dry," contained, require privacy, and offer easy clean-up. With the possible exception of a sink, other water sources and equipment are not located in dry treatment rooms. Wet treatment rooms are designed to accommodate water-based or hydrotherapy treatments. These rooms are private and constructed of tile, stone, or other waterproof surfaces for easy drainage and maintenance. Details regarding the different elements of dry and wet treatment rooms are provided in a later section.

Space Considerations (in general, for treatment rooms)

- Treatment rooms at minimum include a standard-size treatment table (or floor mat), shelving or a small table, a clothing hook, a provider stool, and space surrounding the table (3 feet) for therapist movement. With these minimum requirements, treatment rooms could be as small as 9 feet by 12 feet.
- The ideal spa treatment room size is 10 feet by 14 feet or larger; this size allows considerable storage space for linens, tools and supplies, counter space, sink, small equipment, and room for guests to change and store clothes, and the possibility for an in-room shower.
- Consider designing for couples treatment rooms. The average use of a couples' massage room is 7 percent (Minton, 2002), so for a small facility it may be better to place a movable wall in the space and use it for single massages as well. These larger rooms can also serve as a location for staff training and spa parties.
- For rooms where facials will be offered, direct and indirect lighting are needed.
- Millwork for cabinets must be washable.
- To protect these serene areas, provide extra soundproofing in between rooms and hallways. Consider "floor to slab" wall construction for extra isolation of sounds.
- Use acoustic tiles in room to help absorb sounds.
- When possible, provide an in-room sink with hot and cold running water.
- Select a floor that is nonporous, smooth, washable, and easy on the provider's feet.
  - Consider cushioned flooring, and avoid tile, marble, or granite.
  - Door must be solid, and for privacy, open into the center of the room, similar to a doctor's treatment room.
  - Consider having some type of numbering or lettering for identification and an "in use" sign.
  - For security and safety, all doors need to lock from outside, not inside.
  - For soundproofing, avoid the use of pocket doors.
- Indirect lighting with dimmer control should be placed on wall or overhead at edge of ceiling, not directly over facial lounge or massage table.
- Tables range in size to upwards of 73 inches by 33 inches; select for the comfort of the guest and the treatment room size.
  - For multipurpose rooms, select a table that can convert from lying-down to sitting-up position.
  - Select tables based on their strength, stability, and degree of adjustability.
- Select fabrics that offer abrasion and tear resistance, are easy to clean, soft, and have a great memory to retain shape (Gemmill, 2006).
- Provide in-room storage for small equipment and linen.
  - Consider each room having the ability to accommodate a daily supply of materials and linens.
- Provide adequate counter space and shelving for supplies, tools, and equipment.
- Don't forget the esthetic of the ceiling—that's where your customer will be looking, at least part of the time.

- For rooms with electrically adjustable tables, install floor outlet with dry lock centrally located under the table.
- Place wall outlets on side walls.
- Place outlets at counter height or inside cabinets for selected pieces of equipment, such as a sterilizer, waxing unit, or essential-oil diffuser.
- Require an in-room phone or intercom for proper communication in larger facilities.
- Select a centrally or locally located sound system with speakers in each room. Each room needs an individual volume control or, if possible, individual channel control.
- Use lever-type hardware on doors, as the provider's hands may be too slippery for knobs.
- All rooms should have a chair and hooks for a client's personal items, such as robes and/or towels.
- Consider placing a soiled laundry dispenser in the room.
- Locate near laundry or place a laundry drop directly outside rooms when possible, preferably dropping into chute or carts.
- Lounge and wait area should be within close proximity to the treatment rooms.

Dry Treatment Rooms

Activities
- Body massage requiring a table, such as Swedish, deep tissue, Rolfing, and Reiki.
- Body massage requiring a floor mat, such as Thai massage and acupressure.
- Body treatments requiring a table, such as dry brushing or waxing.
- Treatment that requires a seat or a table with seating capabilities, such as facials, cranial sacral work, or reflexology.

Space Considerations
- Consider the supplies for common dry treatment room offerings. It is usual to have in the room a towel heating unit, product warmers such as hot stone grills or pots and paraffin bowls or warmers, sheets for the table, towels for the treatment and draping the client, head rests, face cradles, and bolster pillows in the room. Treatment products and mixing bowls and utensils should also be available.
- Consider dry rooms to be multifunctional "suites" for semiwet or dry treatments, making tables convertible for facial or massage work.
  - Some treatments lend themselves to these wet-to-dry crossovers, such as body exfoliation using evaporating products, body masks using a paraffin-based product, lotion-based body tanning, and chamber hydrotherapy cabinets.

Wet Treatment Rooms

Activities
- Body massage and treatments requiring a table, such as Vichy shower, body masks, scrubs, and wraps.
- Body treatments requiring standing or specific vertical equipment, such as body spray tanning, Swiss shower, and Scotch hose.
- Body treatments requiring specific seated or reclining equipment, such as private tub, steam chamber, or spa pedicures.

Space Considerations

- Same layout and needs as the dry rooms, but with selected hydrotherapy equipment and constructed with materials that can get wet without damaging the space.
- Because of the nature of hydrotherapy treatments, turnover of the space is typically more difficult than in a dry room. Consider selecting equipment, materials, and supplies that ease in the efficient turnover of the room.
- Design a sloped floor and insist on a central quick draining system.
  - Depending on the products selected for treatments, drain traps may be needed.
  - Consider placing a drain grate in the threshold of the door to the guest corridor.
- Wall and floor materials must be waterproof.
  - Waterproof areas can stop at a 5-foot height or can go floor to ceiling.
- Ceiling materials need to be water-resistant.
- Consider showers inside room for guest rinsing during body scrubs, masks, or wraps.
- Electrical outlets need to be covered.
- Provide a hand-held hose for cleaning the space and equipment.
- Minimum size of room for a Scotch hose treatment is 8 feet by 12 feet, with equipment placed on the 8-foot wall or in the corner.
- In choosing a Vichy shower, consider water-conserving heads.
- In-room towel storage is necessary, as body treatments with hydrotherapy double or triple the amount of towel use.

Exercise/Movement Studio

Activities

- Group fitness classes
- Space for selected personal training offerings

Space Considerations

- Self-contained, with all equipment needed to complete a class, which might include mats, weights, balls, bands, etc.
  - Equipment can be kept in a connected storage room.
- May be designated specifically for equipment-based classes, such as spinning or Pilates.
- Often exercise studios have mirrors on the wall behind the instructor.
- Consider bars for dance offerings and stretching.
- Provide self-contained in-room sound system, music player, and possibly microphone.
- Self-service water should be available with cups and trash dispensers, or a drinking fountain.
- For safety, provide telephone or intercom equipment.
- Provide display space for towels.
- Provide storage for towels and cleaning supplies.
- Low on space? Consider using the outdoors for additional exercise space.

Fitness Equipment Studio

Activities

- Self-guided fitness workouts.
- Space for personal training offerings.

Space Considerations

- May consider 24/7 access.
- For entertainment during workouts, provide group or individual TV monitors or Ipod docking stations. An alternative is a music sound system.
- The amount of space will define how much equipment to put in, and the market will tell you what equipment to select (Singer, 2009a).
- Plan for easy supervision of space.
- Place weight resistance equipment close together.
- Consider placing weight resistance and aerobic equipment in separate spaces.
- To aid in the proper use of equipment, mirrors may be important in this space.
- Self-service water should be available with cups and trash dispensers or a drinking fountain.
- For safety, provide telephone or intercom equipment.
- Provide display space for towels.
- Provide storage for towels and cleaning supplies.

Back-of-the-House Staff Areas

Administrative Offices

Activities

- Space for managers and workers to complete the administrative tasks associated with operating the spa.
- Interviewing potential employees.
- Meeting with current employees.
- Storage of guest records.
- Storage of some operational supplies and personnel records.
- Display and/or storage of spa permits and licenses.

Space Considerations

- Place general office equipment such as desk, chair, drawers, shelving, files, telephone, computer, printer, etc.
- Place electrical outlets adequate for office equipment.
- Provide locked storage for personnel and guest files.
- Provide adequate lighting for administrative work.
- Consider placing one-way windows for confidential viewing of common guest areas.

Staff Lounge

Activities

- Staff break-time relaxation.
- Space for eating and drinking.

Space Considerations

- Employee areas serve two purposes, establishing boundaries between clients and employee spaces and providing an opportunity for positive employee relations (D'Angelo, 2006).
- Fill with tables, chairs, phone, and a wall clock.
- Provide food storage and preparation equipment such coffee maker, refrigerator, microwave, etc.

- Provide storage for meal supplies.
- Provide sink for hand and small dish washing.
- Consider a dish washer.
- Consider placing staff mailboxes and announcement posting area.

Staff Changing Area

Activities
- Storage area for staff personal items.
- Staff restroom, vanity, and changing area.

Space Considerations
- Consider separate entrance for staff.
- Provide staff lockers, showers, and toilets.
- Place coat rack or hooks for damp clothing or large coats.

Storage/Dispensary Areas

Activities
- Storage of clean linen, tools and supplies, spa products, and cleaning supplies.
- Possible holding location for covered soiled linen.
- Area for dispensing and mixing spa products.
- Possible location of staff meetings.
- Holding location for product deliveries.

Space Considerations
- Place in location with easy access to all treatment providers.
- Provide counters and utility sink(s) for hand washing, small utensil and dish clean-up.
- Consider separate entrance for deliveries.
- Provide covered storage of spa supplies, tools, and products.
- Include locked storage for items such as hazardous and valuable materials.
- Material Safety Data Sheets (MSDS) must be easily available, stored and/or displayed according to OSHA regulations.
- Plan for the space to be independently temperature-controlled to extend shelf life of spa products.

Laundry/Housekeeping

Activities
- Washing, drying, and sorting all spa laundry, including linens, towels, robes, shoes, and uniforms.

Space Considerations
- Select commercial-grade washing and drying equipment, adequate for the amount of laundry generated in the spa.
- Consider that it is typical to use 12 pieces of linen, 1 guest robe, and 1 pair of slippers for each treatment (Lumley and Glover, 2008).
- Provide area for ironing and ironing equipment.
- Place shelving and/or cabinetry on all possible walls for storage of towels, linens, robes, and uniforms.
  - Consider full height for cabinet storage of seldom-used products and equipment.

- Select appropriate electrical outlets for selected laundry room equipment.
- Segregate clean and spoiled laundry in separate areas or rooms to avoid cross-contamination.

Equipment Storage and Utility Spaces

Activities
- Storage of spa equipment.
- Access to facility utility panels.

Space Considerations
- Common spa equipment that may require ample storage includes water heaters, hydrotherapy pumps, and equipment. Some equipment can be placed in guest view, i.e., sauna equipment; others will be better hidden.

⟶ REFERENCES

Capellini, Steve (2008). Expanding Your Practice into a Day Spa. *Massage & Bodywork,* May/June, pp. 37–40.

Cornell, Jack (2007). Saving Space. *American Spa,* June, pp. 86–90.

Elliott, Marilee (2007). Jumping the Curve. *Resort + Recreation,* Winter, pp. 36–39.

Gimmy, Arthur, and Woodworth, Brian B. (1989). *Fitness, Racquet Sports and Spa Projects: A Guide to Appraisal Market Developing and Financing.* Chicago: American Institute of Real Estate Appraisers.

Krismanic, Tom (2006). A New Brand of Design. *American Spa,* May, pp. 42–46.

McCarthy, Jeremy, and James, Jennifer (2006). *FabJob Guide to Become a Spa Owner.* Seattle: FabJob, Inc.

Mills, Robert Christie (2008). *Resorts: Management and Operation,* 2nd ed. Hoboken, NJ: John Wiley & Sons.

Stipanuk, David M. (2006). *Hospitality Facilities Management and Design,* 3rd ed. Lansing, MI: Educational Institute of the American Hotel and Lodging Association.

Urban Land Institute (2008). *Resort Development,* 2nd ed. Washington, DC: Urban Land Institute Development Handbook Series.

Note: Some "design considerations" come directly or are adaptations from the above sources.

Standard Operating Procedures

→ LEARNING OBJECTIVES

At the end of this chapter, readers will be able to:

- Develop and design standard operating procedures (SOPs).
- Understand the purpose of policies and procedures.
- Assess the best implementation strategy for new procedures.
- Assess the cost and return on SOP development.

The secret of success is to do the common things uncommonly well.
                  —John D. Rockefeller

A **standard operating procedures** (SOP) document is a tool for communicating the way your business will operate to deliver the product and services to the client as promised. Sometimes called an **operations manual, employee manual,** or **policies and procedures guide,** the SOP document is a collection of materials used to promote training and education as well as assist with efficiency, productivity, consistency, and quality. SOPs are typically presented and maintained in a printed manual format and include:

- ▶ Process maps
- ▶ Spa policies
- ▶ Procedures for performing tasks
- ▶ Supporting forms and checklists
- ▶ Sample letters and notices
- ▶ Blank templates for creating new content

(See also the online resources for a full, more detailed version.)

SOPs are among the most important assets in the spa. Though the tide may be turning, many owners, managers, and employees have not always seen these documents as a valuable tool for their operation. This may be because the SOPs have not been developed correctly or maintained to reflect a changing business. To be effective and remain a dynamic asset of the business, SOPs must be updated as the business changes and procedures are refined and improved.

POLICIES AND PROCEDURES

The foundations of the SOP document are the **policies** and **procedures** for the spa. Both policies and procedures are developed to communicate to employees how the organization operates. A business's operations can malfunction if the policies and procedures are not correctly understood. The following definitions are provided to illustrate the key, distinct qualities of each concept and to help ensure that your SOPs are documented and maintained effectively.

Policies are the set of rules, regulations, standards and strategy that employees must follow. They dictate:

- ▶ When a procedure must be followed
- ▶ Who may or may not enact a procedure
- ▶ Which external standards and regulations must be followed, including legal requirements health standards, etc.
- ▶ Management requirements and expectations
- ▶ Behavior expected from employees of the organization
- ▶ Terms for clients of the organization

Procedures specify a sequence of tasks for conducting a specific activity. A procedure is a fixed set of steps that one or more individuals perform to achieve a result of value to the business. Procedures:

- ▶ Capture industry best practices
- ▶ Capture spa best practices
- ▶ Maximize efficiency
- ▶ Provide a guideline for employee training
- ▶ Help the operation to maintain consistent service and quality standards

Many spas have a written description of what employees should be doing every day. It is the primary resource used to orient a new employee to the unique tasks of the spa and a reference for existing employees. Policies are in essence the "spa laws" and how they are enforced, and the procedures are the steps we take to ensure compliance.

SOPs include components that relate directly to the daily operations of the facility and include everything from the employee compensation structure to the spa's recycling policy. Simply acquiring these documents so you can check them off your list is not nearly as important as the foundation created in your diligent design of these materials for the business.

INDUSTRY BEST PRACTICES

Policies and procedures should represent the industry's best practices. The most efficient and effective way to run a business is to follow **industry best practices**. These practices will change over time as new methods are developed or existing techniques are refined and improved. For this reason, it is important to ensure that SOPs do not remain static; rather they must be followed on a daily basis to ensure that your spa remains competitive. Typically, procedures may need to be updated periodically to capture the latest industry best practices and in-house best practices. Changes in policy occur less frequently.

The spa industry is a relatively young and fast-growing industry, so best practices are constantly being refined and improved. However, even with an industry as young as the spa industry, many practices have been implemented for ample time to create the groundwork for spa management.

Best practices provide:

- ▶ The most effective way to perform a task
- ▶ A method to maximize operation and training effectiveness
- ▶ Risk reduction for the business, including controlling the risk of litigation and protection for effects of the loss of a key employee
- ▶ Consistent quality standards when multiple employees perform the same activity or when multiple spas operate under the same brand name.

Maximizing Operational Effectiveness

SOPs minimize inefficiencies and confusion that can result from a lack of definitive direction established by owners and managers. For example, the most costly employees in a spa business are managers. So, it is expected that managers will be the most productive employees and will provide the greatest return on that investment. If SOPs are utilized properly, they will minimize unnecessary interruptions by employees seeking guidance, confirmation, or management approval for issues that can be clearly outlined in a procedural document.

By having clear procedures available to spa staff, the number of management engagements can be reduced. Employees will feel empowered to act, as they will know exactly what to do and how to do it according to the SOPs. The employee can feel confident that the task is being completed properly and that expectations are being satisfied. A good manager and proper training can never be replaced by a SOP document; however, it can be the catalyst for excellence in every position in the spa.

Maximizing Training Effectiveness

A comprehensive set of SOPs allows new employees to familiarize themselves with a number of important activities and provides answers to many of the frequently asked questions of new recruits. When a new employee is recruited, there is a time period during which they must be trained in how the spa operates. During this time, their productivity will be well below the peak they will achieve once they are fully trained. In addition, the cost involved in using existing employees to provide in-house training to new staff members has to be considered.

SOPs can fast-track the productivity of new employees, reducing training and supervision time required from existing staff. When new employees are hired, they should be given their own set of SOP and be asked to review them prior to beginning their on-site training program. To minimize paper consumption, many spas make their SOPs available on CDs or through website access. With a solid foundation created through these documents, new recruits will be more effective when they reach the on-the-job stage of training.

REALITY CHECK

It is a common misconception that a new employee can be handed a "manual" to read and then report to work fully prepared for success. The spa environment is, at its core, a "touch" business. New employees must be given the opportunity to "shadow" your best employees and experience the products and service that are offered in the spa. This adds a layer of complexity to the training procedures that must be implemented.

Staff Retention

The loss of an employee is always a challenge. This loss inevitably means investing time to find and train a replacement. Employee loss can also mean the loss of **intellectual property**—the knowledge needed to perform specific tasks that may only be known by the employee who has left.

Documenting how the business tasks are performed via SOPs provides a level of insurance for the spa that it will be able to continue if a key employee leaves. It is not uncommon for spas that have relied on the business owner as a key person in the daily operations to be forced to close down after a sudden illness or another event forces that person to leave the business. This risk highlights how critical a current set of SOPs is to any business.

Minimizing Legal Risk

Although any legal advice can only be truly applicable for a particular case, the key requirements and principles of litigation are fairly similar in all cases. We can use past scenarios to understand the implications of liability when something goes wrong within the spa and how a SOP can help.

▶ Scenario #1: An esthetician burns a guest with hot wax.
▶ Scenario #2: A spa owner dismisses the spa manager, who has recruited several new employees into the business without permission.

These events (and many more) could end up in court, with someone seeking damages from your business. In each case, the court will try to determine if the individual is at fault or if the business is at fault. For example:

▶ Scenario #1: If the esthetician was correctly following the treatment procedure outlined in the SOPs when the client was burned, he or she would not be held individually responsible and the focus will be on the spa. The court would then decide if the procedure for the treatment being performed was flawed. If, however, the employee was not following the spa's procedures, then there is a risk of the employee being personally responsible for his or her actions and the results.

▶ Scenario #2: If the spa manager wants to pursue legal action for unfair dismissal, the case will rely on the following: Did the spa manager follow the correct procedure for recruiting? If there is not a formal recruitment procedure or the procedure does not require the spa manager to seek approval, then the spa manager will have a very strong case. If the spa manager failed to follow the correct procedure and complete the correct forms, then the spa manager will likely be found at fault.

These are only two examples of the many things that could devastate a spa business if it resulted in a court case. The basic principles remain:

▶ Spa owners and managers must protect themselves by having an effective, current, and available set of SOPs.

▶ Spa owners and managers must ensure that *all* employees have access to, understand, and follow the SOPs.

▶ Employees must protect themselves by following the procedures of the business at *all* times.

There are some common misconceptions about the need for a spa to have SOPs. The first is that SOPs are unnecessary, because only qualified people are hired. Many spas attempt to hire the best people with the most experience in the hope that they will always "know what to do." This is an unrealistic expectation, however, because every operation is different. The best employee from one spa does not necessarily know what to do in another. If you want all your employees to be as good as your best employee, capture what your best employee does in your SOPs and give them to all your employees.

Some believe that everything will take longer if procedure must be followed. In reality, the most efficient way to perform a task will be the one documented in the SOPs. If there is a more efficient way of doing something, then it is time to update that procedure. It is not necessary that employees open the procedures manual and read each step every time they perform the task. Once employees becomes familiar with a procedure, they will be able to perform it from memory or by referring to the supporting checklist. Using the SOPs also ensures consistency from employee to employee.

The most disturbing misconception is that employees hate to follow procedures. Humans by nature like structure and routine. SOPs provide employees with a structured environment and a familiar routine. Procedures, defined by SOPs, encourage employees to maintain the high standards also being met by their peers. Once employees have worked in a structured environment, the majority will feel very uncomfortable working in a less structured workplace. The SOPs become an attraction for the business and reflect the level of professionalism at which it operates.

Many spas choose to operate without SOPs in place under the misconception that developing and implementing SOPs is expensive.

Depending on how they are implemented, SOPs can be costly in terms of money, time, staff commitment, consultant fees, and opportunity cost. However, the actual cost of inefficiency and waste created by inconsistent, unprofessional, and ineffective practices will outweigh the investment of developing SOPs over time.

DEVELOPING SOPS

There are several ways to develop SOPs, and there are advantages and disadvantages to each approach. Time and money are the main factors that will influence the decision of how to develop SOPs for your business. At the end of this chapter is a special section that summarizes options and details needed for this decision. In general, a spa manager is looking at four different options:

1. Develop 100 percent of the SOPs in house.
2. Purchase an SOP outline and use it to guide in-house development.
3. Purchase a comprehensive, customizable, ready-to-use SOP document.
4. Commission a consultant to develop the SOPs.

With the exception of the last option, all choices are available to a reader of this text, as a sample outline and a customizable SOP document is available in the online resources. In addition, Chapters 6, 7, and 8 all include examples of the SOP information related to each topic area. For a full collection of materials, see the online resources for this book.

SUCCESSFUL SOP IMPLEMENTATION

Every implementation process will be different, and there are more possibilities than can be covered in this chapter. However, a common set of activities can be performed to reduce the overall cost and time of implementation, while dramatically increasing the chances of success. If these actions are taken seriously, spas will be able to fully meet the business goals that drove the decision to develop or overhaul existing SOPs.

Management Commitment

All managers in the spa must be committed to implementing SOPs in the interest of positively affecting the way the business operates. If any manager, at any level, is less than 100 percent committed to implementing change, then the probability of success decreases dramatically. As human nature dictates our ability to create habits, it is always easier to avoid change than to embrace it, even when we are aware of a better process. Employees will be looking to management for any sign to bypass the new procedures and go back to the old routine. Consider offering incentives to each manager who gives 100 percent support to implementing change. Managers play a key role in affecting change, and when the business experiences the financial rewards of new SOPs, management's persistent efforts will be well worth the investment.

Stage the Implementation

Implementing anything new can be overwhelming. It can be especially difficult when changing the way tasks have been performed for years. It is usually possible to break down the implementation into stages to ease the pressure on employees and reduce the disruption to daily operations. This allows employees to focus on one element or area at a time, and staging implementation allows a test of each phase's success before embarking on the next area. If there are many new procedures to learn, it may be more palatable for employees to memorize a small number at a time.

Consider focusing first on the area that needs most urgent attention. If there are multiple urgent areas, rank them by urgency and importance to help prioritize the activities. For example, if the existing spa has received an increase in complaints or a decrease in repeat visits recently, you may choose to focus on client-related areas, such as raising service standards. If the spa is looking tired and needs a spring cleaning, housekeeping procedures may be more urgent. If the spa is experiencing high staff turnover, human resources and administrative procedures may be a higher priority.

Implementation Approach for Larger Spas

Unless you have a very small team, trying to implement new SOPs across all staff members at the same time can be risky. It can be difficult to provide motivation to a large group of people at the same time, so a staged rollout will allow you to focus your efforts and ensure success. Start by selecting a small team of two to five people who will be the initial users of your new SOPs. The people in this team should have the following attributes:

- ▶ Understand the business very well
- ▶ Are proactive and motivated
- ▶ Are more likely to embrace change than reject it
- ▶ Have skills to become leaders of the remaining employees

The initial team will be the first of the employees to use your new initiatives and provide constructive feedback. Use the initial team to refine your procedures and iron out the kinks. Allow for plenty of opportunity to refine your manuals, as writing or customizing procedures in an office will rarely uncover all the steps and exceptions that will happen once you get out into the spa.

Once the initial team has refined, accepted, and embraced the new SOPs, make them team leaders for the next group of people who will adopt the SOPs. Each of the original team will now act as trainer and mentor for the new team, being able to speak with experience about the benefits of the new work methods. Following the same process, you can continue to divide and create change within the organization.

→ SOP TRAINING

All employees must have easy access to the SOPs that relate directly to their job roles and responsibilities. When new SOPs are developed, ensure that employees are allocated training time to review the new SOPs and, where appropriate, practice the new procedures before they are expected to implement them with clients present. When individual SOPs are updated over time, training should be provided for all affected employees, and the remaining employees should be notified during employee meetings. Updated copies of the SOP must be circulated and inserted into printed SOP manuals located around the spa.

→ OPPORTUNITIES FOR FEEDBACK

It will be valuable to ask employees using the new tools if they are efficient and practical so the procedures can be fine-tuned with time. Create an environment in which employees can provide feedback and make suggestions for improvements. A spa manager will need to manage change requests. Just because someone believes there is a possible improvement does not always mean there is one. All suggestions for improvement need to be considered by the individual who best understands the particular business need. A clear process and time frame for reviewing suggestions and planning the implementation will ensure that employees contribute their best ideas and feel valued.

→ MEASURE THE RESULTS

Develop a process to measure the effectiveness and success of your SOPs. This will enable you to identify how the spa benefited from implementing the new procedures as well as identify additional opportunities for improvement. Examples of key metrics include:

- ▶ The number of customer complaints relating to poor service from employees, cleanliness of the spa, or ambience within the spa—for example, music levels and air conditioning temperature
- ▶ The repeat visitation ratio, if the spa is located in a community environment
- ▶ The level of staff turnover, state of staff morale, and number of sick leave days taken
- ▶ Annual expenses relating to product waste, laundry costs, and retail theft

Calculating Return on Investment

Calculations of the return on investment for your spa will depend largely on your current situation and should incorporate:

- ▶ Increase in revenue due to:
  Increased customer satisfaction
  Increased repeat visitation
  Improved sales techniques
- ▶ Cost reduction due to:
  Reduced training costs
  Reduced supervision costs
  Reduced staff turnover
  Reduced compensation for unhappy customers (free treatments or products)

▶ Business risk reduction:
   Business continuity after loss of a key staff member
   Reduced risk of business failure in a competitive market
   Reduced risk of litigation
▶ Increase in business value:
   Resale value of the business
   Ability to open additional spas using the same business model
   Franchise or branding opportunity

Evaluation Checklists

The following evaluation checklists are designed to:

▶ Assist a spa with existing SOPs to assess current procedures and determine if the spa is receiving the full benefits from a quality set of SOPs, or if there are gaps that need to be filled where some procedures may not be currently documented.
▶ Assist a spa that does not currently have documented procedures to identify the key content and supporting items in SOPs.

There are no right and wrong answers to developing SOPs, as every spa is different and the checklists are not exhaustive. Rather, aim to promote your thinking and highlight the fundamental elements of SOPs. The decision to replace or update existing SOPs may be influenced by your answers to the checklists below and will need to be considered relative to the drivers, risks, opportunities, and constraints that face the business.

SOP CONTENT: EVALUATION OF BASIC REQUIREMENTS

- Was SOP updated during the last six months?
- Are the policies listed separately from the procedures?
- Are the procedures comprehensive enough that new employees can follow steps they have never seen before and achieve the desired result?
- Do your SOPs include supporting forms?
- Do your SOPs include supporting checklists?
- Do your SOPs include sample letters?
- Do your SOPs include sample notices?
- Do your SOPs include supporting process maps to assist training?
- Do your SOPs cover all aspects of how to operate your spa?
- Are all your employees trained to use the SOPs?
- Do all employees have access to relevant sections of the SOPs at all times?
- Do all employees follow the SOPs at all times?

KEY TERMS

Employee manual

Industry best practices

Intellectual property

Operations manual

Policies

Policies and procedures guide

Procedures

Standard operating procedures

REVIEW QUESTIONS

1. What is the difference between a policy and a procedure?
2. Would you prefer to work in a business that has current SOPs in place? Why or why not?
3. How do SOPs maximize training efficiency?
4. Why do some spas choose not to have SOPs?

REFERENCE

Rockefeller, John D. (n.d.). Retrieved June 22, 2010, from www.onepotmeal. com/?tag=success-sayings.

OPTIONS FOR DEVELOPING SOPs

Time and money are the main factors that influence the decision of how to develop SOPs for a business. In general, there are four primary options:

1. Develop 100 percent of the SOPs in house.
2. Purchase an SOP outline and use it to guide in-house SOP development.
3. Purchase a comprehensive, customizable, ready-to-use SOP document.
4. Commission a consultant to develop the SOPs.

It generally takes several hundred hours of work to develop a complete and practical set of SOPs. For this reason, many start with an existing SOP template, which can cut months of work from the overall project. The cost of the development options varies significantly, so it is important to research the available options and calculate their respective costs to assist your decision.

Whether you are starting from the beginning or already have a documented SOP manual that needs to be updated, there are several options to consider. If you already have an existing set of SOPs, conduct an assessment of their quality and completeness and compare them to the cost of purchasing a complete new set. Any savings from not purchasing SOP may be negated very quickly if the labor-hours required to update and reformat your existing SOPs becomes significant.

Option 1.   Develop 100 percent of the SOPs in house.
It is possible to develop SOPs from the beginning if there is a staff member who is very knowledgeable about the spa or if a number of employees with a particular expertise take sections individually. The advantage of this option is that there is little or no direct outlay of expenses. However, one of the main disadvantages is that this option requires a significant amount of time. The hidden cost of taking employees away from other staff responsibilities, and ultimately generating spa revenue, may be significant and detrimental to the business. Also note that the SOPs will only be developed to the standard of the employee(s) who write them and some industry best practices may be missed, negatively impacting the competitive position of your spa.

Option 2.   Purchase an SOP outline and use it to guide in-house SOP
                   development.
If you have time to dedicate to the project and you decide to develop the SOP in-house, you may want some base guidelines to give you ideas and inspiration. You can readily purchase a template online and use it to guide your in-house development. The advantage of this option is that the guidelines typically offer suggestions for content and give brief descriptions of key items to include in your SOPs. Some of the available packages are offered in editable electronic format, enabling easier customization. The main disadvantage is the generic tone of the outline and spending the time to sift through all of the information making the appropriate modifications and creating forms to suit your business. Even though this sounds like a lengthy process, however, it still may be significantly shorter than complete in-house development. The current products available begin at

approximately $150 and generally include the guidelines for a Policy and Procedures Guide, Employee Manual, Human Resources Manual, and a Housekeeping Manual.

Option 3.   Purchase a comprehensive, customizable, ready-to-use SOP document.

Comprehensive SOPs are usually provided in a professional table format in a ready-to-implement state, containing written detailed policies and procedures, as well as supporting forms, checklists, and samples. Though the wording may be a bit generic, this saves hours of development time as resources are only needed to customize the standard policies, procedures, and supporting items for the unique aspects of the particular business. The key advantage of using a ready-to-implement SOP is that they incorporate industry best practices and effectively allow acting as your own consultant. When an editable version is available, it enables customization. Although there is an up-front cost to purchasing ready-to-use SOPs, approximately $1000, development time is much faster, and the result is detailed and complete.

Option 4.   Commission a Consultant to Develop the SOPs

Consultants who help develop SOPs typically use their own collection of procedures, or they purchase "off-the-shelf" SOPs from a third-party organization to use as the foundation. If either of these solutions applies, the most important factor will be to ensure that you have the proper user license and copyright agreements in place so that use of the newly delivered document is not restricted or illegal. It could prove very costly and caustic to your business if, after investing time and money into the project, it is discovered that the consultant's previous client owns the copyright because the consultant used their documents as the basis for your SOPs. The consulting agreement should state the terms of use and ownership of the deliverables of the project, and specify if an editable, master document will be provided so you clearly understand how to update the SOP. In addition, you will need to consider whether additional consulting fees should be budgeted for the consultant to return to make updates, or if you will be able to make changes in house.

The main advantage of this option is that an expert dedicates time to customize the SOPs for the requirements of the specific business, which can reduce the time required by employees to work on the project. However, time must still be allocated to brief the consultant, liaise with him or her during the project, and review the draft SOPs that are presented. The major disadvantage is the significant cost of hiring the consultant. The rates are determined by the individual firms and are generally $15,000 to $60,000 for customized SOP development on a new project. Though it may seem an indulgent expense, the demands of a large project can be significantly reduced with the addition of a qualified spa consultant. Large consultancies typically have very impressive credentials, a large team of professionals, and a global perspective on the industry, whereas a smaller firm may have a thorough understanding of a particular local market or type of facility. Do the research and ask for references. The value a trusted industry professional will add to the process can far exceed the extra dollars spent.

Determining the Cost of SOP Options

In considering a budget for developing and implementing SOPs, it is critical to place a value on your own time and that of your employees. Determine the opportunity cost of having yourself and your employees involved, as every hour that is dedicated to the project is an hour that is not generating revenue in the spa. Estimate the number of hours needed for the project and calculate the value of that time based on the cost of taking them away from revenue-generating activities, such as delivering a one-hour massage or assisting a customer with a reservation or a retail purchase. Also, identify the price of acquiring off-the-shelf SOPs and/or consulting fees so you can accurately compare the costs of each scenario.

Option 1:   Develop 100 percent of the SOPs in house

- To develop comprehensive SOPs from the beginning, including supporting items such as checklists and forms, realistically takes between 500 and 1000 hours, depending on the size and complexity of the business.
- If therapists or technicians develop the SOPs, calculate the revenue lost while they are not able to deliver treatments (e.g., the price of a massage) as well as the compensation cost of their employment. If other types of employee do the work, calculate the value based on the cost of not completing the activities they are primarily employed to conduct, which may indirectly generate revenue, in addition to the compensation cost of the employee.

Option 2:   Purchase an SOP outline and use it to guide in-house SOP development.

- The number of development hours saved by using a guidelines publication is not significant, because you still have to create the format and the entire content of the SOP yourself. Some time may be saved, however, by reducing the search for additional ideas to assist in identifying the topics to include in the SOPs.

Option 3:   Purchase a comprehensive, customizable, ready-to-use SOP document.

- The amount of time needed to customize existing, comprehensive SOPs is significantly less compared to developing the SOPs from the beginning.
- Refinements and updates may be quickly implemented based on employees' comments and feedback.
- Paying significantly more for a set of base SOPs may not necessarily provide proportionally more content or quality. Understand the content of the SOPs before purchasing to ensure that the additional cost will result in significant time savings.

Option 4:   Commission a Consultant to Develop the SOPs

- Consulting fees vary dramatically based on the size of the consulting firm, the type of related experience the consultant has, and the length of time he or she has been consulting.
- Out-of-pocket expenses, such as travel, should also be estimated and factored into the total consulting costs. The consultant should take less time to develop the SOPs compared to developing 100 percent of the SOPs in house (Option 1), because consultants should be able to refer to other SOPs developed for previous clients and use them as a foundation for the new SOPs. However, they still have to allocate time to learn about the business to develop and customize the SOPs to address the unique needs of the spa, as well as format the SOPs so they comply with the spa's brand identity.
- A spa employee also needs to allocate time for the project, for example, to meet with the consultants and provide them with an overview and the

direction of the spa business, liaise with the consultants during the project and gather necessary information, review and give feedback on the first draft of the SOPs, approve the final draft, and coordinate the implementation of the new SOPs.

Calculating the Cost

Data may vary from the described example based on the size and complexity of your business, the internal cost of labor and price of services, consultant fees in your area, and the actual cost of available base SOPs. Calculating the real cost of the various options will clearly highlight which option is best suited to your situation, as well as enable you to calculate the return on investment.

Spa Human Resources

→ LEARNING OBJECTIVES

At the end of this chapter, readers will be able to:

- Distinguish among the common positions of employment in a spa.
- Comprehend laws established to govern human resources.
- Understand the elements of a thorough hiring plan for a spa business.
- Be aware of strategies used when composing an employee selection tool.

The best executive is one who has sense enough to pick good people to do what he wants them to do, and self-restraint enough to keep from meddling with them while they do it.

—Theodore Roosevelt

Much of the knowledge related to human resources is constant across any business. Consequently, there are many resources available to individuals involved in recruiting, managing, and providing direction for the people who work in an organization. However, there are a few qualities of spa personnel that make human resource procedures different from those of many other businesses. First, a spa has a unique personnel makeup. Each spa position has a dramatically different role in the spa, and each must rely on others for success. Second, often in smaller spas, which have fewer on the leadership team, managers take on a multitude of responsibilities. Human resource tasks are one of the most important. Unfortunately, spa managers too often have no formal training or education in these practices. This chapter provides an overview of structures and workforce positions unique to the spa industry. In addition, the basics of human resource law and hiring practices are also discussed.

→ THE ORGANIZATIONAL STRUCTURE OF A SPA

Before reviewing general hiring practices, it is essential to understand the typical composition and structure of a spa. An **organizational structure** is a visual representation of the hierarchy of a business. An organization can be structured in many different ways, depending on the philosophy, size, and offerings of the organization. The structure of an organization helps facilitate working relationships among various entities in the organization and improves the efficiency of the operation by setting the structure for order, control, and supervision of personnel and processes.

In general, a spa staff includes managers, providers, and support staff. Managers may be responsible for the entire spa or just a portion of the operation. Managers are the individuals who are ultimately responsible for all elements of the business, including human resources. They may hire staff, assess employee performance, contract and work with vendors, and schedule workers. With these responsibilities, it is reasonable to find the management staff at the top of the organizational structure. Depending on the type of spa, the individual at the top of the organization may have the title of owner, spa director, or spa manager. The topmost person in charge at a resort, hotel, or destination spa is typically referred to as the **general manager**.

The destination spa structure, Figure 6.1, reflects those areas common to many lodging establishments, including operations, finance, human resources, and executive branches. In the sample provided, fitness, wellness, and beauty are the focus of the spa services. The Golden Door in Escondido is a forty-guestroom spa that opened in 1958. In destination spas, other specialties areas such as golf, counseling, medicine, or adventure activities may be recognized in the leadership structure.

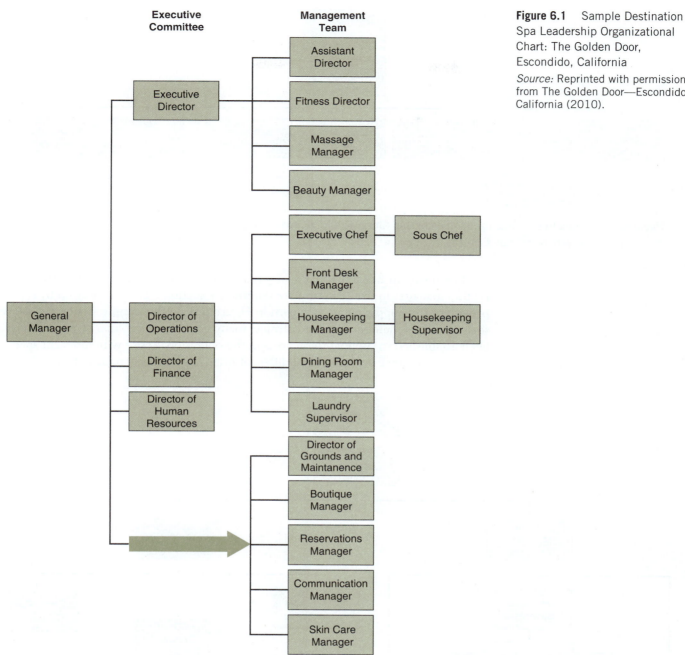

Figure 6.1 Sample Destination Spa Leadership Organizational Chart: The Golden Door, Escondido, California

Source: Reprinted with permission from The Golden Door—Escondido, California (2010).

In a resort/hotel it is typical to see the person responsible for the spa serving on the executive committee and reporting directly to the general manager. In this case the title **executive spa director** is common. Spa functions and personnel who are not members of the executive staff are typically part of the Rooms Division, as shown in Figure 6.2. The Ritz-Carlton, Naples, is a 450-room luxury beach resort with a wide range of amenities. In addition to dining, the resort also features on-site tennis, pool, beach, fitness, nature, family, and children's activities and facilities, as well as off-site golf. The operations of the resort amenities also fall under the Rooms Division in the organizational hierarchy, but they are separate from the spa operation and management.

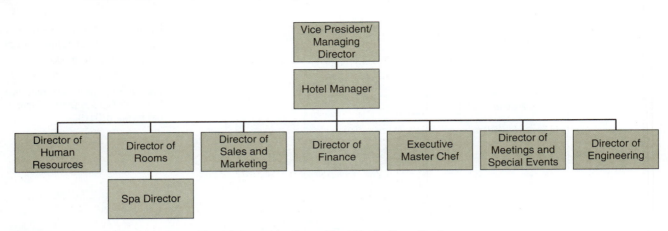

Figure 6.2   Sample Resort Organization Leadership Chart: The Ritz-Carlton, Naples
Source: Reprinted with permission from The Ritz-Carlton, Naples, Florida.

In a resort or hotel that has a large, full-service spa, those just below the spa director/manager in the structure are commonly section leaders, followed by service providers and support staff as shown in Figure 6.3. In the sample structure, the resort spa offers memberships and attracts many conference groups, so positions have been established to support these areas of the operation. Those with different specialties will have other personnel and different branches on the structure. Figure 6.3 can

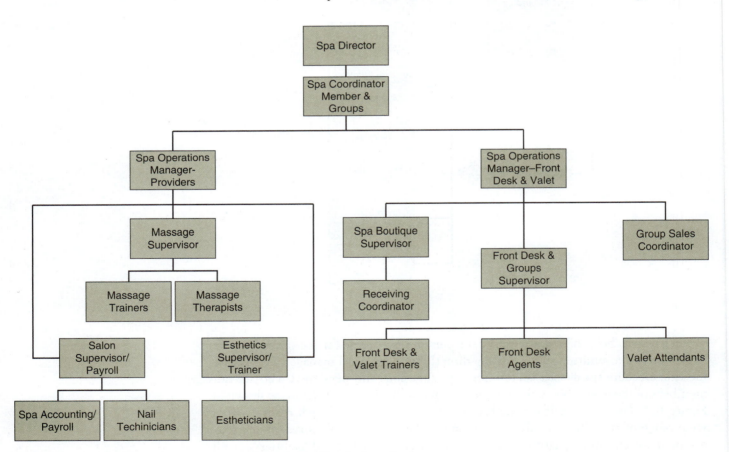

Figure 6.3   Sample Resort Spa Organizational Chart: The Ritz-Carlton, Naples
Source: Reprinted with permission from The Ritz-Carlton, Naples, Florida.

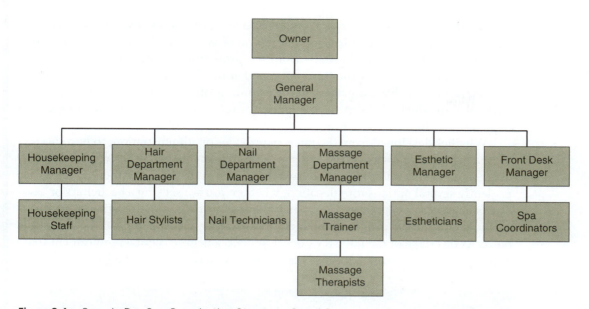

Figure 6.4   Sample Day Spa Organization Structure: Grand Spa
Source: Reprinted with permission from The Grand Spa—Dallas, Texas.

also be a model for any full-service spa that can be adjusted depending on the spa of-ferings and personnel.

In smaller spas, service providers usually appear just below the general manager in the organizational structure, as shown in the day spa sample in Figure 6.4. The sample shown represents a full-service spa with a staff of sixty-five employees.

SPA PERSONNEL

In the organizational structure of any spa, there are three primary staffing areas: managers, service providers, and support staff. Each is essential to the operation, and each relies on the other areas to accomplish their tasks. A description and com-mon personnel found in the area, along with the responsibilities and qualifications of each position, follow.

Managers

Managers are full-time employees who are generally present every day the spa is open. The spa owner may also serve as spa director or play a management role, but this is not always the case. Internally, managers oversee daily activities; communi-cate with employee and guests; develop, oversee, and enforce all policies and pro-cedures; and oversee all human resources functions of the spa. Externally, managers market and sell the spa; contract with vendors, work to understand and serve the spa client, and recognize and adapt to changes in the industry.

Management may have several levels in the organizational structure. Working on the management team may be division managers/directors, such as hair, nail, esthet-ics, massage, front desk, fitness, housekeeping, retail, and others. These assistant managers are generally responsible for all the management functions in a designated area, thus providing the lead manager with additional time for external duties and responsibilities.

Spa managers have a unique blend of business skills and knowledge of spa services. They generally enter management in one of two ways. They have been service providers and learned the business from the ground up, or they worked their way into management in another industry and moved to operating a spa. Service providers tend to have a greater understanding of spa offerings and personnel, whereas individuals with little spa experience tend to have a greater understanding of general business practices.

Whether developed from the ranks of provider or administration, to be a successful spa manager, knowledge and skills in both areas are essential. Driven by demand, degree and certification programs have developed across North America. There are presently several options for education, whether you are seeking a bachelor's or associate's degree or a certificate in spa management. For a complete listing of spa management educational programs in North America, see the Appendix at the end of the book. At this stage of the industry's development, a degree is not a requirement to be a spa manager, but rather a means of acquiring the necessary knowledge.

HISTORY FACT

Although several practitioner-focused associations existed previously, it was not until 1991 that the first national professional associations were formed to support spa managers. The International Spa Association (ISPA) and the International Day Spa Association were both founded in the United States in 1991, followed in six short years by the Leading Spas of Canada.

Service Providers

Spa service providers vary based on their treatment specialty; however, there are several commonalities. Providers must have a foundation of knowledge and skills related to their expertise. Because of the physical nature of the work, they must possess both strength and stamina. Service providers spend the greatest amount of time with spa guests, so they must have effective communication skills.

The industry has divided service providers into four groups: licensed technicians, licensed therapists, medical personnel, and specialty/fitness personnel. Those generally included in the division of cosmetology are technicians, those in the health department are therapists, and those with a medical degree are medical personnel. Specialty and fitness personnel can have from no to several governmental regulatory bodies, depending on the area of expertise.

Licensed Spa Technicians

Spa technicians focus on skin, hair, and nails. Spa technicians must be licensed based on the laws of the state. To acquire a license, spa technicians are typically required to complete an education program, pass a state exam, and have a specified minimum number of training hours. Training times range from 240 to 2000 hours, depending on the state and the type of license (ASCP, 2010; Find a Beauty School, 2010). See online links to state regulation sites in the Appendix for more information. The following is a listing and general description of common categories of spa technicians. Additional categories may include makeup artistry, electrolysis (regulated by the board of medicine in some states), hair design, permanent makeup, laser technicians, body wrapper, and others.

Licensed Esthetician

Esthetics concerns treatment of the epidermal layer of human skin. Esthetic practice may include, but is not limited to, skin cleansing, exfoliation, and hair removal. Exfoliation procedures may include microdermabrasion, chemical exfoliation, light-based therapies, or the use of instruments or products. Skin care treatments can be applied either on the face or the entire body and typically include services such as facials (back and face), body wraps, body scrubs, and fango (clay) treatments. **Estheticians**, sometimes licensed as *facial specialists,* can also apply makeup. Some estheticians may be licensed to practice partial massages, nail services, and hydrotherapy. Unlike medical personnel, estheticians are not allowed to offer dermatological diagnosis or prescription.

In the United States, skin care practitioners are licensed in forty-nine states (not in Connecticut), as well as in Washington, D.C., Puerto Rico, and the U.S. Virgin Islands. Utah, Virginia, and the District of Columbia have two-tier systems, with general esthetician and master esthetician licenses. Additional training and licensure allows estheticians a wider set of treatments, including electrolysis, airbrush tanning, laser hair removal, and micropigmentation (permanent makeup).

Licensed Hairstylist/Cosmetologist/Barber

Cosmetologists, hair stylists, and barbers work with the scalp and hair. Treatments include haircuts, styling, braiding, chemical services (highlighting, coloring, permanent wave, relaxing), and therapeutic hair and scalp treatments. These practitioners can also shave and implement temporary hair-removal techniques using depilatories and waxing. Cosmetologists are generally licensed to provide a wider range of services, including makeup application, skin treatments, and limited nail services.

Licensed Nail Technician

As the name describes, "nail techs" provide natural and artificial nail services, such as manicures, pedicures, polishing, nail extensions, and nail art. **Nail technicians** can also perform professional hand and foot treatments, including basic hand and foot massage.

Spa or Salon Assistant/Attendant

Treatment assistants can be very useful in a busy spa. As the title suggests, these employees assist service providers in the preparation of the guest. This may include shampooing the guest, assisting in product preparation, readying equipment, or selling retail. In addition, some types of spa therapy that do not involve physical touch may be practiced without a license in some states. In this instance, assistants may help guests with self-administered or private hydrotherapy treatments, such as still or whirlpool tubs, steam, and sauna.

Licensed Spa/Massage Therapists

Spa therapists focus on the mind, body, and spirit. Like estheticians, **massage therapists** must be licensed based on the laws of the state. All but two of the United States have regulations in place for massage therapy; see Figure 6.5. In Canada, only the provinces of Ontario, New Brunswick, and Newfoundland/Labrador regulate massage therapists.

Pedicure Service

States Regulating Massage Therapy

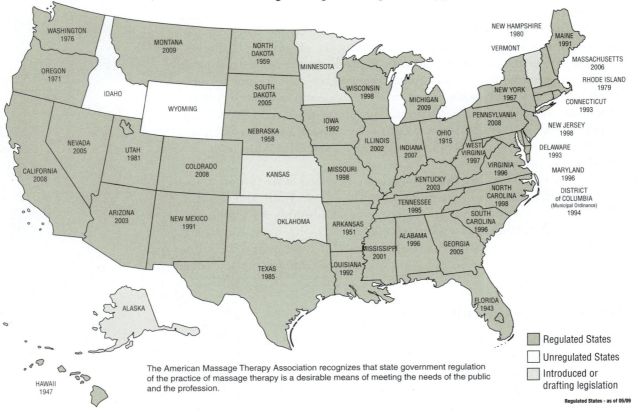

The American Massage Therapy Association recognizes that state government regulation of the practice of massage therapy is a desirable means of meeting the needs of the public and the profession.

- Regulated States
- Unregulated States
- Introduced or drafting legislation

Regulated States - as of 05/09

Figure 6.5   States That Regulate Massage Therapy

Source: AMTA (American Massage Therapists Association) (2009). States Regulating Massage Therapy. Retrieved January 4, 2009, from www.amtamassage.org/pdf/Regulated_States.pdf.

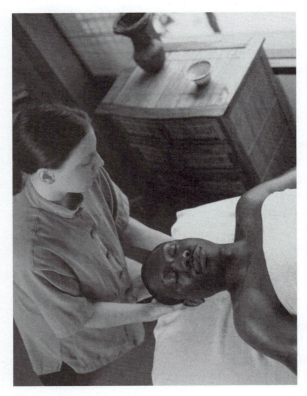

Massage Therapy

To acquire a license, spa therapists are typically required to complete an education program, pass a state exam, and complete a specified number of training hours. Some states also require first-aid and CPR training. Training times range from 250 to 3000 hours, depending on the state/province and the type of license (AMTA, 2009). Continuing education, beyond the initial certification, is generally a requirement for maintaining a massage therapist license. Details on individual state and provincial regulation can be found online. The number of licensed massage therapists is growing; as reported in 2010 by the Associated Bodywork and Massage Professionals, U.S. therapists numbered 293,531.

Some organizations offer multilevel license offerings, such as the American Medical Massage Association (AMMA), which offers three levels ranging from an entry-level program to a postgraduate diploma program for those seeking to extend their education. See the Appendix for links to more information.

Massage involves manipulating soft tissue, such as muscle, connective tissue, tendons, and ligaments, using pressure, tension, motion, or vibration. Massage can be applied with the hands, fingers, elbows, forearm, feet, or mechanical aids. Massage therapists are educated in basic therapeutic massage techniques; however, many expand their skills to include other specialty massage techniques, such as shiatsu, Thai, trigger point, sports massage, Reiki, Rolfing, reflexology, and so on.

Medical Professionals

There are a variety of alternative and conventional medical professional groups throughout North America. Physicians, dermatologists, dentists, nurses, psychologists, psychiatrists, chiropractors, and others are licensed and regulated throughout the United States and Canada. Each license requires completion of an education program, including internships and an examination. Those wishing to practice acupuncture and traditional Oriental medicine will find varying forms of regulations in all but two of the United States and in British Columbia, Ontario, and Quebec in Canada (Acupuncture.com, 2010; WFCMS, 2010).

Specialty and Fitness Personnel

The list seems never-ending when trying to identify all the individuals who might be involved in the provision of spa services. Most common are personal trainers, fitness instructors, nutrition consultants, aquatic managers, sports and recreation leaders and instructors, and special-topic educators. A spa might also utilize talents such as artists, astrologers, or even animal handlers to provide guest services. Each specialty area may or may not have licensure or regulations associated with its practice. Spa managers are wise to research federal and state regulations associated with any specialty or fitness personnel.

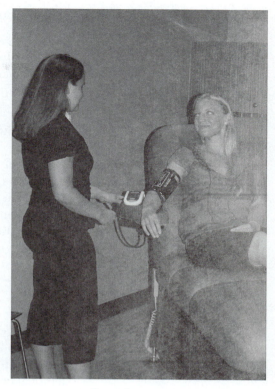

Guest Assessment

Support Staff

A number of staff positions are needed to keep a spa working effectively. Some of these positions have direct contact with spa guests, whereas others do not.

Receptionists/Hosts/Front Desk Agents

These employees are the heart of a spa business. Seldom will a spa flourish without the presence of a skilled front desk staff. Spa receptionists have the ability to orchestrate the guest's entire experience. They answer potential and current guest inquiries, greet spa visitors, schedule and coordinate appointments, handle financial transactions, and are the primary sellers of spa services. They often provide the guests with both the first and last impressions of the spa.

Housekeepers/Locker Room Attendants/Laundry

The housekeeping team keeps the facility neat, clean, and well stocked. They are typically responsible for operational supply inventory for the spa. In smaller operations, the entire staff is responsible for the upkeep of the facility; in larger spas, however, there may be several persons on the housekeeping staff.

Appointment and Billing Specialists

Some spa staff may work strictly behind the scenes. Large spas may have special staff members just to coordinate appointments. Also, with the involvement of medical personnel and increasing numbers of individuals being prescribed spa services, spas need competent staff members to manage medical insurance reimbursement. With the growth of medical spas and spas that work in conjunction with hospitals and rehabilitation centers, this is likely to be a growing need in the industry for such specialists.

Chefs/Cooks/Servers/Stewards

If the spa serves foods and beverages, a number of individuals on the spa staff may support this function. Chefs and cooks are responsible for the preparation of the food. Servers take and serve guest orders. Stewards assist with clearing and cleaning dishes.

⟶ EMPLOYMENT LAWS

Numerous federal and state laws affect the human resources functions of businesses. These laws, generally known as labor or employment laws, address the legal rights of and restrictions on employees and their employers. In this section we discuss the most common labor laws and how they may affect the human resource functions of a spa operation. Understanding and working within the confines of the laws is the spa manager's responsibility.

Equal Employment Opportunity Laws

A number of federal laws address employment standards in the United States. These laws are generally categorized as **equal employment opportunity (EEO) laws**, a term that applies to the laws that guard the rights of a protected group. In the United States, these protected groups include those based on gender (including pregnancy), age, national origin, race, color, religion, disability, and, most recently, genetic information. Table 6.1 summarizes the major EEO laws and their implications for businesses in the private sector. Each of the equal opportunity laws described in Table 6.1 also makes it illegal to retaliate against a person because of their involvement in a charge of discrimination.

Nearly all states and some municipalities have EEO laws that provide much broader protection than the federal EEO legislation detailed in Table 6.1. Managers cannot assume that compliance with federal laws is enough. Some states have enacted laws that protect sexual preference, physical appearance, or political affiliation. Managers are wise to investigate state and local laws before opening their spa. All equal opportunity laws—federal, state, and local—forbid discrimination against protected groups in any aspect of employment, including hiring, firing, pay, job assignments, promotions, layoff, training, fringe benefits, and any other term or condition of employment (EEOC, 2010).

Other Important Labor Laws

There are other labor laws related specifically to wages, benefits, and the workplace environments that may also affect spa businesses:

▶ **The Fair Labor Standards Act** regulates workplace practices related to minimum wage, overtime pay, and child labor.
▶ **Workers' Compensation** provides compensation for on-the-job injuries and illnesses. Some workers' compensation programs also require employers to provide job modifications or alternative assignments.
▶ **The Occupational Safety and Health Act (OSHA) of 1970** sets safety requirements for workplaces (see Chapter 9 for a detailed discussion).
▶ **The Family and Medical Leave Act (FMLA) of 1993** requires employers to offer up to 12 weeks of unpaid, job-protected leave during a 12-month period for birth or adoption; care of an ill parent, spouse, or child; or medical treatment. Eligibility requirements include that the individual

	TABLE 6.1

Major EEO Laws and Their Implications

Civil Rights Act (Title VII) of 1964 and Civil Rights Act of 1991	Bar discrimination based on race, color, religion, national origin, or sex (gender). Amended by the **Pregnancy Discrimination Act** of 1978, Title VII now bars discrimination against a woman because of pregnancy, childbirth, or a medical condition related to pregnancy or childbirth. Title VII also requires reasonable accommodation for an employee's religious practices. Employers with fewer than 15 employees are exempt, except in the case of intentional discrimination. *Sexual harassment* is also prohibited under Title VII, making it unlawful to harass an applicant or employee because of that person's gender. Harassment can include unwelcome sexual advances, requests for sexual favors, and other verbal or physical harassment of a sexual nature. (See Chapter 9 for more information about sexual harassment.)
Equal Pay Act (EPA) of 1963	Makes it illegal to pay different wages to men and women if they perform equal work in the same workplace.
Age Discrimination Employment Act (ADEA) of 1967	Bars discrimination against people over 40 years of age and prohibits retaliation against anyone involved in an ADEA discrimination complaint. All private-sector employers with 20 or more employees must comply.
Immigration Reform and Control Act (IRCA) of 1986	Bars discrimination against applicants on the basis of citizenship or nationality. In addition, the IRCA prohibits recruiting and hiring aliens (noncitizens) who are not eligible for U.S. employment. For employers with four or more employees, the IRCA requires that employers provide a working environment that prohibits verbal or physical abuse based on an individual's national origin.
Rehabilitation Act of 1974 and Americans with Disabilities Act (ADA) of 1990	Prohibit discrimination against a qualified person with a disability and prohibit retaliation against someone involved in this type of discrimination complaint. The ADA requires that employers of 15 or more reasonably accommodate those with known physical or mental limitations, unless doing so would impose an undue hardship on the operation of the employer's business. Beyond what are typically considered to be physical and mental disabilities, obesity, psychological challenges, disease, allergies, and diabetes are also covered.
Genetic Information Nondiscrimination Act (GINA) of 2008	Bars discrimination against employees or applicants because of genetic information. Genetic information includes information about an individual's genetic tests and the genetic tests of an individual's family members, as well as information about any disease, disorder, or condition of an individual's family members (i.e., an individual's family medical history).

Source: EEOC (Equal Employment Opportunity Commission) (2010). Laws Enforced by EEOC. Retrieved January 5, 2010, from www.eeoc.gov/laws/statutes/index.cfm.

has worked for at least 12 months and has worked an average of 25 hours per week. The FMLA applies to businesses with fifty or more employees. FMLA leave can sometimes overlap with Title VII requirements governing leave for pregnancy and pregnancy-related conditions, and with ADA and Rehabilitation Act requirements governing leave as an accommodation for an employee with a disability (EEOC, 2010).

For information on laws that govern other elements of spa operation, see Chapter 9.

→ HUMAN RESOURCES PRACTICES

Human resources practices include methods used to manage people in a business. Sometimes called personnel systems, these techniques include establishing job responsibilities, recruiting, selecting, training, monitoring, compensating, retaining, evaluating, and terminating staff. Human resources practices are common to all businesses, and the processes are fairly standard. In this section, each phase of the hiring process is briefly described, incorporating any elements that may be unique to the spa industry. Details related to training, monitoring, retaining, evaluating, and compensating staff are given in Chapter 7.

Establishing Job Descriptions

Job descriptions are a tool used by salon and spa businesses everywhere. Job descriptions assist employees in understanding the job they have been hired to perform. Spa job descriptions have many functions. They help managers choose the qualifications needed for selecting each position in the spa, provide facts to use in job postings, give employees an overview of their duties and responsibilities, and offer guidance in assessing an employee's performance. Lastly, job descriptions are a "road map" for spa leaders to help direct consistency in the way services are delivered.

A job description should be developed for each position in the spa. Each job description should include a written job summary, essential duties and responsibilities of the position, qualification requirements for the position, required education and experience, physical demands of the work, and details about the work environment. The job descriptions may also include details about place of the position in the organizational hierarchy. Thus each job description illustrates the specific duties of the position, and the standard operating procedure (SOP) manual provide information about how to perform those duties. Visit the online resources for this book for sample job descriptions for key spa personnel.

Many organizations do not use formal job descriptions, though establishing requirements for the position is still necessary. Job descriptions are recommended by human resources professionals and attorneys because they can assist managers to stay on task throughout recruitment, training, and evaluation efforts. The American with Disabilities Act (ADA) does not require employers to have job descriptions, but this type of document can be extremely helpful should a claim be filed under the ADA.

Employees Versus Independent Contractors

An **independent contractor** is just that: someone who provides a service to the business but is not an employee of the business. According to the International Spa Association (2010), 17.4 percent of all spa workers in 2009 were contracted. Day spas have the largest percent of contracted workers (19%) and resorts the smallest (10%). The vast majority of contract workers in the industry are service providers. Before provider positions are posted and the selection process is begun, spa managers must first decide whether they want to hire employees or contracted workers. Most spa providers have a preferred way of working. Some like the independence and self-sufficiency of contract work; others prefer the security, consistency, and medical benefits that are usually associated with employment.

From a spa manager's perspective, there are advantages with either choice. Because different laws govern compensation and tax treatment of independent contractors, it is generally less expensive to contract service providers. The primary advantage of hiring employees is the ability to have greater control over spa services. In the independent contractor scenario, sometimes called *booth rental,* the manager's role is more that of a landlord than a director.

Although spa management decides whether to contract or hire an employee, the Internal Revenue Service (IRS) sets the rules for this determination. When spa managers are weighing their options, their preferred degree of control over the worker must be assessed. There are three categories that the IRS uses to make this determination (IRS, 2010):

- ▶ **Behavioral:** Does the company control what the worker does and how the worker does his or her job? (That is, stipulating hours of work and/or requiring a full-time schedule, permission for absences, or attendance at meetings and training sessions are all means of behavioral control.)
- ▶ **Financial:** Are the business aspects of the worker's job controlled by the payer?
- ▶ **Type of relationship:** Are there employee-type benefits? Is the work performed a key aspect of the business?

There is no set number of factors that establishes a worker as an employee or an independent contractor, and no one factor stands alone in making this determination. According to Skip Williams (2009), a recognized leader in the spa industry, "the IRS [is] looking for spas that violate this rule/law. They have warned us . . . and are coming down hard on the spa and salon business." The bottom line is that if the manager wants control, the best choice is to hire an employee.

Recruiting

Recruiting is the process of attracting, examining, and selecting qualified people for a job. The purposes of recruiting are clear: to increase the pool of job applicants, increase the success rate of selection, and help meet the organization's legal and social obligations regarding diversity in the workforce. Once a staffing need is determined, the first step in recruiting is to announce the availability of the position. This announcement, often called a *job posting,* is the primary tool used to recruit employees. Based on the position and spa policies, postings can be advertised in newspapers, magazines, or online, or sent directly to individuals or educational institutions that specialize in qualifying those in the position being sought. Other means of recruiting may include using internal or external referral programs, partnering with trade schools, creating internship programs at the location, and recruiting at trade shows or professional association networking events. An employment agency may also be contracted to assist in the process.

The key to successful recruiting is targeting your audience. New generations are attracted by a clear and persuasive recruiting message. Frame this message in terms of what you have to offer today, and in the immediate future, and your potential employee will be more apt to be interested in exploring opportunities with your company. Keep in mind that your job posting represents not only you, but also your business. It is likely that not only will job candidates be seeing your position announcement; customers, community members, and competitors will also see it. Several online spa job posting sites may be useful in recruiting; a list is included in the Appendix at the end of the book.

Selecting Candidates

Selection of candidates for a position generally includes several stages: application, interviews, decision, position offer, and hiring the employee. During the initial stage, applicant requirements should be included in the position announcement. This helps eliminate unqualified candidates. Spa managers should also require completion of an application form. Information requested on this form should include contact information, work history, education and training, and references. For manager positions, a résumé is generally requested; and for service providers, proof of licensure. A sample application form is provided in the online resources, in the section on recruitment. The purpose of the application materials is so that the spa manager can assess the eligibility and qualifications of each candidate.

The information requested during the preemployment process should be limited to what is essential for determining if a person is qualified for the job—any information regarding race, gender, national origin, age, and religion is not appropriate. In general, unless the information is essential for assessing whether the applicant can do the job, questions related to height, weight, economic status, marital status, number of children, disability, or an applicant's medical history should be avoided (EEOC, 2010).

Once the applicant pool has been reviewed, interviews with candidates generally take place. Interviews can be conducted over the phone or in person. Personal interviews have the advantage of allowing the interviewer to observe the applicant's communication style, grooming habits, and confidence. Spa managers are typically troubled about what to ask in an interview, but maybe a better question might be what not to ask.

Because of today's legal considerations, there are some general rules to keep in mind during this stage of the selection process. It may help to write a script listing the questions you will ask each candidate. Check the list to make sure all questions comply with EEO laws. Take notes during the interview, and keep the interview notes together with the candidate's paperwork. Be consistent! To assist with the review of candidates after this stage, think of the perfect answer for each of the questions you have prepared and compare the candidates' answers.

When developing the list of questions, consider including situational inquiries. This style of questioning has been very successful in selecting employees for the service industry. *Situational inquiries* ask candidates to provide an example of a past experience to demonstrate their abilities. For example, instead of asking the candidate, "Can you handle a difficult guest?," A question such as, "Tell me about a situation in which you responded to an upset guest, and what was the outcome?," may provide you with actual evidence of this skill instead of just an opinion. The way the candidate has handled such a situation in the past is most likely how he or she will handle the same situation in the future. A list of sample interview question can be found in the online resources.

For service providers, a hands-on assessment is a good idea. In this case, the most effective assessor is a service provider who is experienced in the candidate's area. Hands-on assessments allow for the evaluation of level of customer care, hands-on skills and preferences, professionalism, and the confidence of the provider. More than one assessment may be necessary for a thorough evaluation. These sessions do not need to include a full treatment; an evaluator can generally complete the review in a shortened 15- to 20-minutes session.

Beyond skills, spa managers are wise to also hire based on attitude. Hiring individuals who have a positive attitude, with passion and inner motivation to serve the client, will make it easier to build a winning team. Thinking that you can change the attitude of a new employee, or that the candidate "just needs a chance," can prove fatal to your business. The behavior and attitude that is evident during the interview will likely be the behavior you will get at work.

With a thorough selection process and clear understanding of the suitable candidates, the correct decision can be made and the right candidate hired. The selection process is complete once the spa manager has offered the job, including compensation details, the candidate understands the offer, has accepted the position, and an employment contract is signed.

→ EMPLOYEE POLICIES AND PROCEDURES

General employee policies and procedures are often developed as part of an employee manual or handbook that includes items such as guest service and communication policies, safety and security procedures, and general employee expectations. An **employee handbook**, which may be one of the standard operating procedures documents, is a tool used by managers that outlines the terms and conditions of employment and may reference compensation and job requirements as well as providing guidance on how to achieve the company mission. See the online resources for some sample employee handbook materials and editable template forms for creating new human resource policies and procedures. Employee manual contents available in the online resources are listed in Table 6.2. A sample Recruitment Request Form and a sample Job Advertisement Checklist are provided in Figure 6.6.

Job Advertisement Checklist	
Quantity	Item
	Job title
	Job number
	Employer
	Location
	Job description summary
	Key responsibilities
	Minimum qualifications
	Required experience
	Required skills
	Date applications due
	Name of contact person
	Method of application
	Address/fax/email address/web site form link
OFFICE USE ONLY	
Completed by:	
Authorized by:	

Figure 6.6 Sample Job Advertisement Checklist

SAMPLE RECRUITING POLICY AND PROCEDURE

Recruiting Policy

Recruiting procedures are to be conducted in compliance with applicable regulations. Only employees who are professionally qualified to conduct treatments can perform those treatments. The spa manager must approve all new recruits. The Recruiting Procedure must be followed.

Recruiting Procedure

1. When a potential new employment opening is recognized, the department head must complete the Recruitment Request Form and Job Description Form and submit them to the spa manager.
2. The spa manager must review the Recruitment Request Form and Job Description Form and reply within one week.
3. If approved, the department head is to request existing résumés on file from the spa manager and review them for potential candidates.
4. The department head is to prepare a Job Opening Notice and display it on the internal notice board to find out if employees know any potential candidates.
5. If no suitable applicants are identified, the position should be advertised. The department head is to draft a job advertisement and submit it to the spa manager for approval.
6. The spa manager must review the draft job advertisement and reply within two days.
7. The department head is to review applications received in relation to the job position requirements and sort them according to suitable versus not suitable applications.
8. Letters acknowledging receipt of suitable applications under consideration and applications denied should be sent out within one week after the application submission date.
9. If there are more than eight potential candidates, the department head is to conduct telephone interviews to short-list the potential candidates.
10. The department head is to telephone the short-listed applicants and invite them to attend an interview.
11. The department head should interview the short-listed applicants and identify the top four candidates.
12. The references of the top four candidates must be checked.
13. The remaining applicants should be invited to attend an interview with the spa manager.
14. If required, a personality assessment is to be conducted.
15. If required, a third interview should be conducted with both the department head and the spa manger attending.
16. If applicable, the remaining candidates must perform a treatment demonstration for the department head and the spa manger.
17. The department head and the spa manger must make a decision as to the preferred candidate. After agreement, the department head must telephone the successful candidate and make a verbal job offer.
18. If the candidate accepts, conduct the Employment Contract Procedure.
19. Prepare Application denied letters for unsuccessful applicants and post them after the employment contract is signed and returned.

TABLE 6.2

Standard Operating Procedures
Policy and Procedure Sections for Human Resources

Policies, Procedures, Forms and Maps

Recruitment, including job opening notice, job advertising checklist, interview questions list, and sample letters for applicants under consideration and unsuccessful candidates

Job Descriptions, including samples for the following positions:

Spa Director

Spa Manager

Spa Supervisor

Spa Therapist

Spa Technician

Housekeeping Manager

Spa Attendant

Spa Sales Manager

Spa Receptionist

Employment Contract, including sample job offer and employment confirmation letter

New Employee Orientation

Buddy/Partner System

Probation Period

Performance Warning

Breach of Employment Contract

Employee Resignation

Employee Termination

Exit Interview

Employee Retrenchment

Shift Roster Preparation

Time Recording

Performance Appraisal

Training and Career Development

Employee Counseling

Continuous Improvement Program

Spa Security

Employee Arrival

Employee Departure

Time Sheet, including sample Time Sheet Form

Shift Roster

Leave, including sample Leave Form

Personal Communications and Errands

Employee Access, including Gender-Specific Areas Access Request Form

Non-Public Areas

Client Access

Emergency Evacuation, including a sample Map of Emergency Evacuation Exits

(continued)

TABLE 6.2

(*continued*)

Policies, Procedures, Forms and Maps

First Aid Implementation, including a sample map of First Aid Kit Locations and First Aid Incident Report Form

Operating Equipment and Systems

Smoking

Photography

Lost Items, including a Lost Items Form

Found Items, including a sample Found Items Form

Employee Presentation, including sample Uniform Request Form

Telephone Etiquette

Employee Communication

Employee Meetings

Continuous Improvement, including a sample Continuous Improvement Suggestion Form

Performance Appraisals and Training, including a sample Training Request Form

Employee Benefits

Gratuities

Employee Resignation

KEY TERMS

Cosmetologists

Employee handbook

Equal employment opportunity (EEO) laws

Estheticians

Executive spa director

General manager

Human resources

Independent contractor

Job descriptions

Massage therapists

Nail technicians

Organizational structure

Recruiting

Spa technicians

REVIEW QUESTIONS

1. What are the three categories that comprise the spa staff?
2. In a resort, under what division do you generally find the spa?
3. Who are spa service providers, and in what area does each provider focus?

4. What is the difference between a spa technician and a spa therapist?
5. What group of laws addresses employment standards in the United States?
6. What is the purpose of a job description?
7. What are the key differences between employees and contractors?

REFERENCES

Acupuncture.com (2010). Retrieved January 12, 2010, from www.acupuncture.com/statelaws/statelaw.htm.

AMTA (American Massage Therapists Association) (2009). States Regulating Massage Therapy. Retrieved January 4, 2009, from www.amtamassage.org/pdf/Regulated_States.pdf.

ASCP (American Skin Care Professionals) (2010). Board Information. Retrieved January 12, 2010, from www.ascpskincare.com/become/boardinfo.php#FL.

Associated Bodywork and Massage Professionals (2010). ABMP Releases New Data on Massage Therapist Population. Retrieved May 4, 2010, from www.massagemag.com/News/massage-news.php?id=8992.

EEOC (Equal Employment Opportunity Commission) (2010). Laws Enforced by the EEOC. Retrieved January 5, 2010, from www.eeoc.gov/laws/statutes/index.cfm.

Find a Beauty School (2010). Licenses and Laws. Retrieved December 1, 2010, from www.findabeautyschool.com/site/licenses-and-laws.aspx.

Entrepreneur Press and Eileen Figure Sandlin (2005). *Start Your Own Hair Salon and Day Spa*. Irvine, CA: Entrepreneur Media.

International Spa Association (2010). ISPA 2010 U.S. Spa Industry Study. Retrieved November 29, 2010, from www.experienceispa.com/includes/media/docs/ISPA2010USSpaIndustryStudy.pdf.

IRS (Internal Revenue Service) (2010). Independent Contractor or Employee? Retrieved January 13, 2010, from www.irs.gov/businesses/small/article/0,,id=99921,00.html.

Roosevelt, Theodore (1900). American 26th U.S. Presidential Speech. Retrieved June 22, 2010, from BrainyQuote.com, www.brainyquote.com/quotes/quotes/t/theodorero137797.html.

WFCMS (World Federation of Chinese Medicine Societies) (2010). Retrieved January 12, 2010, from www.wfcms.org/english/detail.aspx?innerID=2009527162133453.

Williams, Skip (2009). Independent Contractors in Spas—Don't Go There!! Retrieved August 19, 2009, from www.spaclique.com/indes.pho/independent-contractors-in-spas-dont-go-there.htm.

7

Spa Facility Operations

⟶ LEARNING OBJECTIVES

At the end of this chapter, readers will be able to

- Understand the components of a spa facility.
- Implement vendor and product selection criteria.
- Use tools for inventory management.
- Understand equipment service life.

Whenever I go on a ride, I'm always thinking of what's wrong with the thing and how it can be improved.

—Walt Disney

↪ WHAT IS FACILITY MANAGEMENT?

In the capacity of managing a spa building, a spa director can frequently wear the "hat" of facility manager. Managing a spa is similar to being a home owner. If you are not familiar with this responsibility, the transition will undoubtedly involve an introduction to many new responsibilities. Along with the thrill of this new endeavor comes the responsibility of understanding how the facility functions to support a spa's amenities. A typical spa has many pieces, fixed and movable, all of which make up the facility. **Movable objects** are the pieces that would hypothetically "fall out" if the building or land were to be turned upside down, such as furniture, supplies, movable equipment, and other building contents. Exterior features, the building, and permanent fixtures and equipment are generally considered **fixed objects**. See Table 7.1 for partial list of facility objects.

TABLE 7.1

Facility Management Elements

Building exterior and land	Parking area, windows, lighting, waste disposal and collection, air conditioning equipment, heating equipment, landscaping, entrances, exits, building facade
Building interior	Electrical outlets and capacity, plumbing, air conditioning and heating zones, thermostats, wiring, outlets for phones and IT, lighting zones, sound system and speakers, fixtures, built-in cabinetry/storage, flooring, walls and ceilings, rooms, hallways, interior finishes, stairs, elevators, doors
Furniture, fixtures, and equipment:	
Public spaces	Furniture, fountains/water features, lighting, sound system and speakers, plants, sculpture and artwork
Salon	Pedicure chairs, pedicure foot spas, stylist chairs, shampoo station, manicure tables and chairs, makeup table and chairs
Treatment rooms	Massage table, hot-towel cabinet, oil/product warmers, shower, facial steamer, tub
Exercise equipment room and wellness center	Treadmill, elliptical trainer, stationary bike, recumbent bike, rowing machine, free weights, stair stepper, circuit training machines, heart rate monitor, pedometer, body fat analyzer, sound system
Fitness studio	Mats, blocks, straps, balls, drinking fountain
Café and juice bar	Café: dishwasher, microwave, refrigerator, cook top; juice bar: extraction juicers, vita-mix blender, refrigerator, specialized counter surfaces, ice machine, oven, freezer, dry storage
Rest and locker rooms	Lockers, cabinetry, sinks, showers, chairs
Laundry	Washer, dryer, steam press, ironer, cabinetry
Administrative space	Computer, reception/reservation computer, printer, fax, copy machine

REALITY CHECK

Medical spas may have additional requirements such as specialized equipment. However, many of the manufacturers of high-tech medical equipment also provide on-site maintenance packages for a monthly or annual fee. Purchasing these packages is advisable because it helps ensure that equipment is properly maintained and eliminates the risk of warranties being voided if maintenance and repairs are not performed by a certified technician. This cost should be calculated into the annual lease or purchase price of the equipment.

REALITY CHECK

In larger facilities, such as a resort or destination spa where the spa is part of a multifunctional operation, there may be a designated facility manager who oversees some or all of the noted responsibilities. As the spa director in this situation, you may think you are off the hook. This is not true. The reality is that you have access to someone with a specialized skill set, and this can be a huge asset if managed properly. However, as spa manager, you remain ultimately responsible for the safety, function, and upkeep of the building and its contents. It is likely that the facility manager has a different set of priorities than you do, and it is your job to communicate thoroughly so that your needs are met in an efficient and timely manner.

WHO HAS THE KEYS?

Whether you are opening a new spa or reorganizing an existing operation, successful maintenance of the facility is dependent on well-developed organizational skills. To start, when staging the facility—that is, creating a physical action plan for the facility—there are several keys to success.

The first key is to keep and file everything. It is likely that every spa document from the beginning of this process to the end will be important. If you are coming into an established spa, do your best to locate the information related to the facility and invest the time to develop a system of organizing the documents. Look back at Table 7.1 and note all of the spa equipment and building systems for which you are accountable. It is likely that each element came with documentation and directions. File every piece of paper that comes in with the equipment and products. This may include a packing slip, warranty information, user manual, maintenance instructions, email addresses, phone numbers, copies of your orders, and other documents. Filing all this paperwork may be tedious if you are taking delivery of everything necessary for a new facility, but it will be well worth your time. Make note that each piece of equipment has its own unique identification number. This may not seem important until you need to order a part for one of the Jacuzzi tubs in the spa and ordering the correct item requires the model number and an identification number that is not visible on the unit after it is installed. If this step is missed, your options may be reduced to opening the wall to find the information or offering a new "soaking treatment" in your nonfunctioning tub. It is much more convenient and also more cost-effective to reach into your desk drawer, pull out the file, and provide the person on the phone with the required information. In this business, as in most, brilliance is realized in the ability to fully exploit the details.

The second key to success is to label everything. Regardless of the size of the facility, the spa manager cannot be everywhere all the time as the spa is being staged. The better you are able to communicate with others even when you are unavailable, the more effective you will be as a spa manager. Think of your labels as the grease necessary for the business to run smoothly. Do your best to mark the placement of everything coming in to the spa with obvious labels so that everyone is aware of the placement of equipment and supplies. If you already have guests in the spa, use your staff members as verbal "signs." Give them the necessary information to direct delivery or installation. A labeling system will also allow easy tracking once the spa is open for maintenance and safety checks.

REALITY CHECK

As deliveries are being made, it is common to have contractors finishing their work, inspectors visiting from the building department, code enforcement and health department representatives all in the space at the same time. Keep a checklist so you know who has been there and who is still scheduled to visit; also keep a list detailing any issues identified by the contractors and inspectors that need attention. If there is more than one person managing the project, maintaining a log book can be helpful in communicating what was accomplished in the other person's absence. In addition, this is a great way to track critical decisions so that when questions arise, you have documented when and by whom the decisions were made.

The final key to successful facility management is the development of standard operating procedures (SOPs) for the facility. This is perhaps the most meaningful key to success, as it encompasses full representation of the business. Develop operating policies and procedures that allow staff, vendor, and client participation. That may sound like a tall order and will require focus in the development phase; however, this is necessary groundwork and will be the most valuable asset of the business.

⟶ MAINTENANCE SAFETY AND SANITATION

In the role of facility manager, the spa manager needs to understand the physical facility, its contents, and also how the contents function. To ensure that the facility is well maintained, the spa manager must have a working knowledge of the laws that govern spa operations and work continuously to stay within the laws. See Chapter 9 for more information about legal aspects.

SAMPLE SANITATION POLICY AND PROCEDURE

Sanitation Policy

Detail products for each task:

1. Walls, ceilings, floors, furniture, and equipment must be free from dust and debris.
2. Showers, steam rooms, toilets, shampoo bowls, sinks, and service sinks must be thoroughly cleansed and sanitized daily.
3. Pedicure/manicure soaking units, hydrotherapy tubs, steam capsules, or wet treatment tables must be thoroughly cleaned and sanitized after each use.
4. Towels, sheets, robes, slippers, and facial wraps must be placed in a covered/enclosed container until properly laundered.
5. The use of any article that is not properly cleansed and sanitized is prohibited.
6. All waste material must be removed daily.
7. Trash will be stored in a covered washable container and not be left in the facility overnight.
8. Professional implements and tools will be cleansed thoroughly with soap and water and sanitized by using approved disinfectants, autoclave, or UV exposure as allowed by the appropriate state agency.
9. Creams, lotions, shampoos, conditioners, soaps, and other cosmetics for use by guests must be kept in sanitary, closed containers.
10. Pets are prohibited in the spa.

Sanitation Procedure

Cleaning the Pedi Spa
1. Start draining process after final foot removal, before prepping feet for polish.
2. After client has left and tub is drained, follow sanitation steps in the Pedi Spa Manual.
3. Clean all product bottles and replace fresh towels that were used during treatment.

Cleaning the Vichy/Wet Treatment Room
1. Escort client from the room, back to waiting area, and offer water or tea.
2. Immediately go back to room and start cleaning process behind closed doors.
3. Rinse table and pad and remove pad to rinse underneath.
4. Spray cleaning solution on table and pad and rinse well; wipe dry.
5. Make sure floor is totally rinsed of product before spraying with disinfectant.
6. Rinse floor well with water and dry as much as possible.
7. Squeegee down walls. Replace towels that were used during treatment.

Cleaning the Facial Room
1. Escort client to waiting area, and offer water or tea.
2. Immediately go back to room and start cleaning process behind closed doors.
3. Remove sheets and deposit them in appropriate covered container.
4. Replace towels used during treatment.
5. Prepare table for next appointment.
6. Wipe all product bottles, steamer, and surfaces.
7. Make sure floor is clean.

Cleaning the Massage Room
1. Escort client to waiting area. Offer water or tea.
2. Immediately go back to room and start cleaning process behind closed doors.
3. Remove sheets and deposit in appropriate covered container.
4. Prepare table for next appointment.
5. Wipe down all oil bottles and bottle warmer with dry cloth.
6. Make sure floor is cleaned and swept.

Figure 7.1   Sample Sanitation Checklist

Example Post Treatment Checklist						
Room	Time	Time	Time	Time	Time	Time
Task						
Treatment						
Remove dirty linens						
Wipe bottles						
Dry counters						
Clean sink						
Replace towels						
Refill products						
Clean mirror						
Replace linens						
Prepare table						
Clean steamer						
Check floor						
Turn off table warmer						
Wipe door handle						
Turn off towel warmer						
Office use only						
Complete by:						
Checked by:						

The physical aspects of the business—the facility and other assets—should present an inviting retreat environment for the health, wellness, and beauty-minded. Each team member should continually be proactive in efforts to maintain a meticulously clean and inviting spa environment. Maintaining cleanliness standards that guests expect and are required by law takes the effort of every staff member.

Not only will strict adherence contribute to the goal of providing guests with an exceptional experience, it will ensure the safety of both guests and staff. Sanitation guidelines are commonly part of the SOP manual provided to all employees and vendors working in the spa.

There are many sources to consider when establishing SOPs for the facility, such as the local or state department of health (establishment licensure), OSHA (the federal Occupational Safety and Health Administration), the state board of cosmetology, and the fire chief in your district, as they can provide valuable training and materials. Figure 7.1 provides an example of spa policy, procedure, and a task checklist for maintaining spa sanitation. Table 7.2 highlights additional SOP facility operation materials that are available in the online resources for this book. Also included in the online resources are editable template forms for creating new policies and procedures.

TABLE 7.2

Standard Operating Procedures
Policy and Procedure Sections for Facility Operations

Policies, Procedures, Forms and Maps

Process Maps for Treatment Rooms, Stations, Reception, Relaxation Room, Locker Room, Supporting Facilities, Stock
  Requisition & Monitoring, Laundry, General Spa Ambience
Policies, Procedures, and Task Checklists for each of the following:
  Spa Cleaning and Presentation
  Spa Opening—Treatment Rooms
  Posttreatment Preparation—Treatment Rooms
  Spa Closing—Treatment Rooms
  Spa Opening—Stations
  Posttreatment Preparation—Stations
  Spa Closing—Stations
  Spa Opening—Reception
  Spa Presentation—Reception (including Locker Usage Status Form)
  Spa Closing—Reception
  Spa Opening—Relaxation Room
  Spa Presentation—Relaxation Room
  Spa Closing—Relaxation Room
  Spa Opening—Locker Room
  Individual Locker Restock
  Spa Presentation—Locker Room (including Locker Room Toiletry Items Checklist
    Format)
  Spa Closing—Locker Room
  Spa Opening—Supporting Facilities
  Spa Presentation—Supporting Facilities
  Spa Closing—Supporting Facilities
  Store Stock
  Professional Stock
  Retail Stock
  Stock Monitoring
    Master Stock List
    Stock Status Report Format
    Stock Requisition Form
  Linen
  Laundry
  Food and Beverage
    Approved Food and Beverage Menu Format
    Approved Food and Beverage Ingredients List Format
  Reading Materials
  Music (including Approved Music List Format)
  Diffusing Oils (including Approved Diffusing Oils List Format)
  Repairs and Maintenance (including Repairs and Maintenance Log Form)
  Back-of-House

EQUIPMENT LIFECYCLES

Each piece of equipment that is purchased for the spa has a **service life** expectancy. Knowing when to anticipate replacement costs will avoid unwanted surprises related to operations and finances. Table 7.3 highlights the life expectancy of common spa equipment.

TABLE 7.3

Common Spa Equipment Life Expectancy and Replacement Cost

Equipment	Average Life Expectancy (Years)*	Average Replacement Cost, 2010 ($ US)
Hydraulic treatment table	6	4,200
Hot cabbie	2	200
Heating blanket	3	80
Facial steamer	3	550
Lotion warmer	2	45
Wax heater	2	130
Vichy shower	4	5,800
Hydro tub	4	10,500
Pedicure chair	5	3,200
Nail dryer	1	80
Hair dryer	1	150
Experiential shower	8	7,400
Whirlpool	8	5,500
Sauna-dry	7	6,000
Steam room	7	4,500
Cardio—treadmill	3	4,300
Cardio—stepper	3	4,000
Cardio—elliptical	3	2,200
Cardio—bike	4	1,500
Cardio—recumbent bike	5	2,200
Fitness—water cooler	2	180
Strength equipment	7	2,000 per muscle group
Impact mat	2	10 per sq ft
Yoga mat	1	15

*Assumes moderate use and regular maintenance.

REALITY CHECK

If your building is owned by someone other than you, it is important to determine in the lease agreement who is responsible for maintenance and replacement costs associated with the "big ticket" items, specifically, air conditioning, heating, electrical wiring, and plumbing. If you are responsible for any or all of these systems, be proactive by having a contractor assess replacement, repair, and annual maintenance costs so you have the financial reserves required. Malfunctions in any of these systems close a business, at least temporarily. If you do own the building, this assessment will have been done during your property inspection. Regular maintenance and conservative plans for failure of these items will need to be incorporated into business planning.

VENDOR SELECTION

With a clear picture of the needs of the operation, it is now pertinent to determine what other company relationships can add value to the vision of the spa. This process is called **vendor selection** and **product selection**. If you have been thorough in outlining the SOPs for the business, appropriate vendors will be apparent, because their mission and philosophy will be aligned with that of the spa. The commitment that is made bringing a manufacturer's products into the spa should be reciprocated. For example, the vendor should offer training for the staff so they fully understand how to use the product or equipment. The list of vendors that are required to open and operate the spa can be lengthy, and care should be taken in choosing them.

REALITY CHECK

I am constantly amazed every time I enter a spa and see portable massage tables when thousands of dollars worth of seldom-used equipment sit dust-covered in a corner. On average, 55 percent of a spa's revenue is generated by massage services. Put your equipment dollars where they will best generate revenue for the business. Treatment tables should be the best the spa can afford!

There are thousands of companies that service the spa industry. Some produce products for a specific use, such as a manufacturer of laundry equipment. Other companies offer a catalog of products featuring several manufacturers that create similar products. Price is always a consideration when selecting equipment and products, though care should be taken to select quality, especially in equipment that is used daily. When beginning the process, do not attempt to contact everyone who offers spa products. Use the Internet, referrals, and recommendations to create a short list, and contact only those companies in which you are truly interested.

Be considerate. A lot of time, materials, and resources are used by companies to provide you with information about their products and services. Use this time to develop relationships with the companies you have chosen, because a quality partnership will aid the success of your business. Many product vendors will provide both a professional and a retail component that support the treatments performed in the spa. The retail availability of the products used in the treatment room is a critical piece of the guest experience.

⟶ INVENTORY MANAGEMENT

A Harvard Business School Study (Watson, 2008) concluded that the most important factor considered by the consumer when purchasing a product is the availability of the product. It only takes two incidents when a product is out of stock for a guest to look elsewhere. Guests who look elsewhere for products will eventually go elsewhere for services. **Inventory management** is a critical function: Make a commitment to have the products your guests want to purchase always on hand.

Many spa product vendors require minimum quantities (or case packs) when placing product orders. Although it is impossible to maintain minimum quantities at all times, Table 7.4 provides some guidelines on quantities of treatment products that should be kept on hand in a moderate-sized spa. Following these guidelines can help ensure that the spa meets the product demands of its customers.

Many spas use a software package that offers various inventory solutions combined with point-of-sale (POS) features. When product is received at the spa, it is entered into the software program; every time a product is sold, it is automatically deducted from the inventory. If the procedure for inventory management is clearly outlined in the SOPs, it is possible to share responsibility with staff to ensure that physical inventory (product actually on the shelves) and system inventory (what was entered into the computer minus what was sold) balance. This will assist in minimizing "shrinkage" and allow any necessary actions to control it.

As the industry develops, the tools available improve and change to meet the needs of a wide range of operations. Several companies now provide hardware, software, training, monthly maintenance, appointment booking, payroll services, and much more. Your needs might be as simple as an appointment book application that will run on a phone or as complex as a spa with multiple locations and a Web-based reservation system, as is common with resort spas, that all needs to interface with the proprietary management software. There is something available to meet almost any need in most any price range.

Retail Consultation

TABLE 7.4

Quantity Guidelines for Spa Inventory (Moderate-Size Spa)

Item	Recommended Quantity	Minimum Quantity
Basic facial cleansers	6–12	3 of each type
Basic facial toners	6–12	3 of each type
Basic facial moisturizers	6–12	3 of each type
Eye creams	6–12	3 of each type
Facial specialty care items	3–6	3 of each type
Basic body cleansers	6–12	3 of each type
Basic body moisturizers	6–12	3 of each type
Basic body exfoliants	3–6	3 of each type
Body specialty-care items	3–6	3 of each type
Spa apparel	1–3 of each size	1 of each size
Spa accessories	3–6	3 of each type
Candles	3–6	1 of each scent
Music CDs	6–12	3 of each
Videos/DVDs	6–12	3 of each
Books	3–6	1 of each
Small items (travel sizes, lip balms, etc.)	12	3 of each type
Teas, tonics, and other items	3–6	1 of each type

KEY TERMS

Fixed objects

Inventory management

Movable objects

Product selection

Service life

Vendor selection

REVIEW QUESTIONS

1. What is facility management, and why is it important to a spa business?
2. What is the difference between fixed and movable elements of a spa facility?
3. What kind of tool can be used for determining when to budget for new equipment?
4. What should be considered when selecting a spa vendor?

→ REFERENCES

Disney, Walt (n.d.). BrainyQuote.com. Retrieved June 25, 2010, from
    www.brainyquote.com/quotes/quotes/w/waltdisney131639.html.
Watson, Noel (2008). *Exploring Inventory Trends.* Boston: Harvard Business School.

Spa Client
Management

→ LEARNING OBJECTIVES

At the end of the chapter, readers will be able to:

- Understand the needs of the spa guest.
- Know the components of a successful client management program.
- Have the ability to ensure consistency of service delivery in the spa.

Electric communication will never be a substitute for the face of someone who with their soul encourages another person to be brave and true.

—Charles Dickens

Constancy in love is a good thing; but it means nothing, and is nothing, without constancy in every kind of effort.

—Charles Dickens

SPA CLIENT PROFILE

Spas serve approximately 25 percent of the North American population, with more new customers every day. The average spa customer is female, in her mid-forties, married, and Caucasian, with a college degree and an average household income of over $50,000. The average spa guest visits the spa alone to relieve stress, decrease pain, and increase her overall well-being During her first visit to a spa, the selected treatment is likely a massage or facial (Coyle Hospitality Group, 2009; Day Spa Association, 2010; ISPA, 2006).

Spa visitors vary according to the type of spa they visit. According to the Day Spa Association (2010), 95 percent of day spa visitors are females, whereas studies that included visitors to different types of spas have shown men averaging from 25 to 31 percent of visitors (Coyle Hospitality Group, 2009; ISPA, 2006). The majority of spa goers are in their thirties and forties, and whereas most women have their first spa experience in a day spa, men are more likely to visit a resort or hotel spa on their inaugural visit. For the Coyle Hospitality Group's Spa Sentiment Research Report (2009), the group surveyed 1300 spa goers and found that all had visited a spa within the past twelve months, though the largest number of respondents had visited only one to two times (38 percent), as opposed to only 9 percent who reported more than ten visits during the same period. Referrals or "word of mouth" was the number-one reported reason that a potential customer selected a particular spa to visit the first time (74 percent). There is only one chance to make a first impression!

WHAT IS CLIENT MANAGEMENT?

Client management is a term that is used frequently to reflect the many aspects of a client's spa experience. Successfully managing each element of a client's visit is essential to the success of the business. A great deal of time and money is dedicated to attracting clients to visit our spas. The true measurement of how well a product is delivered is reflected in the number of first-time guests who become loyal and regular customers.

There are inherent differences in the types of services at spas, as described in Chapter 3. Whatever the distinguishing features may be, however, there are many similarities among spas. Whether we call the people who purchase spa services guests, clients, customers, or patients, they return regularly because we are delivering on our promise and meeting their expectations.

Various "tools" for managing client information (databases, software packages, etc.) can make the job much easier, but such tools alone cannot determine the success or failure of the spa. Whatever success the business achieves is always a direct result of the consistency and quality of the product delivered.

Quality—An essential and distinguishing attribute of something or someone; a degree or grade of excellence or worth (Dictionary.com, 2010).

If they are asked, most people will define a quality product as something of high value, or something without imperfections. These are suitable definitions in all businesses and across all industries, but the delivery of quality is generally assessed by consistency. Consistency builds a spa's reputation and reinforces the strength of the brand.

Consistency—Harmony of conduct or practice with profession (Merriam-Webster Online Dictionary, 2010).

Consistency is a crucial requirement to any successful enterprise (Williams, 2010). Excellence may be defined as consistency in delivering the product, but the product must also meet the needs of the customer. Consistently producing a bad hair cut, for example, will create brand identity but not customer satisfaction.

How does the spa industry define quality? Is it excellence? Is it consistency? Is there a true advantage to measuring our ability to deliver a product? It is surely recognized that something is wrong when two of the same services rendered in the same facility are delivered differently. Spa treatments are definitely not "one size fits all." Therefore, consistent quality combined with a customized and personal experience is what makes the experience superior. Customized and consistent are not mutually exclusive.

Service providers with their own unique way of performing services can distinguish themselves as professionals in private practice. The business is consistent by simple virtue of having only one person perform the treatment. However, even in this scenario, failure to provide consistent service is possible. In a spa, where there are multiple providers, there can be discrepancies among employees' level of service as a result of differences in experience, training, or other factors.

If the spa is delivering excellent service, is there a problem? This issue has many layers, but at the core the spa will be spending time and dollars attempting to market an unknown product. If a protocol is being followed to perform a particular treatment, expectations may have been met, but will they continue to be? To have a successful business and an identifiable brand, high-quality, consistent service needs to be delivered to the client.

REALITY CHECK

Staff retention is, unfortunately, a common complaint of spa owners and managers, which can inevitably have an overall impact on consistency.

It is important not to isolate the need to be consistent as a task just for the treatment providers. It is actually the treatment providers who have the most flexibility for customization. The term *consistent service* should refer to the full experience of the customer when interacting with the business, from anticipation to recollection. See Figure 8.1 for a model of the spa client experience (Clawson and Knetsch, 1966).

The guest experience begins when the potential client starts gathering information for a spa visit an ends only long after the guest leaves the spa. Spa personnel have the opportunity to make or break a customer's spa experience during any stage in the experience.

Taking the time to create a unique product and fully outline the policies and procedures for each spa process is necessary. The spa can measure consistency using

Figure 8.1   The Spa Client
Experience
Source: Based on a model originally
developed by Marion Clawson and
Jack L. Knetsch in *Economics of
Outdoor Recreation* (Baltimore:
Johns Hopkins Press, 1966).

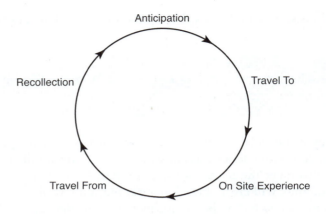

the guidelines established by its policies and procedures. Dedication to training and a commitment to measurement and evaluation are the keys to superior client management. It should not matter which attendant is working today, whether the service was performed by Tricia or Mark, or who answered the phone to schedule the appointment—the client's experience must be the same every time. If it is not, there will never be a business strategy that moves beyond hoping that everyone is on task and committed to excellence today!

It is a well-accepted concept in most businesses that the phone should be answered in a certain way every time. It is also understood that the layout of the retail area should conform to certain guidelines. So, why is it that a constant focus on the way the staff interacts with guests is not resulting in consistency? Is it difficult to achieve consistency? Are we capable of achieving consistency in every customer encounter?

WHAT DOES IT TAKE TO BE CONSISTENT?

Achieving consistency is a challenge. Consistency truly separates successful from unsuccessful businesses. In all industries, attention to detail is required: It takes a combined effort; it takes training; it takes regular inspection and testing; and it always takes a genuine commitment to quality. If it seems more difficult to create consistency in the spa it is not because it cannot be done, but because we have not thoroughly utilized the tools that are available.

Three tools are essential to achieving consistency:

▶ Standard operating procedures
▶ Training
▶ Evaluation and testing

In this chapter we discuss standard operating procedures and training in terms of achieving consistency; evaluation and testing is discussed in Chapter 12.

Standard Operating Procedures

One of the most important tools for achieving consistency is your **standard operating procedures (SOPs)** documents. As described in Chapter 5, SOPs spell out the policies and procedures to be followed in carrying out all tasks of the operation, including client interactions. SOPs contain elements such as maps of potential client interac-

Spa Guest Journey: Reservation and Scheduling Flow

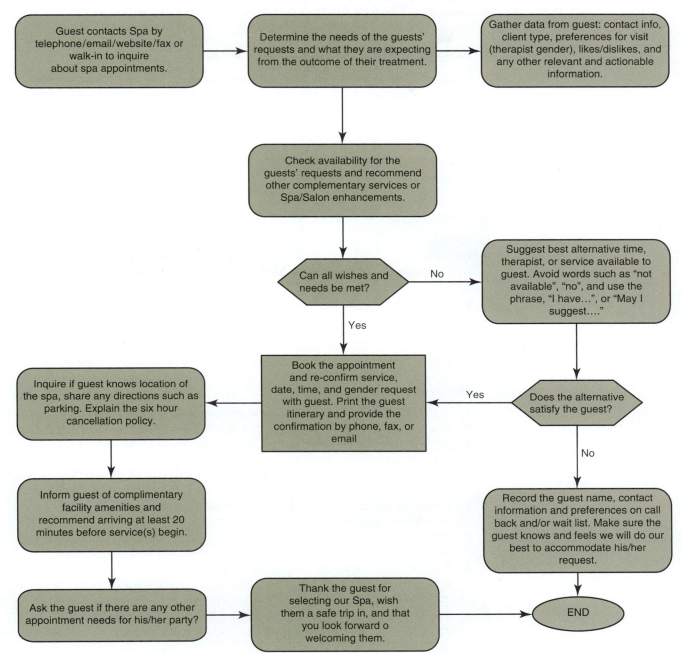

Figure 8.2 Client Interaction Process Map—Reservations

tions (see Figure 8.2 for a sample process map), policies and procedures, and forms and templates to use when completing tasks, as shown in the example in Figure 8.3. Standard policies and procedures for spa client interactions are listed in Table 8.1, all of which are provided in full in the online resources.

To help achieve consistency in client treatments, two different documents are commonly used. A **treatment protocol manual** is a detailed procedural document for each of the treatments and services offered in the spa. It includes descriptions of the products used and the timing and steps each treatment follows. A **product description manual** provides a list of ingredients for every product used or sold in the spa. It can include uses, benefits, and contraindications. Sample content from each of these documents can be found in the online resources for standard operating procedures.

Consistency in Process and Product

Everything done in a business is considered a **process**, and everything provided in a business is a **product**. In the business of spa management, the primary product is **service**. Spa employees share (sell) time, interest, passion, skill, and knowledge with the commitment that the next time a client visits the spa, the employee will again

SAMPLE RESERVATION IN PERSON POLICY AND PROCEDURE

Reservation in Person Policy

Reservations must be processed according to spa procedure and by authorized employees. An existing reservation can only be altered if requested or authorized by the subject client. The Reservation in Person Procedure must be followed.

Reservation in Person Procedure

1. . . . Ask "Which day and time would you prefer and I'll see if it's available."
2. Ask "Do you already know which treatment you would like to experience?"
3. If the client knows the treatment, document the name of the treatment and state the description to confirm it is correct.
4. If the client does not know the treatment, ask "What type of experience would you prefer?"
5. When the client decides, document the name of the treatment and state the description to confirm it is correct.
6. List and describe relevant treatments based on the client's response.
7. Ask "Would you like to request a particular therapist by name or gender?"
8. Document the client's response and repeat it to confirm it is correct.
9. If the client's preferred date, time, treatment, and/or therapist is not available, assist to identify a mutually acceptable reservation.
10. Ask for and insert all appointment details into the Appointment Schedule, including the client's name, daytime contact number, and, if applicable, the client's membership number.
11. Summarize the appointment details to confirm they are correct.
12. Advise the details of the spa's cancellation and no-show policies and conduct Request Credit Card to Confirm Booking Procedure.
13. Advise the client that someone will call him or her two days before the appointment to reconfirm the reservation.
14. Advise the preferred arrival time, including arriving up to an hour before the appointment time if the client would like to use the spa's water and steam facilities free of charge, or to arrive 15 minutes before the appointment time to ensure the client has enough time to prepare for the treatment.
15. If applicable, advise the client to bring swimwear.
16. If required, advise location and parking details.
17. Ask "Is there anything else I can assist you with at this stage?"
18. If yes, address the query.
19. If no, say "Thank you for visiting. I look forward to seeing you again. Good bye."

Action	Reservation Checklist
	Appointment date
	Appointment time
	Treatment(s)
	Requested therapist name
	Requested therapist gender
	Membership number
	First name
	Second name
	Telephone number
	Email address
	Cancellation and no-show policies
	Reminder confirmation call two days before
	Reminder arrival time
	Reminder bring swimwear
	Advise location/parking
	Completed by
	Date

Figure 8.3 Sample Reservation in Person Checklist.

TABLE 8.1

Standard Operating Procedures
Policy and Procedure Sections for Client Management

Policies, Procedures, Forms and Maps

Client Greeting (telephone, in person)
Reservation (telephone, in person now, in person later)
Confirmation
Cancellation
No-Show Policy
Client Arrives Late
Therapist Arrives Late
Therapist Not Available
Check In
Client Profile Form
Privacy Policy
Terms of Entry and Spa Etiquette
Mobile Phones and Pagers
Receiving Clients—Treatment Room
Receiving Clients—Station
Releasing Clients—Treatment Room
Releasing Clients—Station
Check Out
Retail Assistance and Sales
Terms of Sale
Product Samples
Payment (credit or debit card, cash, check, gift voucher, electronic funds)
Client Farewell
Product Returns
Complaints (in person, telephone, written correspondence)
Spa Tour Booking
Guest Book
Spa Brochure Request
Purchase Gift Certificate (in person, telephone)

offer (sell) time, interest, passion, skill, and knowledge. By providing our product consistently, our clients experience wellness, relaxation, education, balance, beauty, and peace. When one of the staff deviates, or does not meet expectations, clients are expected to pay for a product they did not wish to purchase—resulting in stress, discontent, discomfort, and frustration.

The typical response to delivering a spa product poorly is to offer the guest another service at a discount or free of charge, or to provide the current experience at no charge. Although this is a useful gesture, how will you ensure that the same poor experience does not happen again?

Taken to its purest form, a client's visit is merely a process. From the way the spa is marketed, asking people to visit the spa, to welcoming them when they arrive, facilitating check-in, performing the treatments/classes/assessments, selling retail products, collecting payment, and scheduling their next visit are all processes. It is the efficiency of the processes and the ability to ensure that the processes are utilized that guarantee a spa's success.

REALITY CHECK

The discussion of creating consistency always begins in the spa with great intentions and often ends with everyone feeling unappreciated for the quality, skill, and talent they bring to the business. We tend to hear the word "consistency" and envision some kind of assembly line with no personalized elements.

Approach this conversation instead with the following data: The result of experiencing consistency creates a positive reality for our guests. Our guests respond positively to our consistency, describing us as stable, reliable, genuine, professional, and committed. Clients have reported that they may try every one of your treatments and every service provider to find the right fit before looking elsewhere if the quality of the service (not just the treatment) they receive is consistent.

Training

You are your own best employee. **Training** is the example you model every day. It may be called leading, mentoring, parenting, coaching, guiding, encouraging, or teaching, but no matter how you structure it for your team, the example you set will determine the level at which they function. Without trekking down the path of personal exploration, it is well understood that the old adage, "Do as I say, not as I do," will reap only sorrow and pain.

Maintaining a sense of humor while providing training to staff is essential. Also, remember what is at stake when the team is watching every step you take and how you take it.

Spa operating procedures will provide a definitive outline for what training will need to be provided, but what will determine technique? What will be most effective when imparting information to such a diverse group of individuals? Learning in the spa is not just an important topic for employees; it is a critical piece in the success of the business. We ask that employees not only be exceptional students, but also compassionate teachers. It is often assumed that this will occur by simply hiring great people. The misstep is often the hope that something magical will transform new employees from a pool of talented professionals to a fully functioning team. While the hope is an important motivator, it is not a suitable foundation for creating consistency.

Often, training is approached with the expectation that learning is best accomplished through repetition. Although repetition is definitely helpful when refining what has been learned, time is better spent creating understanding, competence (depth of knowledge), and organizing the information in a way that facilitates retrieval and application.

Investing in training and motivating employees is vital to the progress of the spa. Employee training and development today means more than just meeting course requirements. The very definition of training has evolved into a recruiting tool, an effective retention resource, and something that can become an industry differentiator as you create great employees.

No matter whether you are just beginning to create teaching tools or you have a fully established "learning management system," the defining factor in training success is creating an environment and a spa culture in which learning is valued. By providing multiple teaching resources and courses that are relevant to your employees' training needs, it will quickly become evident that the spa values its employees and the refinement that is gained through ongoing training. (See the online resources for sample training formats.)

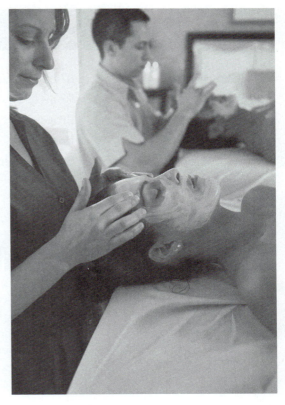

Facial Training

RESORT SPA RATINGS

Although spa clients generally make spa selections using references and word of mouth, spa travelers use a wide variety of methods to select their spa destination. Hospitality rating systems have been assisting individuals with their leisure and travel destination selections for years. Ratings are generally unveiled annually and assist consumers to understand the wide range of spa hospitality offerings, as well as recognize those at the top of their game. Hospitality ratings are one approach that potential spa clients can take to review the quality of a potential spa experience and make an informed spa vacation decision.

There are many different approaches to hospitality ratings. Ratings may be based on reader polls, online consumer traffic, opinions of industry professionals, member ratings, or even advertising commitment. Spa ratings are common in many industry trade publications. Some of the more popular include *American Spa, Condé Nast Traveler, DAYSPA, SpaFinder,* and *Travel and Leisure.* Although the methods used can provide insight for the consumer, some of them may be misleading if the consumer does not understand the sampling technique used.

When it comes to hospitality ratings there are two that have withstood the test of time and for over 50 years have provided the most comprehensive and objective hospitality ratings. The two most recognized and influential in the industry are AAA's diamond ratings and Forbes, formerly Mobil, star ratings. Both rating systems have been in existence for decades, and each has earned a strong reputation for quality and accuracy. In fact, millions refer to these travel guides in researching and selecting their restaurants, hotels, and resorts. While AAA has stuck to its traditional roots of rating hotels and restaurants, several years ago, while still under the ownership of Mobil, star ratings took a dramatic leap into the resort spa industry. To learn more about the Forbes Travel Guide's Spa Star Ratings, see the special section at the end of this chapter.

KEY TERMS

Client management	Quality
Consistency	Service
Process	Standard operating procedures (SOPs)
Product	Training
Product description manual	Treatment protocol manual

REVIEW QUESTIONS

1. What has to occur during your first visit to a business for you to consider returning? What would get you to refer a friend or family member?
2. What type of training do you expect to receive from your employer?
3. What does it mean to be consistent?
4. Why is excellence unlikely without consistency?

REFERENCES

Coyle Hospitality Group (2009). Spa Sentiment Research Report 2009. Retrieved June 20, 2010, from www.coylehospitality.com.

Day Spa Association (2010). Online Spa Consumer Survey. Retrieved June 20, 2010, from www.dayspaassociation.com/index.htm.

Dickens, Charles John Huffam (n.d.). BrainyQuote.com. Retrieved June 22, 2010, from www.brainyquote.com/quotes/quotes/c/charlesdic132524.html (quote #1).

Dickens, Charles John Huffam (n.d.). In *Bleak House*. Retrieved December 9, 2010, from www.goodreads.com/author/quotes/239579.Charles_Dickens?page=3 (Quote #2).

Dictionary.com (n.d.). Quality. Retrieved June 25, 2010, from http://wordnetweb. princeton.edu/perl/webwn?s=quality.

ISPA (International Spa Association) (2006). ISPA 2006 Spa Goer Study. Retrieved June 20, 2010, from www.experienceispa.com//includes/media/docs/ ISPA-2006-Spa-goer-Study.pdf.

Merriam-Webster Online Dictionary (2010). Consistency. Retrieved June 25, 2010, from www.merriam-webster.com/dictionary/consistency.

Williams, Skip (2010). Resources and Development. Retrieved June 20, 2010, from www.resourcesanddevelopment.com/Quality.htm.

FORBES TRAVEL GUIDE'S SPA RATING SYSTEM

The Forbes Travel Guide program began rating hotels and restaurants in North America in 1958. For over 50 years, the Travel Guide has been a consumer advocate for travelers, providing them with helpful resources and a rating that helps decide the hotel or restaurant that will best meet expectations. Recognizing that the resort spa industry had yet to be formally rated or inspected and that spa visitors did not have a reliable source of unbiased information, resort and hotel spas joined the list in 2005 (mobiltravelguide.com, 2007).

Only spas located on a hotel or resort property are rated. Directors of spas located in a hotel or resort will likely already be quite familiar with the rating system and its power. A manager developing a new spa or working on a major renovation needs to have a thorough understanding of the rating process to be well prepared for an upcoming rating inspection. A manager of a spa that is already rated needs to understand the meaning behind the rating and the responsibilities related to deserving and maintaining the rating.

Spa Star Ratings

Hotels and restaurants receive ratings from one to five stars. Ratings of one and two stars are generally based on an assessment that these operations are quick, efficient, clean, and well maintained. Forbes has elected to rate spas only on a scale from three to five stars; spas that receive less than three stars are not rated in the Travel Guide. Gina Taylor, director of operations at Forbes Travel Guide (2010), says that the Travel Guide looks at spas as a luxurious experience, and because a spa experience is so experientially driven, just being efficient, clean, and well maintained is not enough. Table 8.2 lists the Forbes Travel Guide definitions of three-, four-, and five-star spas.

TABLE 8.2

Forbes Travel Guide Star Definitions

★★★★★**Forbes Five Star Spas**

Stepping foot in a Five Star spa will result in an exceptional experience with no detail overlooked. These properties wow their guest with extraordinary design and facilities, and uncompromising service. Expert staff to cater to your every whim and pamper you with the most advanced treatments and skin care lines available is to be expected. These spas often offer exclusive treatments and may emphasize local elements.

★★★★**Forbes Four Star Spas**

Four Star spas provide a wonderful experience in an inviting and serene environment. A sense of personalized service is evident from the moment you check in and receive your robe and slippers. The guest's comfort is always of utmost concern to the well-trained staff.

★★★**Forbes Three Star Spas**

These spas offer well-appointed facilities with a full complement of staff to ensure that guests' needs are met. The spa facilities include clean and appealing treatment rooms, changing areas and a welcoming reception desk.

Source: Forbes Travel Guide, Rating Criteria: Spa. Retrieved October 15, 2009, from www.forbestravelguide.com.

REALITY CHECK

Where do destination spas fit in? Are they rated as resorts or as spas? In the Forbes structure, the most common scenario is a spa rated within a rated hotel. So, for example, The Mayflower Spa at the Mayflower Inn, a destination spa in Connecticut, is rated as a hotel and spa separately.

Achieving a five-star spa rating is not easy. In the first year that spa ratings were published, no spa rated five stars; for 2011, only fifteen spas in North America rated five stars (Forbes Travel Guide, 2010). The first five-star spa resort was the Spa Montage at Montage Resort in Laguna Beach, California, which received the five-star rating in 2006. In 2007, the Spa at Mandarin Oriental in New York joined the list.

Asked what makes these five-star spas stand out from the rest, Gina Taylor (2010) said, "From reservation to the reception to the therapist and the nail technician... it comes down to how the guest was treated. Were they comfortable? Was the staff engaging? How fluid was the experience?" In a five-star experience, the process needs to be flawless and the guest must be led through the spa experience by staff that is genuine and sincere.

In 2010 there were 107 four-star spas. As is apparent in the rating descriptions, even a three-star rating is a compelling achievement and will help consumers recognize the quality of the facilities and services of the spa.

A spa is rated separately from the hotel. During a hotel rating, there are upwards of 500 attributes that are evaluated. During a spa visit, the attributes evaluated are completely different. Consequently, there can be and are four-star spas in three-star hotels, for example, and vice versa. The spa evaluation is influenced only by time spent in the spa, the public spa areas, the locker rooms, treatment rooms, lounge, and the like.

The Rating Process

Forbes offers two separate hospitality services, ratings and consulting. Although there is no fee for the rating service, there is a fee for consulting. Most hotels and resorts will hire a Forbes consultant to complete a service evaluation report on the entire operation prior to a rating evaluation. The consultation can be scheduled just for the spa alone; however, it is more common for properties to include the whole operation, including the hotel, restaurants, and spa (Taylor, 2010).

Consulting will contract to visit during a certain quarter or month. Then management will know when, in general, the rating will occur. With the consultation, the properties are able to review the service standards and receive information on how they performed prior to when a different inspector visits to complete an actual rating. Unlike other rating systems, to maintain the anonymity of the inspector, there is no wrap-up meeting with management at the end of either the consulting or the inspection visit.

There is no formal application process for receiving a star rating. As Forbes Media is quite familiar with hotels and resorts across the country, their research often uncovers spas in need of ratings. According to Gina Taylor (2010), every so often consumer feedback or direct contact from a spa manager will trigger a visit. However, having completed over six years of resort spa ratings, if there are new spas or spas undergoing major renovation, Forbes will know.

As with the consultations, most inspector ratings take place at the same time, meaning the visitor rates the hotel, restaurants, and spa all on the same visit. Forbes has incorporated a process of visiting the property initially to do a facility inspection and, if warranted, later a service inspection; this pattern is followed with spa visits as well. The Forbes team of experts visits anonymously to evaluate properties. There are between fifteen and twenty full-time, year-round inspectors. Interviewers often have extensive hospitality and/or food and beverage backgrounds. Ratings are announced in November for the following year. Rating visits, or the rating season, can come any time after the November announcement up until six weeks prior to the next year's announcement (Taylor, 2010).

The Inspection

The vast majority of the rating effort takes place while the visitor is on site. There is the possibility of some attribute ratings occurring outside the spa visit, such as booking treatments or reviewing spa marketing materials prior to arrival. Although the hotel or restaurant inspectors may utilize a number of tools, such as cameras, stopwatches, and measuring tapes, during their evaluation, because of privacy issues, and to help maintain anonymity, no such tools are used in a spa inspection.

Forbes Travel Guide considers 230 attributes in their star rating evaluation. Because not all the attributes may be applicable to a given operation, in general, around 200 ratings are collected for any one analysis. After the visit, inspectors tabulate scores for each spa. For a five-star rating, a spa must achieve a score of 92 percent or above; for a four-star rating, 82 percent or above; and for a three-star rating 72 percent or above, with high ratings for attributes such as the sense of luxury, cleanliness, and condition. Because of the particular importance of these attributes, a spa may score 75 percent, but if it received a lower score for cleanliness and condition, according to Taylor (2010), it would likely not be awarded a star rating. Spas are automatically disqualified if an injury or ailment occurs, or if there is a gross indiscretion or lack of proper hygiene in the practices or facility (Mobil Travel Guide, 2007).

All attributes are intended to mirror the average traveler's needs and expectations. The following experiences or elements are evaluated:

- Reservation
- Spa reception
- Spa paper and electronic marketing materials
- Public areas, including locker rooms, lounges, and pretreatment spaces
- Treatment One—body or massage
- Treatment Two—facial or nail service

Over the years there have been some changes to the standards used to rate a spa. In 2009, for example, elements of the fitness center were removed from the spa rating. As this element was already incorporated into the hotel rating, the redundancy was removed. Prior to 2010, the emphasis on the review of marketing materials was on the paper versions of the menu and brochures of the spa. In 2010, a change was made to reflect the change in technology that resort spas are embracing, and the ratings now incorporate a greater emphasis on electronic items. The spa facility is a portion of the analysis; however, it appears year after year that the service features of the spa are becoming more prominent.

Rating the Spa Facility and Design

Facility attributes are important, but the rating is not based solely on the physical ambiance or designed spaces of the spa. For example, some kind of pretreatment offering is important, generally hydrotherapy such as steam, sauna, and/or whirlpool.

However, a property that does not have a whirlpool but may have steam, sauna, and/or experience showers would be sufficient. Every such attribute is weighted with a point value, so a spa can still achieve sufficient rating points with alternative pretreatment offerings. Five-star spas most likely have a full range of pretreatment offerings. As another example, gender-specific locker facilities were a previously mandated attribute. Although a majority of spa rated properties do have them, Forbes inspectors can positively assess guest comfort and convenience without these attributes.

Privacy is an issue when it comes to spa design and thus when it comes to star ratings. So items such as the placement of locker facilities is analyzed, including checking the pathways of robed guests to ensure that they are not entering into public hotel spaces. To ensure that the experiences of both genders are of quality, both male and female inspectors are used.

In the analysis, Forbes Travel Guide seeks spas that are clearly distinguished from the other areas of the hotel. Serenity, calm, and inspiring the senses are key. The concept of the spa does not need to reflect that of the hotel to receive a positive rating. For example, the Encore, Las Vegas, has a strong Asian influence in the hotel; inside the spa, however, the influence is Middle Eastern. For the Forbes inspectors, that is fine. As a matter of fact, the Spa at the Encore received the prestigious five-star spa rating in 2010.

Rating the Client Experience

Inspectors analyze the client experience to ensure that whether the client is a first-time or a seasoned spa visitor, the experience is one of quality. Treatment menus should include offerings for the beginner as well as enough variety for the avid spa customer.

Body and beauty treatments are experienced by each service inspector. There are attributes that assess the knowledge of the therapists and technicians. Was the treatment carried out as the therapists said it would be? Did they seem knowledgeable? Were the treatment providers confident in their abilities? Was the guest escorted from the lounge to the treatment room and back to the lounge or locker facility? As mentioned earlier, inspection attributes are developed to reflect the average spa user's experience, and therefore the treatments selected are typically those in the mainstream. For example, massage selections will likely be Swedish, therapeutic, hot stone, or sports. Although these inspectors have likely received hundreds of these treatments and can easily recognize a good one from a bad one, the analysis does not get into detail regarding the technical execution of the treatment. In reviewing the treatment, the inspector is generally looking at factors such as enjoyment level, benefits received, and elements such as whether the massage therapist maintained quiet during the massage if the inspector did not initiate conversation.

Many of the Forbes Travel Guide attributes focus on the guest experience. Elements of comfort, convenience, personalization, technical proficiency, skill, knowledge, cleanliness, condition, ambience, and sense of luxury are all key elements. Table 8.3 lists some common service details selected from a 2009 Forbes Travel Guide online publication.

When asked what advice she had for spa managers seeking a star rating, Gina Taylor (2010) stated, "You can have the most fabulous, esthetically pleasing facility, but if your staff isn't warm, and approachable and doesn't make the effort to make the guest feel taken care of; that beautiful space suddenly feels cold. If they don't feel welcome and comfortable, and if they aren't led through the process in a seamless and kind manner, then you don't even notice the physical beauty and all the attributes the spa may have.... It trickles down to the staff selected and training to make every guest feel special."

TABLE 8.3

Spa Service Details

- Staff is well groomed, with neat, professional, and well-maintained attire.
- Staff members encountered are pleasant, thoughtful, and professional in their demeanor.
- Appointments are booked efficiently, with staff assisting and guiding the guest.
- Staff knowledgeably describes treatments and their benefits.
- Guests do not need to wait or wander after arriving.
- Treatments begin and end on schedule.
- The therapist describes the treatment and inquires about any special requirements or medical concerns.
- Throughout the treatment, the therapist appears to be genuinely an expert.
- The spa atmosphere is relaxed, quiet, private, and comfortable.
- In treatment rooms and locker rooms, hygiene is outstanding and general tidiness is very good.
- Following treatments, complimentary refreshment is offered, or self-service refreshments are immediately available and recommended by staff.
- The therapist is aware that a guest has scheduled multiple treatments.
- Staff can answer detailed questions about the products used in treatments
- There is a comfortable area (not in the locker room) in which guests can relax semiprivately after treatments.
- The spa has a marketing brochure with a list of services offered.

▶ REFERENCES

Clawson, Marion, and Knetsch, Jack L. (1966). *Economics of Outdoor Recreation*. Baltimore: Johns Hopkins Press.

Forbes Travel Guide (2010). Annual Star Awards 2011. Retrieved December 9, 2010 from www.forbestravelguide.com/five-star-spas.htm.

Forbes Travel Guide (2009). Rating Criteria: Spa. Retrieved December 9, 2010, from http://static.howstuffworks.com/pdf/spa-criteria.pdf.

Mobil Travel Guide (2007). Helping You Find a Spa That Delivers on Its Promise of Relaxation and Rejuvenation. Retrieved November 1, 2007, from http://mobiltravelguide.howstuffowrks.com/mtg-inspect-rate-spa.htm.

Taylor, Gina (2010) Director of Operations, Forbes Travel Guide. Personal communication, May 5, 2010.

PART IV
Business Skills and Knowledge

9

Spa Operations and the Law

Types of Spa Ownership
The Business License
Naming the Spa
Provider Licenses
The Americans with Disabilities Act
Insurance for the Spa
Operational Practices
    Alcohol Licensing
    Music Licensing
    Taxes
OSHA
Marketing
Security Cameras
Waivers and Release Forms
Under-Age Clients
Sexual Harassment
HIPAA and the Duty to Warn and Protect
Spa Equipment and Product Safety
Medical Spa Practices
    Physician Supervision
    Medical Insurance Billing
Risk Management
    Discovery
    Analysis and Control
    Implementation
Key Terms
Review Questions
References

⟶ LEARNING OBJECTIVES

At the end of this chapter, readers will be able to:

- Identify the primary laws associated with opening and operating a spa.
- Recognize the operational policies and practices necessary to protect employee and customer safety in the spa.
- Classify the different licenses and permits needed to operate the variety of spa areas, elements, and personnel.
- Appreciate the large number of agencies that regulate the spa industry.

Obedience of the law is demanded; not asked as a favor.
—Theodore Roosevelt

In today's society, it is essential for spa managers to be familiar with and follow the laws established for daily spa operations. When establishing a spa business it is advised that as the owner and/or manager you seek legal counsel for guidance on the many legal elements associated with establishing and operating a spa. This chapter will introduce you to the most common laws established to assist spa owners and managers in creating the business, developing operating practices, and protecting the employees and customers of the spa.

TYPES OF SPA OWNERSHIP

Although there are several types of business ownership, spas generally operate under one of three legal structures: sole proprietorship, partnership, or corporation. Under a **sole proprietorship** structure, the spa has one (or a marital community) owner. As the owner, you are ultimately responsible for all elements of the business. The owner selects the business name, acquires the license, set ups the financial accounts, and so on, and basically establishes the business independently. Under a **partnership** structure, two or more individuals share the responsibilities of the business. Sharing may be equal or, as in a limited liability partnership (LLP, described below), one member of the partnership may be responsible for the operation, the other for the working capital. The partners generally sign a contract outlining each individual's responsibilities and then carry out the functions necessary to establish the business. LLPs are not recognized by every state, and some states allow LLPs only for those that offer select professional services. Setting up a business under a sole proprietorship or partnership structure is a fairly simple process, but both carry **unlimited liability**, meaning that the owners are personally responsible for the business.

Under a **corporation** structure, the spa is a legal entity totally separate from the owners. There are two types of corporations. A **C corporation** is the most common form of business ownership and offers limited liability protection for the owners, tax benefits for health and life insurance deductions, and ownership transferability. A **Subchapter S corporation** (named for the section of the U.S. tax code in which it is defined) is similar, but has some advantages over a C corporation for small business owners. With a C corporation structure, your business is taxed as a corporation, then the owners are taxed again on their profits. With an S corporation, there are more restrictions on how the business is run, but the business itself does not pay taxes; all earnings are "passed through" to the owners, who pay personal income taxes on their gross earnings (Entrepreneur Press, 2005). Thus, there is no double taxation as with a C Corporation.

A corporation or partnership can be structured so the owners have limited liability. A **limited liability corporation (LLC)** or **limited liability partnership (LLP)** protects the owners from the personal liability found in sole proprietorships and general partnerships. There are advantages and disadvantages to each form of ownership. An attorney can help match your situation to the most effective structure for your spa. Whichever structure is chosen, this selection must be made before filing for a business license. Table 9.1 provides a brief overview of the various forms of business ownership.

THE BUSINESS LICENSE

All spas must hold a current establishment license. Rules related to the licensing of businesses are found in the state's cosmetology and massage laws, typically regulated by a state's board of cosmetology and/or department of health. Some states do not have state-wide regulations but do have city, county, or local requirements. It is typical for full-service spas to hold three separate licenses: a business license, a

TABLE 9.1

Forms of Business Ownership

Basic Business Structures	
Sole Proprietorship	The sole proprietorship is a simple, informal structure that is inexpensive to form; it is usually owned by a single person or a marital community.
Limited Liability Company (LLC)	The LLC is generally considered advantageous for small businesses because it combines the limited personal liability feature of a corporation with the tax advantages of a partnership and sole proprietorship.
General Partnership	Partnerships are inexpensive to form; they require an agreement between two or more individuals or entities to own and operate a business jointly.
C Corporation (Inc. or Ltd.)	A C corporation is a complex business structure with more start-up costs than many other forms. A corporation is a legal entity separate from its owners, who own shares of stock in the company. Corporations can be created for profit or nonprofit purposes and may be subject to more licensing fees and government regulation than other structures. Corporations should always be assisted by a qualified attorney.
Subchapter S Corporation (Inc. or Ltd.)	This structure is identical to the C corporation in many ways, but it offers avoidance of double taxation. If a corporation qualifies for S status with the IRS, it is taxed like a partnership; the corporation is not taxed, but the income flows through to shareholders, who report the income on their individual returns.

Special Structures	
	The following business structures are available in some states, but not all. You will need to determine which structure makes the most sense for your business and then see if that structure is available in your state.
Limited Liability Partnership (LLP)	LLPs are organized to protect individual partners from personal liability for the negligent acts of other partners or employees not under their direct control. LLPs are not recognized by every state, and those states that do recognize LLPs sometimes limit LLPs to organizations that provide a professional service, such as medicine or law, for which each partner is licensed.
Professional Service Corporation (PS)	A PS must be organized for the sole purpose of providing a professional service for which each shareholder is licensed. The advantage here is limited personal liability for shareholders. This option is available to certain professionals, such as doctors, lawyers, and accountants.
Limited Partnership (LP)	LPs have complex formation requirements and require at least one general partner who is fully responsible for partnership obligations and normal business operations. The LP also requires at least one limited partner, often an investor, who is not involved in everyday operations and is shielded from liability for partnership obligations beyond the amount of his or their investment. LPs do not pay tax, but they must file a return for informational purposes; partners report their share of profits and losses on their personal returns.
Nonprofit Corporation	Nonprofits are formed for civic, educational, charitable, and religious purposes and enjoy tax-exempt status and limited personal liability. Nonprofit corporations are managed by a board of directors or trustees. Assets must be transferred to another nonprofit group if the corporation is dissolved.

Source: U.S. Small Business Administration (2010). Choose a Structure. Retrieved January 15, 2010, from www.sba.gov/smallbusinessplanner/start/chooseastructure/START_FORMS_OWNERSHIP.html.

cosmetology/salon license, and a massage therapy license. In addition, if part of the hydrotherapy offerings of the spa will include operating a pool (including Watsu, whirlpool, or hot tub), a permit will be necessary. These pool permits are generally provided by the state department of health. Each license or permit requires compliance with specific rules defined by the regulating agency.

REALITY CHECK

Be thoroughly familiar with all applicable regulations before designing a project. Consult those in charge of compliance as early in the process as possible. Written regulations are not always clear to the reader, and mistakes in interpretation will be very costly once construction is underway.

NAMING THE SPA

There is more to naming a business than just coming up with something that sounds good. Thought must be given to state and local requirements and to make sure that there is no infringement on the rights of someone else's business name. The name of a business should be related directly to its vision and concept. Choose words that create an accurate image in the minds of potential clients—words that tell them what the business offers. Naming a business requires both creativity and knowledge of the target market.

To file a business license, you will be required to supply a business name. For these purposes, this can be your personal name, something to use temporarily, or the name you will actually use for the business. If you are the sole owner of your business, its legal name is your full name. If you use your personal name, your Social Security number will appear on the business license. If your business is a partnership, the legal name is the name in your partnership agreement or the last names of the partners. For limited liability corporations (LLCs) and corporations, the business's legal name is the one that was registered with the state government (business.gov, 2009).

Once the spa name is chosen, registering the name is the next step. Only one business at a time can possess a name. To ensure the distinctiveness of the selected name, the name will need to be registered by filing a "doing business as" (DBA) statement. There will be a small fee for this filing, which will allow you to operate under your DBA. Once filed, the government entity of your filing will search to make sure the name is not already in use. Duplication is fairly common, so you should have a backup name or two ready just in case. Registration of your business varies by state. Visit www.business.gov for state-by-state details.

For many businesses that have a presence on the Internet, the trade name is synonymous with the domain name, such as Amazon.com or Monster.com. Domain names are not registered through state or local government; rather, they can be obtained from numerous online businesses, most of which will allow you to conduct a name search before you buy the domain name, to be sure your chosen name is not already taken.

PROVIDER LICENSES

In the United States, health-care licensing is a matter of state law. There is great diversity among the states as to how providers are licensed, who can be licensed, and the scope of that practice. In the United States, members of several licensed professional groups work in the spa industry. The most common are massage therapists, cosmetologists, estheticians, barbers, and nail technicians. Other licensed professionals include chiropractors, practitioners of acupuncture and Asian medicine, and naturopathic physicians. Although several states have attempted to regulate fitness instructors and personal trainers, no states presently regulate fitness professionals (National Board of Fitness Examiners, 2008). Providers must work within their scope of practice. In states in which spa services are regulated, it is a misdemeanor violation for any provider or spa to provide services without a proper license. It is also unlawful to practice beyond the scope of a particular license, which varies by state.

An establishment is always regulated by its highest-level license. For example, if a spa employs a chiropractic physician, the spa must comply with all requirements of that license. In this case the state department of health and board of chiropractics are the regulating agencies. Many states also have requirements detailing what types of licensed practitioners can provide services in a particular type of establishment. For example, to employ an acupuncturist, the spa must register and meet all of the guidelines issued by the department of health to operate as a "clinic," and must obtain the appropriate establishment license.

Hair, nails, and esthetics are generally governed by the state board of cosmetology. Massage therapy and body treatments typically are governed by the state department of health. In accordance

Water Aerobic Instruction

with your local regulating agency, all providers' licenses need to be conspicuously posted at their primary work station. Licenses vary by state, so providers need to understand their scope of practice. For example, in California, unlike other states, estheticians are not allowed to dye or tint lashes (Crossett and Gordon, 2009). Copies of all current business and provider license documents are required to be on site at the spa.

⟶ THE AMERICANS WITH DISABILITIES ACT

In 1990, the **Americans with Disabilities Act (ADA)** was signed into law by President George H. W. Bush. The purpose of the law is to prohibit discrimination against people who have disabilities. The ADA is not just about physical accessibility, although the law does address these elements, as discussed in Chapter 4. It is also not just about equal rights in employment, as covered in Chapter 6. The law also addresses equal access to services. For spa managers, this means looking at how services are delivered to ensure that policies and procedures do not prevent someone with a disability from experiencing a service.

The ADA protects not only the physically challenged, but also the blind and deaf, individuals with learning disabilities, mental health problems, and those suffering from serious medical conditions—all of whom can benefit from a spa's offerings. Completing an accessibility audit on the spa's full menu of services is a requirement for any operation. For instance, what would you need to consider if you offer a body scrub in a treatment room with a private stand-up shower? Table height, room signage, allergies to products used, rigor of the treatment, added accommodations for sitting up, dressing, using the rinsing shower, and communication before and throughout the treatment experience are all possible considerations.

INSURANCE FOR THE SPA

Insurance is necessary to protect your spa operation from loss. Although insurance expenses may seem high, the costs associated with vandalism, theft, fire, or a liability lawsuit can debilitate a spa. An insurance broker can help assist with determining the level of coverage needed for your business. Compare prices and plans to ensure that you are not over- or underinsuring your operation. Several types of insurance should be considered for a spa operation.

Liability insurance is the single most important coverage the business needs. It protects business assets against damages and lawsuits resulting from general negligence. Liability insurance covers against injuries and accidents that may happen at the spa. The cost of this insurance is determined by the size of the business, including assets, number of employees, and actual size of the facility. Additionally, **malpractice insurance** protects against loss resulting from negligence, errors, omissions, and wrongful acts that can be attributed directly to your professional practices.

All businesses may suffer loss as a result of natural disasters. Fire, flood, and storm damage can create a loss for any spa. **Casualty (property) insurance** covers the business against these natural occurrences, as well as against loss resulting from vandalism.

Worker's compensation insurance compensates employees for work-related injuries and illnesses. This mandatory business insurance offers reparation to employees without the necessity of suing the spa business.

Many other forms of insurance are also available to a spa business. Fidelity bonding protects the business against theft. Business interruption insurance can protect your spa in the event of an unexpected closing because of natural disaster, theft, vandalism, and other events. Providing health, life, and disability insurance to employees is common practice in larger spas. To protect specific business assets, personal property insurance (furniture, fixtures, and equipment), automobile insurance, and other forms should be considered. Insurance for real and personal property should cover at least 80 percent of the value of these assets. Business interruption insurance should pay at least 50 percent of fixed operating expenses (Gimmy and Woodworth, 1989).

Certainly, spas should take preventive measures to reduce the likelihood of lawsuits, such as providing suitable levels of training, issuing appropriate warnings to guests, establishing and complying with operating protocols and procedures, and evaluating customers before they receive a service. However, should a suit be filed, the spa must have insurance to cover possible losses.

OPERATIONAL PRACTICES

Alcohol Licensing

To sell alcoholic beverages, you need a liquor license. The procedure for acquiring a liquor license varies and is typically under the jurisdiction of the state, providence, city, or county in which the spa is located. The process consists of filing an application and paying a fee. Some areas restrict the number of liquor licenses available, so if you are interested, you will need to research your local procedures (including cost, degree of difficulty of acquiring a license, timing, etc.) and proceed accordingly.

If you anticipate serving alcohol only at the occasional spa event, you can acquire a temporary liquor license. The procedure is similar: Request a license by filing an application and paying a fee. Most areas limit the number of temporary licenses any one business can acquire in a year.

If you are not selling but are giving complimentary alcoholic beverages to customers, be advised that, if you have included the cost of alcohol in your spa services, then you are, in essence, selling alcohol and will need a license (Anderson, 2008). Your business can only serve alcohol if doing so is not restricted by zoning or prohibited in your lease.

That's the law. There are also, however, the issues of image, responsibility, and contraindications associated with alcohol intake and spa procedures, which must be considered. Starting with image, spas have always been places for health and wellness, and alcohol is not often seen as a healthy endeavor. Be warned that you may be jeopardizing the spa's healthy image if you serve alcohol. Next, there are added business responsibilities. Serving alcohol means that your business must face the inevitable liability concerns, increased insurance premiums, safe-serve training, and oversight. In addition, you will have new product and equipment inventory, including alcohol, glassware, dishwashers, and refrigerators/ice machines. Finally, management will need to address the mixing of alcohol with the provision of spa services. The consumption of alcohol increases body temperature. Under these circumstances, some spa treatments may be contraindicated.

Music Licensing

In an industry that prides itself on providing full sensory experiences, music is essential. Music can help define the ambiance of your spa, put your customers at ease when they have to be placed on hold, calm the serene areas, and liven up your social spa spaces. If you choose to play music at your spa, you will need to obtain the proper permission.

Music may be played if the business has a license from one of or all three performance rights societies: the American Society of Composers, Authors and Publishers (ASCAP), Broadcast Music (BMI), and the Society of European State Authors and Composers (SESAC). Permission is then granted from the copyright holders to allow the spa to play music without paying any performance rights. These licenses are called *blanket licenses* and usually cover almost any song available. These licenses are not only convenient, they are fairly inexpensive. Spas that play music without a license may be subject to fines.

Another option is to acquire your spa music from a music service such as AEI, DMX, Satellite, or Muzak. Spas that subscribe to these services rely on these contracted companies to hold the blanket licenses. Custom or branded CDs are also an option. Branded CDs or music clear both the master and publishing rights. Spas can also legally play music without obtaining a license if they also sell the music to their clients (LaCour, 2008).

Taxes

Sales Taxes

All businesses must have a sales tax identification number. This can be acquired by applying to the revenue division of the state in which the spa operates. The finance division of the city (or county) sales tax division will provide the spa with the requisite sales tax license and policies for recording spa sales. Sales taxes are commonly charged on sales of products, but they can also be charged on the sale of services. So, at the time of purchase, a state-determined sales tax is typically added. Some jurisdictions may also have an additional city, local, or county sales tax. Reporting and submitting this income to the government agency that charges the tax is a responsibility of the spa owner.

Taxes on Wages

As a business employer, you are required to withhold several different types of taxes from employee wages, including federal and state income taxes, Social Security (FICA) tax, and Medicare tax. These funds are then turned over to the appropriate agency. Business employers are also required to pay a payroll tax on each employee. The business must pay a matching portion of the FICA. Federal and state unemployment taxes are also paid by the business. The amounts vary by state.

Tipping of service providers is common practice in a majority of spas. As a result, the spa also has the responsibility to report employee's tips and to withhold federal, state, and local taxes on this income. Employees use forms in IRS Publication 1244 (Employee's Daily Record of Tips and Report to Employer) to record tip income.

Vanity Taxes

In September 2005, New Jersey made history by becoming the first state to enact a tax on cosmetic surgery and Botox injections. Since the 6 percent tax was passed, a growing number of states are considering a so-called *vanity tax*. Washington, Illinois, Texas, and several other states have considered similar measures. In 2009, as the U.S. government considered health–care reform, proposals included taxes on elective cosmetic surgery and on indoor tanning (Hansen, 2009; Vaughan, 2009). This volatile issue has yet to be resolved.

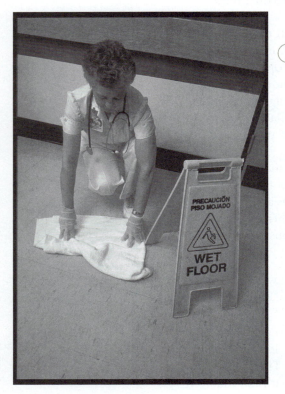

Resolving a Workplace Hazard

OSHA

The federal Occupational Safety and Health Act was enacted in 1970 to help provide a safe working environment for all workers. The **Occupational Safety and Health Administration (OSHA)**, established by the act, is under the jurisdiction of the U.S. Department of Labor. Any business has the duty to protect employees from injury when using hazardous chemicals, and OSHA has established specific protocols for handling these substances.

Companies with fewer than eleven employees are not required to follow OSHA guidelines, but the policies established by OSHA are important for managers of any size spa to understand. OSHA's safety program involves management practices and policies, workplace hazard analysis and record-keeping, hazard control and prevention, and training for all workers (Ochsner, 2009). OSHA regulations supersede any state cosmetology or massage laws. OSHA has also established specific requirements that employers must meet regarding the facility and equipment used on the premises; these requirements were discussed in Chapter 4.

REALITY CHECK

Federal Law Trumps State Law
The Universal Precautions Standard for OSHA states that everyone should be "considered contaminated" and that service providers who are, or have the potential to be, exposed to hazardous materials are required to use preventive measures to eliminate cross-contamination. "Don't wait for your state board to pass this regulation. It's already a federal standard." That means that estheticians, among other things, must wear gloves (McCormick, 2009, p. 21)!

HISTORY FACT

Cleanliness has not always been the norm in the spa industry. In the Middle Ages, the popular Roman bath experience began to be more about hedonism and entertainment and less about health and wellness. There were accounts of mixed bathing, nudity, and immoral acts. Many sites degenerated into brothels and a conduit for the spread of sexually transmitted diseases (Crebbin-Bailey et al., 2005). In hopes of stopping the spread of the bubonic plague in the 1300s and a syphilis epidemic in the 1500s, baths were closed throughout Europe.

MARKETING

States may have laws that govern how you market your services. For example, in Ohio, unless an exfoliation treatment is performed under the supervision of a physician, the term *peel* cannot be used; the treatment must instead be called *resurfacing*. Also in Ohio, there are restrictions on the use of the word *therapy* (McCormick, 2006). Some states specifically exclude Asian bodywork from the category of massage therapy. In these states, providers of Reiki, Shiatsu, Thai massage, and other Asian offerings may only call themselves bodywork therapists, not massage therapists unless they specifically hold that license (Sifleet and Thompson, 2009).

Using the term *natural* suggests that products are free from synthetic ingredients and minimally processed (Pemberton, 2009); however, there is no standardization or certification in the cosmetics industry that assures this (Sellers, 2009). *Organic* refers to the way agricultural products are grown and processed. U.S. Department of Agriculture (USDA) guidelines implemented in October 2002 specify that use of the term is restricted to food products produced without the use of pesticides and/or chemicals (Organic Trade Association, 2009). If a cosmetic product is "food grade," it can legally be marketed as "USDA organic."

REALITY CHECK

It is becoming more common to see labels such as "Organic," "Fragrance-Free," "Hypoallergenic," and "Cruelty-Free" attached to skin care products. The labels sound reassuring, but consumers should be cautious: Too often these labels have little, if any, meaning. Organic foods may be good for your body, but there is not sufficient evidence that organic beauty products are better for your skin. (U.S. Department of Agriculture, 2008).

Although there are no guidelines with regard to the terms *natural* or *organic* in the cosmetic industry at this time, so as not to mislead clients, use of these terms on a spa menu should be associated with treatments that reflect the common definitions. Before developing or marketing your menu of services, make sure you are familiar with your own state and current federal restrictions.

Using testimonials in advertising is a common practice in the spa industry. Testimonials can be very effective, but there are a number of Federal Trade Commission (FTC) guidelines that must be followed if (1) the individual providing the testimonial is compensated in any way for the testimonial, (2) the individual has any connection to spa owners or employees, or (3) a celebrity is endorsing your spa or spa products (Deighan, 2010). If you are considering using testimonials in your advertising, be sure to study up on FTC guidelines before you go to print.

Most spas today have also learned the value of e-mail promotions. However, there are legal issues associated with e-mail marketing. The CAN-SPAM Act of 2004 restricts e-mails for the primary purpose of advertising or promoting products. E-mail sent for marketing purposes must only be sent to individuals who have signed up to receive them. Additionally, spas must use "unsubscribe" links and permission reminders in every e-mail sent.

SECURITY CAMERAS

Whether surveillance cameras may be used in a spa raises issues of privacy law. Placing cameras is dependent on the nature of the business, the placement and kind of cameras, and on state and federal law (Harty-Golder, 2006). Cameras are placed mainly for safety and to prevent loss and damage to property. In general, surveillance cameras are permitted in public areas where there is "no expectation of privacy" or if there are posted notices indicating that cameras are in use. Certainly in a spa, there is an expectation of privacy in many areas, such as treatment rooms, locker facilities, and other areas. However, there may be areas of the spa that might benefit from the placement of a camera. For example, to help ensure the safety of users and aid in an emergency, surveillance cameras have been standard equipment in spa fitness rooms for many years.

Cameras used are typically video only. This is mainly because laws vary regarding recording conversations and generally the laws are in place to prevent the indiscriminate, undisclosed taping of conversations (Harty-Golder, 2006). It is important to recognize that the placement of a camera will lead guests to assume that there is someone monitoring that camera, and this in itself may create legal risk for the employer. A camera raises the expectation that there is someone watching and ready to respond in case of an emergency. Therefore, it is important to know that if a camera is placed, it does have to be continuously monitored by a trained professional. Simply because they provide a false sense of security, decoy cameras are not suggested.

WAIVERS AND RELEASE FORMS

As you learn in Chapter 8, documentation and record keeping are critical to spa service providers. They not only offer a collection of information about each spa customer, they can also protect the provider from legal action. Using waivers and release forms, if they have been developed correctly, help the customer better understand the selected service and recognize the provider's scope of practice (Ochsner, 2009). Release forms and waivers, however, do not protect the business or the treatment provider in the case of negligence. Samples of these forms can be found in the online resources for this book.

UNDER-AGE CLIENTS

The industry has seen an increase in the numbers of children receiving spa services. Because of increased concerns for safety and protection of children, some states have enacted laws to protect both clients and the business. For example, in Georgia, children under 14 must receive their massages from the same gender, and a parent or guardian must accompany them in the room. Older children, between 14 and 17, do not have to be accompanied by an adult, but they must schedule with a therapist of the same gender (Williams, 2009). In many states, all children must have signed consent from an adult before receiving a massage or body treatment.

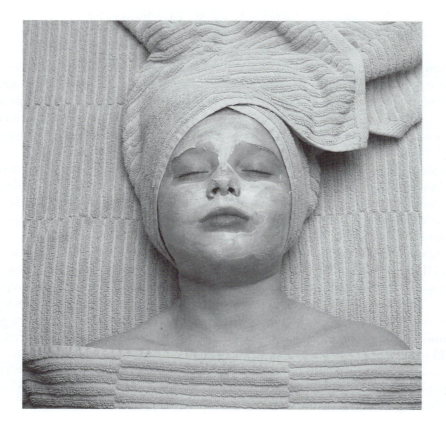

Child Spa Treatment

↪ SEXUAL HARASSMENT

There are very few businesses in which service providers come into such intimate contact with their customers. In preparation for many spa services, guests likely have revealed their medical history, disrobed to the point of nakedness, and may receive a treatment that requires touching. This distinctive environment brings with it a variety of challenges. One that cannot be ignored is sexual harassment. **Sexual harassment** is defined as "intentional or unintentional, unwelcome sexual attention, advance, request for sexual favors, and other verbal or physical conduct of sexual nature by one individual to another" and is illegal under Title VII of the Civil Rights Act of 1964.

A related issue that the industry continuously faces is the stigma of being associated in people's minds with the sexual "massage parlor." It is unfortunate that the spa industry still has to contend with those who use the term *massage* as a cover for operations that offer erotic services. However, as long as these operations exist, massage therapists, and other spa service personnel, have to be prepared to contend with the occasional misled applicant or guest.

In a spa treatment experience, sexual harassment can by instigated by a customer or by the spa service provider. If a therapist is charged with sexual harassment, the therapist will lose his or her license and may be required to register as a sex offender. Therefore, technicians need to be extremely sensitive to the evolution of the spa experience. They need to constantly observe how the customer is responding to a treatment and take the necessary steps to eliminate interactions that might make either the technician or the guest feel uncomfortable. On the other hand, guests have the responsibility to familiarize themselves with the treatment protocol and report to spa management any uncomfortable modifications.

↪ HIPAA AND THE DUTY TO WARN AND PROTECT

In a spa business, personal health information is discussed between the customer and treatment provider to assist with the accurate, safe, and enhanced implementation of a treatment. This information may be shared verbally or in writing. Typically, this information is stored on paper or electronically. Part of the Health Insurance Portability and Accountability Act of 1996 (**HIPAA**) was developed to protect the secrecy of personal health information (U.S. Department of Health and Human Services, 2009).

Health records are among the most sensitive pieces of personal information. The results of an unauthorized disclosure of health records can be devastating and can lead to embarrassment, job loss, and even identity theft. According to HIPAA, any information shared between customer and provider, including demographic information, is confidential and needs to be protected.

Any agency that transmits health-care information electronically must comply with HIPAA standards. This includes health-care providers and, in some cases, spas. If a spa is billing services as medical, for example, direct-billing insurance companies for the services, HIPAA regulations apply. However, even if the spa is not legally required to follow HIPAA regulations, the practices defined by HIPAA are good, common-sense practices for any business in which health information is shared.

In general, HIPAA practices include patients signing an acknowledgment form that lists the privacy practices followed by the business and the business instituting proper protection of any information about a patient that could identify him or her and that is stored in written, spoken, or electronic form.

There are only a few circumstances in which a treatment provider may break a confidentiality agreement with a client. If the spa is in a state that supports the "Duty to Warn and Protect" requirement, and a client confides in a therapist that he or she has been abused, or if there is strong evidence of abuse, the provider has a responsibility to report it to the proper authorities (police or mental health facility) and do what is necessary to protect that individual from further abuse.

SPA EQUIPMENT AND PRODUCT SAFETY

As a spa manager or a member of the staff, you have the responsibility to provide a safe environment for the client and fellow employees. Many spa safety and health issues can be avoided with proper use of products and maintenance of equipment. Users must be familiar with any risks in the operation of spa equipment. Although this may seem obvious, following manufacturer instructions for use and upkeep will help the operation avoid many of the common hazards found in a spa environment.

Providers need to understand the risks associated with spa services and the products used during those services. Conducting safety audits periodically on all materials stored or handled and on all spa equipment is essential to help ensure the safety of employees and clients of the spa. Spa managers are at risk and must understand that if equipment is used or maintained improperly or products are combined improperly or used other than as intended, the spa can be held liable if an injury occurs,.

The term *off-label* refers to the use of a prescription drug or medical device in a manner that is different from, or inconsistent with, the U.S. Food and Drug Administration (FDA) approval for it. The FDA requires a manufacturer of a medical product or device to obtain approval for the item. These products undergo clinical testing to test potency, purity, and stability, and to verify the ingredients to ensure that the item is safe and effective, before they can be introduced to the U.S. market.

Dr. Padraic Deighan (2009), in an article in *MedEsthetics* magazine, describes a popular off-label use of the Botox cosmetic. Botox received FDA approval in 2002 for temporary treatment of moderate to severe frown lines between the brows in people 18 to 65 years of age. Dr. Deighan claims that physicians routinely utilize the product for other areas of the body and in patients older than 65 years of age. Spa managers and service providers need to pay close attention to the manufacturer's instructions for use of products in a spa and ensure their intended use, including not using products that have passed their expiration date.

Many spas integrate aromatherapy into a spa experience. Inhaling and integrating low doses of essential oils into carrier products, such as creams, oils, and lotions, for spa treatments is not presently regulated in the United States, and with an education on the proper use and application of essential oils, can be safe and effective. However, the internal use of essential oils can only be prescribed by a physician.

MEDICAL SPA PRACTICES

Physician Supervision

If a spa is considered to be a medical facility, other rules may apply, depending on the state in which the business is located and the types of services it offers. In a medical practice that is licensed by a state medical board, you can work under a physician's supervision as a medical assistant and have procedures delegated to you by the physician (Warfield, 2009). Physicians in the United States have a very wide scope of practice. Physicians can generally use all methods that their profession accepts as safe and effective to treat a given disease. However, physicians who practice alternative therapies must be properly trained and appropriately credentialed.

As discussed in Chapter 1, medical spas are generally supervised by a medical doctor. State legislation sets the standards of practice for the number of offices certain physicians can supervise. For example, in Florida, physicians can supervise two offices other than their primary practice location, whereas "physician specialists" can supervise four offices. Currently in Florida, dermatologists and plastic surgeons are exempt from these restrictions (Antoline, 2006).

Medical Insurance Billing

Insurance billing for spas at rehabilitation and wellness centers and many medical spas is common practice all over North America. In Canada, mainly because of the nature of the publicly funded health-care system, insurance billing takes place in all types of spas. In the United States, billing services to a client's insurance company is common principally in medical spas.

Insurance regulations and procedures vary from plan to plan, from state to state, and among health-care providers. Before deciding whether insurance billing is appropriate for your spa, consider the following (Thompson, 2002):

▶ If many of your competitors are billing insurance, you may find it difficult to compete if you choose not to do so.
▶ If several people have changed their minds about scheduling with you when they found you didn't accept insurance patients, you may want to consider this change.
▶ If you can afford to wait 30–90 days to get paid—typical turnaround time for insurance reimbursement—you may want to consider insurance billing.

If you choose to go this route, you will need to take the time necessary to learn and integrate suitable procedures into your practice. Ask questions such as:

▶ Which types of health-care providers (HCPs) have primary-care status and can refer customers to your spa services?
▶ Can you bill directly, or must the HCP bill for you?
▶ Which types of insurance will reimburse for your wellness services in your state?
▶ Which therapies are covered under each insurance plan?
▶ What Current Procedural Terminology (CPT) codes correspond with acceptable treatments?
▶ Which conditions warrant manual therapy treatment under each plan, and what are the corresponding Internal Classification of Diseases (ICD-10) codes to be used on the billing form?

In order for insurance companies to reimburse for services, the condition being treated must be medically necessary. CPT codes were developed by the American Medical Association and are updated each year. There are a variety of codes that, for example, a massage therapist might be able to use. An illustration of a CPT code widely used by massage therapists is "97140—Massage, including effleurage, petrissage and/or tapotement (gliding, compression percussion)" (Madison-Mahoney, 2007). As CPT codes are associated with the type of treatment, ICD codes refer to the body location of an injury or ailment. It is important that if your spa chooses to go this route, correct training, keeping up with the changing practices of insurance companies, and meticulous record keeping are essential.

If you choose not to provide billing services for your customers and it is your practice to receive payment at the time of service, spa guests can still seek insurance reimbursement on their own. As stated previously, insurance billing is not a common practice for nonmedical spas in the United States; however, those spas that serve a large international clientele may consider incorporating insurance billing into their practices.

RISK MANAGEMENT

In addition to knowing and following the laws that govern spas, there are other ways to protect a spa operation. Hazards are common to any business; however, some actions can help spa managers minimize threats to the operation. **Risk management** is the practice of protecting a business from loss. As a spa manager, you are at risk. Risks in a spa operation can include slippery floors, equipment malfunctions, ineffective sanitation practices, and poorly trained staff, all of which have the potential to create loss for the organization. Loss can manifest as property damage or as injury and/or suffering of an individual, leading ultimately to financial loss for the spa. A successful risk management program can help to lessen the chance of perilous consequences in a spa operation.

Risk management is a systematic process of assessing hazards and instituting practices to protect the operation from loss. Not all risks can be avoided, of course. However, failing to develop and implement a risk management plan in the current state of litigious uncertainty is just plain irresponsible. In this section we present are the basic steps for developing a risk management plan. Using content developed by Betty van der Smissen, J.D. (1990), this method can be used by any spa manager to develop the foundation for a successful risk management plan. Developing a risk management strategy involves three stages: (1) discovery, (2) analysis and control, and (3) implementation.

Discovery

Before starting risk management planning, several *discovery* questions need to be considered to provide the foundation on which to move into stage 2. If the spa operation is new, this is likely to be a long but enlightening process. If the spa is part of a larger operation or organization, these questions may just need to be clarified by the organization's risk or legal counsel. Whichever the case, a spa manager will need to consider the following issues:

▶ Who is the risk manager? Who is the person ultimately responsible for developing and monitoring a risk management plan?
▶ What elements of the facility offer the greatest risk?
▶ What is the proposed program and service scope? Identify spa offerings with the greatest risk.
▶ What type of risks (and to what extent) will the company be willing to assume without insurance? Or, in other words, what risks will be retained in the spa operation's budget?
▶ What risks will be transferred by contract (i.e., insurance or contracted employees)?

Answers to each of the questions may not be completely clear. If not, clarity may come in stage 2.

Analysis and Control

The heart of the risk management planning process occurs in stage 2: risk analysis and control. In this stage, all potential risks of the spa operation are identified and analyzed. This part of the process consists of three steps: identification of risks, estimation of the level of each risk (using frequency and severity), and selection of approaches to control the risk (van der Smissen, 1990).

Identification of risks may also be recognized as "danger detection." The goal of this stage is to assure a complete assessment. Some risks may be obvious, but don't stop there. A number of tools can be used to identify risks, and it is recommended that many different tools are used to ensure that the evaluation is complete. The methods selected will vary based on the nature of the business. Consider the following:

- ▶ Physical inspections of the spa facility
- ▶ Consulting with external professionals, such as legal counsel, police, engineers, physicians, fire personnel, insurance brokers, etc.
- ▶ Networking with fellow spa leaders, sharing ideas and risk management solutions
- ▶ Discussions with all categories of spa personnel
- ▶ Review of spa records, contracts, financial statements; uncover past claim history
- ▶ Ongoing education related to risk management, literature research, and attending workshops

To facilitate this difficult process, it may be helpful to break down risks into categories. Dr. van der Smissen (1990) identifies four categories: property exposures, public liability (excluding negligence), public liability/negligence, and business operations. **Property exposure** consists of loss or damage to facilities, equipment, inventory, and supplies. To identify these risks, first make a list of all property on your premises. Then estimate what damage or loss could result from occurrences such as fire, vandalism, theft, and natural elements such as hail, tornado, flood, lightning, wind, or rain (Cotton, 1993).

Many different types of risks are categorized as public liability. **Products liability** is one category: hazards associated with products, equipment, or foods. Acts of employees are considered public liability risks, such as malpractice, intentional torts such as libel and slander, assault and battery, invasion of privacy, violation of dram shop and host liquor laws, discrimination, advertisers or contractual liability. **Negligence** is also a public liability and includes bodily injuries that might occur during service provision or while on spa premises. In listing the risks related to negligence, consider identifying the level of risk associated with each of the experiences and offerings available to the guests or exposures of the staff.

REALITY CHECK

Too often spa managers and therapists don't insist on a thorough health history before performing treatments, placing customers at risk. Spa treatments, like many wellness procedures, may be contraindicated, requiring the therapist or technician to adjust, receive medical release, or even refuse to perform the treatment. Consequentially, although spa treatments are designed for wellness, without sufficient client information and proper therapist understanding and reaction, the service may do just the opposite.

TABLE 9.2 Traditional Risk Management Matrix		
	Low Frequency	**High Frequency**
Low Severity	Retention	Retention with loss control/risk reduction
High Severity	Transfer/insurance	Avoidance

Business operations are the fourth and final category in which risks need to be identified. Business operation loss can occur through staff issues such as employee dishonesty, errors and omissions by officers, or the illness of key personnel. Loss of income can occur due to interruption of business because of natural elements, contract, or health issues.

Analyzing risk may seem like a tedious process. However, it is probably the most crucial step in the risk management process. Thorough analysis of all risks can help ensure a comprehensive implementation plan. Keep in mind that a one-time identification of risks is not sufficient. Risk identification must be an ongoing process for spa managers.

Once all risks have been identified, the next step is to measure the extent of the threat associated with each. Traditionally, managers have completed this evaluation step using two primary elements: frequency and severity. *Frequency* relates to the likelihood of an injury, loss, or risk, and *severity* to the seriousness of any injury, loss, or risk. Several other variables may also be important in risk assessment. The size of the organization, the market conditions, and the financial status of the firm can all influence the measurement of various risk management approaches. Starting with the traditional approach, however, can provide a solid starting place from which to make organizational decisions to reduce risk. Using the traditional approach, risk managers often use a matrix to assist with decision making. Once a risk is identified, it is categorized as either high or low in both frequency and severity. The matrix (see Table 9.2) is then used to suggest a possible risk management solution.

In the most basic form, the matrix provides four loss control strategies, depending on how each risk is classified. To help clarify how to use the traditional matrix, an example of how a risk might fall into each of the four matrix quadrants is offered along with the risk strategy to combat or provide protection from that risk.

The first risk strategy described is retention. **Risk retention,** also called *assumption of loss,* implies the route of noninsurance and the spa resolving this risk either in total or in part from its own financing (van der Smissen, 1990). Retention is suggested for a risk with low frequency and low severity. An example might be a front desk worker getting a paper cut while filing. The retention approach, in a nutshell, is to accept that the event may happen and budget to cover any associated costs.

Retention with risk reduction, sometimes called *risk management,* is suggested when a risk is categorized as low severity yet high frequency. A specific spa risk that might have this formula is sore or pulled muscles after a massage or fitness class. With the strategy of retention with risk

Low Risk Assessment

reduction, the emphasis is on managing the operation to decrease the frequency of occurrence. Using the sore muscle example, the spa could implement a variety of practices to decrease the frequency of this occurrence. For instance, spa personnel might be required to institute longer periods of time for stretching in fitness classes or receive additional training on counseling customers to select more appropriate service choices.

Risk transfer is an alternative strategy whereby the financial risk is transferred to another by contract. Most commonly thought to be insurance coverage, other forms of transfer include purchase agreements, lease of premises, contracts for services, and so on. Transfer is suggested when the frequency of risk is low but severity is high. An esthetician or guest having a serious allergic reaction to a spa product or a guest experiencing heart failure when on a guided hike can serve as transfer examples. With proper protocol in place, the chance of this happening is small; however, serious injury will likely be the result of an occurrence. In this case, having suitable insurance to cover any loss may be a route to consider.

The final strategy to consider when using the matrix is associated with high frequency and high severity. In this case, it might be good practice to stay away from this offering. Avoidance or *discontinuance* may be warranted when considering implementation of an untested and extremely rigorous new fitness régime or instituting a new treatment that includes an encounter with a dangerous animal.

The matrix is just a start. In practice, this step in the risk management process is complicated, and assessing the spa accurately takes time and thoughtful consideration. Consider all elements of the operation before taking these steps, and understand that whatever strategy is selected, the ongoing management of your spa operation to reduce risk is essential.

Implementation

Once the risks have been assessed and the control strategies selected, spa managers enter the implementation stage of the process. Risk management strategies generally take on either a financial or an operational approach. As indicated, risks are unavoidable in any operation. Knowing risks will be present, managers must plan for the associated financial implications. As noted earlier in the chapter, purchasing insurance is a financial obligation that is also a spa requirement. Determining the provider, what type, and how much insurance can be clarified through a risk management planning process. In addition to budgeting for insurance needs, funds must also be set aside for other contracts and services and for the cost of risks that are not transferred by contract.

The remaining implementation approaches are operational. Working to eliminate risk in the spa environment is primarily the responsibility of spa personnel. Through the development of appropriate risk management practices and ongoing training of staff, the spa can make great progress toward reducing hazards in the spa. Many examples are provided in the online text support materials. For example, the Spa Operating Procedures Manual contains several sections that outline operational strategies to help minimize risk, such as spa security, emergency evacuation, first aid, operating equipment systems, and employee and client access policies and procedures.

Recognizing the importance of risk management to the spa industry, the International Spa Association has developed a Code of Conduct for spa guests. This document highlights common rights and responsibilities for spa guests but also highlights several statements that, if followed, can assist spa managers in managing risk in the spa.

SPA INDUSTRY CODE OF CONDUCT

As a Spa Guest, it is your responsibility to:

- Communicate your preferences, expectations and concerns;
- Communicate complete and accurate health information and reasons for your visit;
- Treat staff and other guests with courtesy and respect;
- Use products, equipment and therapies as directed;
- Engage in efforts to preserve the environment; and
- Adhere to the spa's published policies and procedures.

As a Spa Guest, you have the right to:

- A clean, safe and comfortable environment;
- Stop a treatment at any time, for any reason;
- Be treated with consideration, dignity and respect;
- Confidential treatment of your disclosed health information;
- Trained staff who respectfully conduct treatments according to treatment protocols and the spa's policies and procedures;
- Ask questions about your spa experience; and
- Information regarding staff training, licensing and certification.

Source: International Spa Association and Resort Hotel Association (2010). Code of Conduct. Retrieved March 24, 2010, from http://experienceispa.com/about-ispa/ethics-and-standards/code-of-conduct.

KEY TERMS

Americans with Disabilities Act (ADA)

C corporation

Casualty (property) insurance

Corporation

HIPAA

Liability insurance

Limited liability corporation (LLC)

Limited liability partnership (LLP)

Malpractice insurance

Negligence

Occupational Safety and Health Administration (OSHA)

Partnership

Products liability

Property exposure

Risk management

Risk retention

Risk transfer

Sexual harassment

Sole Proprietorship

Subchapter S corporation

Unlimited liability

Worker's compensation insurance

REVIEW QUESTIONS

1. What are the three basic types of business ownership?
2. What licenses are required for a spa to operate?
3. What is the purpose of the ADA? OSHA? HIPAA?
4. What are the different forms of insurance, and what elements of the operation do they protect?

→ REFERENCES

Anderson, Peter C. (2008). Toast of the Town. *American Spa,* March, pp. 54–58.

Antoline, Michael L. (2006). Let the Force Be with You. *DaySpa,* November, pp. 34–38.

Business.gov (2009). Business Name Registration. Retrieved December 22, 2009, from www.business.gov/register/business-name/dba.html.

Cotton, Doyice J. (1993). Risk Management—A Tool for Reducing Exposure to Legal Liability. *The Journal of Physical Education, Recreation & Dance,* vol. 64.

Crebbin-Bailey, Jane, Harcup, John, and Harrington, John (2005). *The Spa Book: The Official Guide to Spa Therapy.* London: Thomson Learning.

Crossett, DeeDee, and Gordon, Aimee (2009). Top 10 Errors. *Skin Deep,* March/April, pp. 16–18.

Deighan, Padraic B. (2010). "I Look Ten Years Younger." *MedEsthetics,* January/February, pp. 12–14.

Deighan, Padraic B. (2009). Working Off-Label. *Medesthetics,* May/June, pp. 9–10.

Entrepreneur Press and Eileen Figure Sandlin (2005). *Start Your Own Hair Salon and Day Spa.* Irvine, CA: Entrepreneur Media.

Gimmy, Arthur E., and Woodworth, Brian B. (1989). *Fitness, Racquet Sports and Spa Projects: A Guide to Appraisal, Market Analysis, Development and Financing.* Chicago: American Institute of Real Estate Appraisers.

Hansen, Inga (2009). No Taxation. *MedEsthetics,* September/October, p. 2.

Harty-Golder, Barbara (2006). Privacy and Surveillance Cameras in the Workplace. *Medical Laboratory Observer,* 38(3): 48.

LaCour, Lenny (2008). Music in the Spa Industry. *Pulse,* July, pp. 24–26.

Madison-Mahoney, Vivian (2007). CPT Coding Issues and Answers. *Massage and Bodywork,* February/March, pp. 96–99.

McCormick, Janet (2009). Double Dipping? *Skin Deep,* July/August, pp. 20–23.

McCormick, Janet (2006). Time for a Checkup. *Les Nouvelles Esthétiques,* August, pp. 129–134.

National Board of Fitness Examiners (2010). Dr. Dorette Nysewander, Director of Information, National Board of Fitness Examiners, Personal communication, June 16, 2010.

National Board of Fitness Examiners (2008). States Licensing of Personal Trainers, August 20, 2008. Retrieved June 28, 2009, from www.nbfe.org/news/press_releases/stateLicensing_082008.cfm.

Ochsner, Deborah (2009). *The Massage Therapist's Guide to Client Safety and Wellness.* Clifton, NY: Milady, Cengage Learning Publishers.

Organic Trade Association (2009). Organic Agriculture and Production. Retrieved December 22, 2009, from www.ota.com/definition/quickoverview.html.

Pemberton, Christine (2009). Organic vs. Natural Skin Care Products. *MedicalSpas,* August, pp. 72–78.

Roosevelt, Theodore (n.d.). BrainyQuote.com. Retrieved June 16, 2010, from www.brainyquote.com/quotes/quotes/t/theodorero147890.html.

Sellers, Rebekah (2009). Digging for Answers: The Topic of Organics Can Be Messy. *Pulse,* May, pp. 40–46.

Sifleet, Jean D., and Thompson, Elizabeth Greene (2009). Wellness Management: Avoid the Legal Pitfalls of Multi-Service Spas. *Pulse,* June, pp. 56–58.

Thompson, Diana L. (2002). *Hands Heal: Communication, Documentation, and Insurance Billing for Manual Therapists,* 2nd ed. Philadelphia: Lippincott Williams & Wilkins.

U.S. Department of Agriculture (2008). National Organic Program. Retrieved April, 2008, from www.ams.usda.gov/AMSv1.0/nop.

U.S. Department of Health and Human Services (2009). Health Information Privacy. Retrieved June 25, 2009, from www.hhs.gov/ocr/hipaa.

van der Smissen, Betty (1990). *Legal Liability and Risk Management for Public and Private Entities.* Cincinnati: Anderson.

Vaughn, Martin (2009). Cosmetic Surgery Tax Out, Tanning Tax In for Sen Health Bill. Retrieved December 22, 2009, from www.spaclique.com/professional-interest-spa-news/90-legal-issues/2314-dow-jones-newswiremartin-vaughn.html?tmpl=component&print=1&layout=default&page=.

Warfield, Susanne S. (2009). Top 5 Legal and Liability Issues of Medical Spas. Retrieved May 11, 2009, from www.multibriefs.com/briefs/sdss/top5.htm.

Williams, Nicole Marie (2009). Georgia Spa Laws. Retrieved December 22, 2009, from www.spaclique.com/professional-interest-spa-news/90-legal-issues/1694-georgia-spa-laws.html.

Spa Financial Management

→ LEARNING OBJECTIVES

At the end of this chapter, the reader will be able to:

- Comprehend financial statements used for spa management.
- Understand staff compensation options.
- Utilize the tools for measuring and monitoring business.

Beware of the person who can't be bothered by details.
—William Feather

The subject of financial management often gets sidelined when discussing spa operations. The spa mission statement may be filled with lofty aspirations, but the practical financial knowledge required to keep the business solvent is too important to ignore. Several areas of the spa business are guided by standard accounting practices:

▶ Forecasting and budgeting
▶ Staff compensation
▶ Financial statements

All businesses must maintain an ongoing report of their financial picture. There are four main financial statements for any business: (1) balance sheets; (2) income statements; (3) cash flow statements; and (4) statements of shareholders' equity. In a nutshell, a **balance sheet** shows what a company owns and what it owes, at a fixed point in time. An **income statement** shows how much money a company made, and spent, over a given period of time. A **cash flow statement** shows the exchange of money between a company and the outside world, also over a period of time. A statement of shareholders' equity shows changes in the interest of the company's owners or shareholders over time. This section will focus on the first three of the four statements, as they are most common in the spa industry.

THE BALANCE SHEET

A balance sheet, sometimes called a *statement of financial position,* provides detailed information about a company's assets, liabilities, and shareholders' equity. The balance sheet provides a snapshot of the spa finances at a specific point in time, the final day of the accounting period.

Assets are anything that the spa owns that has value. This can include cash, investments, inventory, equipment, trademarks, patents, and physical property. **Liabilities** are what the spa owes. This category includes rent, payroll, taxes, repayment on loans, and payment to vendors for products purchased. Also categorized as a liability is the obligation of future payment on gift cards, gift certificates, and series or packages sold.

On a balance sheet, assets are generally listed according to how quickly they can be converted into cash. Items that the business expects to convert to cash within the year are referred to as *current assets.* The best example in a spa is professional product inventory and retail items. Most spas expect to convert their inventory into cash within a twelve-month period by performing treatments and selling products. *Long-term assets* are items that are typically not for sale in the spa. A treatment table is a good example, as is other furniture and computers.

Liabilities are listed as current or long-term. As with current assets, *current liabilities* are obligations that the spa anticipates having to resolve within the year. *Long-term liabilities* have a due date more than one year in the future.

Net worth is the money that would be left if a company sold all of its assets and paid off all its liabilities. This leftover money belongs to the shareholders or owners of the company. A balance sheet is an explanation of the equation, Assets − Liabilities = Net Worth. In a balance sheet, the assets are listed at the top, followed by the liabilities and owners' equity/net worth at the bottom, as shown in Figure 10.1 (Bplans, 2010). Note that a balance sheet does not show the cash flow into and out of the accounts during the period. See the online resources for a Spa Balance Sheet template.

Assets	FY 2006	FY 2007	FY 2008	FY 2009	FY 2010
Current Assets					
Cash	$313,263	$393,531	$514,568	$647,351	$797,823
Accounts Receivable	11,123	11,899	11,378	12,876	12,421
Inventory	11,441	10,357	12,868	13,577	14,132
Other Current Assets	33,095	33,095	33,095	33,095	33,095
Total Current Assets	$368,922	$448,882	$571,909	$706,899	$857,471
Long-Term Assets					
Long-Term Assets	$ 0	$ 3,000	$ 6,000	$ 6,000	$ 6,000
Accumulated Depreciation	0	150	200	250	300
Total Long-Term Assets	0	2,850	5,800	5,750	5,700
Total Assets	$368,922	$451,732	$577,709	$712,649	$863,171
Liabilities and Capital					
Current Liabilities					
Accounts Payable	$ 80,790	$ 47,265	$ 49,650	$ 52,002	$ 53,681
Current Borrowing	22,600	17,200	7,800	1,400	0
Other Current Liabilities	0	0	0	0	0
Subtotal Current Liabilities	$103,390	$ 64,465	$ 57,450	$ 53,402	$ 53,681
Long-Term Liabilities	$ 0	$ 0	$ 0	$ 0	$ 0
Total Liabilities	$103,390	$ 64,465	$ 57450	$ 53,402	$ 53,681
Paid-in Capital	$150,000	$150,000	$150,000	$150,000	$150,000
Retained Earnings	(90,450)	39,528	103,232	304,328	445,277
Earnings	119,978	103,705	161,221	140,949	162,101
Total Capital	$179,528	$292,233	$414,453	$595,277	$757,378
Total Liabilities and Capital	$282,918	$356,698	$471,903	$648,679	$811,059
Net Worth	$179,528	$292,233	$414,453	$595,277	$757,378

Figure 10.1 Sample Spa Balance Sheet

THE INCOME STATEMENT

The income statement, or the statement of activities, details the revenue the spa earned during the reporting period. This report also outlines the costs associated with earning the revenue. The last line, or *bottom line,* of the statement is the amount the spa earned or lost over the reporting period. The income statement is often described as a series of steps that lead to the bottom line (U.S. SEC, 2010). The first step is the revenue generated from sales during the period. Each succeeding step is a deduction for the costs associated with earning the revenue. At the bottom of the stairs, after deducting all the expenses, is the amount the spa earned or lost during the accounting period, as shown in Figure 10.2 (Bplans, 2010)

The total amount of money earned from the sale of products and service each month is shown at the top of the income statement. This top line is call **gross revenue** or *gross sales.* If there is money the spa does not expect to collect on certain sales, because of promotions, discounts, or returns, this amount is subtracted from gross revenue to arrive at *net revenue.* If no discounts, promotions or returns occurred during the period, a net revenue may not be posted, as in the example in Figure 10.2. Moving down the statement, there are several postings that represent operating expenses. Although these lines may be reported in different order, the next line after gross revenue is the **cost of sales**. This number is the amount the spa spent to

Figure 10.2 Sample Spa Income Statement

	FY 2006	FY 2007	FY 2008	FY 2009	FY 2010
Gross Sales/Gross Revenue	$825,702	$827,009	$901,070	$966,000	$992,000
Direct Cost of Sales	68,344	59,925	73,175	86,400	99,575
Massage Therapists' Commissions	289,306	302,488	308,964	312,150	329,000
Aestheticians' Commissions	70,992	72,013	74,221	74,430	75,080
Other Services Commissions	15,340	17,550	19,500	22,750	24,050
Total Cost of Sales	$381,720	$375,033	$425,210	$470,270	$464,295
Gross Profit	$443,982	$451,976	$475,860	$496,730	$527,705
Gross Profit %	53.77%	54.65.%	52.81%	51.31%	53.20%
Expenses					
Payroll	$137,510	$145,000	$155,000	$160,000	$167,000
Marketing/Promotion	7,500	5,000	5,000	8,000	5,000
Depreciation	0	50	50	50	50
Rent	66,000	66,000	66,000	66,000	66,000
Utilities	3,000	3,100	3,200	3,300	3,400
Advertising	3,000	3,000	3,000	3,000	3,000
Insurance	1,500	700	700	700	700
Payroll Taxes	0	0	0	0	0
Phone	1,500	1,600	1,700	1,800	1,900
Software Support	0	495	495	495	495
Other	6,700	6,700	6,700	6,700	6,700
Total Operating Expenses	$226,710	$231,645	$241,845	$250,045	$254,245
Profit Before Interest and Taxes	$217,272	$220,331	$234,015	$246,685	$273,460
EBITDA*	217,272	220,381	234,065	246,735	273,510
Interest Expense	2,132	1,568	980	392	49
Taxes Incurred	40,610	44,207	52,103	56,822	58,992
Net Profit	$174,530	$174,606	$180,982	$189,521	$214,469

*EBITDA is Earnings Before Interest, Taxes, Depreciation, and Amortization.

offer the treatments, products, and services it sold during the accounting period As shown in Figure 10.2, cost of sales includes direct costs and commissions.

The total cost of sales is subtracted from the gross revenue to arrive at a subtotal called **gross profit**. It is still considered "gross" because indirect expenses have yet to be deducted. The gross profit percentage is simply the gross profit divided by the gross sales.

The next section of the income statement shows operating expenses. **Operating expenses** cannot be linked directly to the production of the products or services being sold. These expenses include marketing, research and development, insurance, utilities, salaries for administrative employees, and so on.

Depreciation is another expense that is deducted from gross profit. **Depreciation** takes into account the wear and tear on some assets, such as equipment, tools, and furniture, which are used over the long term. Depreciation allows the spa to spread the cost of these assets over the period of time during which they are used. The "charge" assessed for these assets during the period is a small percentage of the original cost of the asset.

Profit Before Interest and Taxes is the operating profit—the amount retained after all operating expenses are deducted from gross profit. This is often called *income from operations*. The spa must also account for interest income and interest expense. *Interest income* is the money the spa will make by keeping cash in interest-bearing savings or checking accounts, money market funds, or other interest-bearing investment vehicles. *Interest expense* is the money the spa paid in interest for money borrowed. Interest income and interest expense are then added to, or subtracted from, the operating profits to arrive at the operating profit before income tax. The line labeled EBITDA is the total amount the spa earned before adjusting for interest, taxes, depreciation, and **amortization** Amortization is paying off debt in regular installments over a period of time.

Finally, after income tax is deducted, the bottom line shows **net profit (or loss)**, also called *net income* or *net earnings*. This number shows how much the spa actually earned or lost during the accounting period.

THE CASH FLOW STATEMENT

A cash flow statement is simply a report of the cash that came in and the cash that went out of the spa business. It is especially important because the business needs to have enough cash available to pay its expenses and make necessary purchases. The income statement tells you whether the spa made a profit; the cash flow statement tells you whether the spa generated cash with which to conduct the business.

The cash flow statement shows the net increase or decrease in cash for the period. Generally, cash flow statements are divided into three main sections. Each section includes the cash flow from one of three types of activities:

▶ Operating activities
▶ Investing activities
▶ Financing activities

Operating Activities

As described by the U.S. Securities and Exchange Commission (U.S. SEC, 2010), the first part of a cash flow statement analyzes a spa's cash flow from net income or losses. This section of the cash flow statement reconciles the net income to the cash the company received from or used in its operating activities. To do this, it adjusts net income for any noncash items (such as adding back depreciation expenses) and adjusts for any cash that was used or provided by other operating assets and liabilities.

Investing Activities

The second part of a cash flow statement shows the cash flow from all investing activities, which generally includes purchases or sales of long-term assets, such as property and equipment, as well as investment securities. When the spa buys a piece of equipment, the cash flow statement reflects this activity as a cash outflow from investing activities because it used cash. If the spa decides to sell off some investments from an investment portfolio, the proceeds from the sales appear as a cash inflow from investing activities because it provided cash.

Financing Activities

The third part of a cash flow statement shows the cash flow from all financing activities. Typical sources of cash flow include cash raised by selling stocks and bonds or

Figure 10.3 Sample Spa Cash
Flow Statement

Cash Received	FY 2006	FY 2007	FY 2008	FY 2009	FY 2010
Cash from Operations					
Cash Sales	$699,524	$720,306	$855,901	$893,641	$933,664
Cash from Receivables	16,928	29,015	29,436	31,002	32,543
Subtotal Cash from Operations	$716,452	$749,321	$885,337	$924,643	$966,207
Additional Cash Received					
Sales Tax,	$ 0	$ 0	$ 0	$ 0	$ 0
New Current Borrowing	0	0	0	0	0
New Other Liabilities (interest-free)	0	0	0	0	0
New Long-term Liabilities	0	0	0	0	0
Sales of Other Current Assets	0	0	0	0	0
Sales of Long-term Assets	0	0	0	0	0
New Investment Received	0	0	0	0	0
Subtotal Cash Received	$716,452	$749,321	$885,337	$924,643	$966,207
Expenditures					
Expenditures from Operations					
Cash Spending	$129,610	$135,060	$149,229	$155,050	$162,100
Bill Payments	497,291	507,796	602,659	634,928	651,037
Subtotal Spent on Operations	$626,901	$642,856	$751,888	$789,978	$813,137
Additional Cash Spent					
Sales Tax, Paid Out	$ 0	$ 0	$ 0	$ 0	$ 0
Principal Repayment of Current Borrowing	6,200	6,200	6,200	6,200	6,200
Other Liabilities Principal Repayment	0	0	0	0	0
Long-term Liabilities Principal Repayment	0	0	0	0	0
Purchase Other Current Assets	0	0	0	0	0
Purchase Long-term Assets	0	2,000	2,000	0	0
Dividends	0	0	0	0	0
Subtotal Cash Spent	$633,101	$651,056	$611,088	$796,178	$819,337
Net Cash Flow	$ 83,442	$ 98,265	$125,249	$128,465	$151,870
Cash Balance	$220,463	$318,728	$443,977	$572,442	$724,312

borrowing from banks. Likewise, paying back a bank loan appears as a use of cash flow. See Figure 10.3 for the layout of a cash flow statement (Bplans, 2010).

Although the cash flow statement is easy to follow, it is important to understand how it is structured. The cash coming into the spa from business operations is listed first. This is followed by any additional cash, possibly from the sale of an asset such as a CD (certificate of deposit) or stocks. The remainder of the statement is the cash spent during the reported period. The bottom line of this statement is the immediate cash on hand. This statement is most similar to the accounting for a personal checking account. It can be created and be useful as a daily, weekly, or monthly report. Historical cash flow statements can be a benefit when forecasting the operating budget for the coming year.

⟶ FORECASTING, BUDGETING, AND BUDGETARY CONTROLS

Forecasting is the first step in the development of an operating budget. Creating an accurate forecast requires reviewing historical results, market conditions, and conditions specific to the spa. If historical data for the business is not available, industry statistics and averages can be used to predict future performance.

An operating budget has many purposes. It is a planning tool, used to map out the coming period of time in monetary terms. It establishes financial goals, allowing managers a way to control costs. Budgets are a useful tool for communicating the financial status of the operation at any given time. A budget can also provide the spa a benchmark by which to evaluate the business and even its managers.

It is helpful to define the type of budget using one of three philosophies: top-down, bottom-up, or zero-based. A **top-down budget** begins with a gross revenue goal determined by the owner or manager of the spa. The manager is then responsible for structuring costs to achieve the revenue objective. A **bottom-up budget** is the reverse, in that the owner or manager may set a net income goal and the budget is then prepared to supply enough revenue less expenses to achieve the net income goal. A **zero-based budget** creates a mini-forecast for each business cycle and uses available data to justify the projected expenses. There are concerns and benefits to each budget method (Dummies, 2010).

▶ **Top-down:** Created by top management. This type of budget outlines the goals and expectations of the heads of the organization. This format can be somewhat unrealistic, however, as there is no contribution from those that will ultimately implement the plan.

▶ **Bottom-up:** Developed by managers and forwarded to top management for approval. This format tends to have more successful implementation, as there is significant input from those who will supervise the process. Employees take more responsibility for the results, as they have had an active role in the process.

▶ **Zero-based:** Developed by each manager and submitted to top management. This format assumes that there no funds have been allocated and the manager prepares the budget with a justification for each proposed expense. Because each dollar requested must be justified, there is careful consideration of each request, and waste is minimized.

A budget is not a static document, meaning that it is not a picture in time as other financial documents. A budget is an educated guess of the future financial activities and therefore must constantly be monitored and adjusted. Budgetary controls include monthly reviews of the forecast to determine variances between the budgeted amount and the actual cost of operations. An analysis of the variances, if any, will assist in determining the appropriate corrective action.

An annual budget for a spa most closely resembles the income statement in format. However, for better control throughout the year, it may include more detail than an income statement. For example, net revenue and direct expenses may be broken down into each of the revenue streams of the spa, such as:

▶ Massage
▶ Skin Care
▶ Hair
▶ Nails
▶ Fitness
▶ Aquatics
▶ Food and Beverage

> ▶ Health and Wellness Education
> ▶ Retail
> ▶ Rentals
> ▶ Sports and Recreation
> ▶ Other Activities
> ▶ Memberships (for a club spa)
> ▶ Rooms (for a destination spa)

A variety of budget analysis techniques and calculations are used to provide greater insight into the financial strength of a spa operation. Managers commonly complete a **vertical analysis**, comparing and contrasting categories within a budget or financial statement, but horizontal analysis is also common. **Horizontal analysis** is a comparison of current or future budget projections with the past year's performance in the same categories.

Calculations and ratios are also used to gather insight regarding the spa's financial performance and to benchmark against other similar operations. Table 10.1

TABLE 10.1

Sample Financial Analysis Calculations

$$\text{Average revenue per guest} = \frac{\text{total spa revenue generated}}{\text{number of guests in the spa}}$$

$$\text{Revenue per available treatment room (RevPATR)} = \frac{\text{total spa revenue generated}}{\text{number of spa treatment rooms}}$$

$$\text{Revenue per available treatment provider (RevPATP)} = \frac{\text{total spa revenue generated}}{\text{number of available treatment providers}}$$

$$\text{Revenue per square foot} = \frac{\text{total spa revenue generated}}{\text{square feet of spa space}}$$

$$\text{Average treatment rate} = \frac{\text{total treatment revenue generated}}{\text{total number of treatments}}$$

$$\text{Treatment room utilization} = \frac{\text{number of treatment room hours used}}{\text{number of available room hours}}$$

$$\text{Service provider utilization} = \frac{\text{service hours performed}}{\text{service hours available}}$$

$$\text{Number of treatments per guest visit} = \frac{\text{number of treatments}}{\text{number of guests in spa}}$$

In a resort spa there are several other opportunities for further operating data analysis:

$$\text{Capture rate} = \frac{\text{number of guests in resort}}{\text{number of guests in resort spa}}$$

$$\text{Spa revenue per occupied hotel/resort room (RevPOR)} = \frac{\text{total spa revenue generated}}{\text{number of occupied hotel rooms}}$$

$$\text{Spa revenue per available hotel/resort room (RevPAR)} = \frac{\text{total spa revenue generated}}{\text{number of available hotel rooms}}$$

Each figure used in the calculation is for a given period of time—a day, a week, a month, etc. Each calculation with a room (R) calculation can be converted to station (S) calculations, for example, revenue per available station (RevPAS), when used to analyze technician services.

includes a sampling of common ratios used to analyze the performance of a spa operation and its personnel.

STAFF COMPENSATION

At present, the debate about compensation structure in the spa is reaching a peak, and the opinions, depending on the holder's role in the spa, are varied. One fact that cannot be avoided is that spa owners are closing their doors at a rate that can be considered an epidemic. The fear of restructuring the current compensation plan is trumped only by the fear that the business in its present state is not sustainable.

Although the economic climate is always a factor to be considered, the current decline in demand has challenged even the most seasoned spa professionals to find creative ways to drive revenue and reduce costs. Many have had to reduce the size of the staff as well as offer premium services at sale prices.

Spa is not the first industry to hit the proverbial wall and be forced into serious analysis of the way the business operates. The discussion of how employees are compensated has been happening, sometimes covertly, for several years. The pressure to conform to "industry standards" has swayed many savvy business owners to make decisions that were not financially sustainable. Though the current compensation structure is widespread, all are best served with a discussion that outlines the best practices. The industry norm was adopted from the salon business and was primarily commission-based (60/40 split). Variations have evolved over the years, but it has become clear that this structure is not suitable for the "team-based" strategy that is becoming more popular and is proving more effective in achieving business goals.

REALITY CHECK

Letter from a spa consultant in response to an inquiry about the worth and compensation of a spa therapist:

Thanks for writing and your interest in this topic. First let me say no amount is too much if all parties are being served, i.e. the customer gets great value for their money, the therapist makes a decent living, AND the owner stays in business AND makes a decent return on their investment.

You say "overhead for a spa is not that much". On this point I could not disagree more with you. Rent on a 4000 sf spa averages at $10,000 a month, advertising averages at $1500-$2500/mo, front desk wages average at $4000 a month, utilities average at $800 a month, insurance $200/month, etc etc etc. The average day spa has $15,000 to $30,000 in overhead costs each month. I can say this with confidence since I review the income statements for about 100 spas each year.

Now let's take your 60/40 split, I assume the therapist is getting 40% now the owner needs to pay an additional 7-9% for worker's comp, 8% min for employer's share of taxes, and to complete each service the business also spends over $10 for supplies and laundry costs. That leaves a whopping (sarcastic) 25 cents out of each dollar to pay the overhead mentioned above. Let's assume the low end of $15,000 overhead. That means the owner's breakeven point would be $60,000 worth of business before they make their first dollar.

Now I understand you've got 10 grand invested in your education, but this is not unusual in most businesses that require college education or special education, employees make this investment all the time in their future.

(continued)

But more importantly is that the owner has several hundred thousand invested in their spa (and we didn't even talk about repayment of this debt in our above example of overhead). If they fail they lose their home, have to file bankruptcy, AND they cannot collect unemployment.

If you lose your job, as tragic as that would be, you get another job or collect unemployment.

I understand you want "incentive" but most jobs simply pay a living wage and people get up every day to go to work and perform admirably. They get pay raises (more per hour) when they do a good job and fired when they don't. Further, the gratuity and the retail commissions are great monetary incentives! That is something that most employees don't have.

Listen, with what I am preaching, I am not recommending pay cuts for anyone that the business can afford to keep employed. Instead I am recommending that we pay everyone equitably by the hour, like every other employment situation, AND that we help your employers stay in business so that they can continue to keep everyone employed. I also want employers to begin to pay for benefits as soon as they can afford to do so.

One last point: If what I was saying was wrong, and you were right, we would not be seeing thousands of spas going out of business as we have in the last 18 months. This industry is crashing and we need to fix it. Providers are not happy and owners are losing their businesses AND consumers are not coming because the pricing is too high, this position is untenable for everyone!

Further, if you still think I am wrong and that you are being "taken advantage of" you should go into business yourself so that you are not "exploited". (You will soon learn how hard and how expensive it is to get clients through the door.)

Providers ARE super humans, I agree, I want to keep them employed and I would never advocate treating them like "sub humans" but rather as well respected professionals like other businesses do. . . .

Source: Williams, Skip (2009). What Is a Spa Therapist Worth? *Resource and Development eNewsletter,* June 2009.

High compensation rates and low profit margins are rampant across all types of spas. Many spa operators are caught in the status quo of compensation structures for service providers that would be suitable for an independent contractor. However, based on the cost of an employee with full-time employment, this structure has endless pitfalls. If the business is to survive, the "per treatment pay" must be replaced with a motivational straight-pay compensation plan with incentives based on targets and performance. Without placing judgment on existing compensation plans, it is easy to focus on what works. (See Sample Compensation Plans in the online resources.)

Revenue management, also known as **yield management**, is the process of understanding, anticipating, and influencing consumer behavior to maximize revenue or profits. We are at a turning point in the spa industry. As spas undergo more and more scrutiny in terms of development, costs, and economic performance, the focus is turning to growing the spa numbers rather than growing the number of spas. There has been a shift in the need for consultants to design and build new facilities to those with a strong background in business systems and maximizing profitability. It is not enough to compare your performance against your budget or last year's actual numbers. You need to know how your spa is performing compared to others in your area or competitive set. Several key metrics need to be gathered, monitored, and measured if you expect to manage the spa as an economically viable business venture.

As an industry, we have developed to the point at which optimal growth can occur only by fully understanding the specific factors that drive the spa business model. We require more economic accountability. Accurate spa metrics can assist in moving many underperforming assets into business-oriented profit centers.

KEY TERMS

Assets	Income statement
Balance sheet	Liabilities
Bottom-up budget	Net profit (or loss)
Cash flow statement	Net worth
Cost of sales	Operating expenses
Depreciation	Revenue or yield management
Gross profit	Top-down budget
Gross revenue	Vertical Analysis
Horizontal analysis	Zero-based budget

REVIEW QUESTIONS

1. What elements are needed to create an accurate forecast and budget?
2. Which financial document shows a snapshot of the assets of the business?
3. What items in the spa may be depreciated over time?

▶ REFERENCES

Bplans (2010). Day Spa Business Plan. Retrieved June 22, 2010, from www.bplans. com/day_spa_business_plan/financial_plan_fc.cfm.

Dummies (2010). Choosing a Budget Method. Retrieved February 6, 2010, from www.dummies.com/how-to/content/choosing-a-budget-method.html.

Feather, William (n.d.). BrainyQuote.com. Retrieved June 22, 2010, from www. brainyquote.com/quotes/quotes/w/williamfea382216.html.

U.S. SEC (Securities and Exchange Commission) (2010). Beginners Guide to Financial Statements. Retrieved June 20, 2010, from www.sec.gov/investor/pubs/begfinstmtguide.htm.

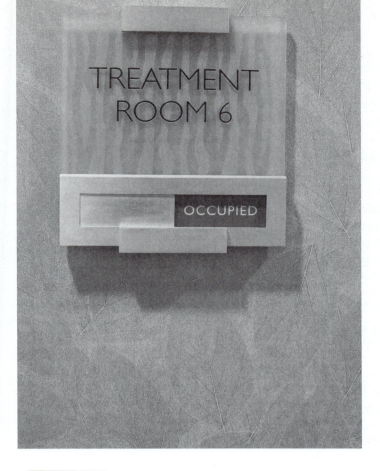

Spa Marketing and Promotion

LEARNING OBJECTIVES

At the end of this chapter, readers will be able to:

- Define marketing theory as it applies to the spa industry.
- Develop and implement a basic marketing plan.
- Identify actions that can be taken to market and promote the spa.

The aim of marketing is to know and understand the customer so well the product or service fits him and sells itself.

—**Peter Drucker**

To be successful in the industry, spa managers must be able to attract and retain satisfied customers. The purpose of marketing activities is to convince people to visit and make purchases at the spa. Spa owners and managers will be wise to carefully develop marketing strategies to keep their market presence strong.

WHAT IS MARKETING?

Marketing is the process by which goods and services are delivered, from conception through to the customer use. **Marketing management** is a business discipline focused on the practical application of marketing techniques and the management of resources and activities to attract or retain customers (U.S. SBA, 2009). A marketing manager may have a variety of responsibilities, depending on the size and culture of the business and on the strength and norms of the industry. The scope of marketing management is quite broad: Marketing management encompasses all factors that influence a company's ability to deliver value to customers. Hence, virtually any activity or resource the spa uses to acquire and manage customers is within the scope of marketing management.

Many spas operate with a much more limited definition of marketing. To some, marketing encompasses only traditional sales activities, such as advertising and public relations. Consider, however, the roles of the spa receptionist, therapist, and locker room host: Their influence in creating and retaining customers may be of even more value to the operation. All successful marketing activities and strategies result not only in matching the right product with the right customer but also create a satisfying customer experience.

When it is done right, marketing produces a win—win situation, as customers receive a product that meets their needs and the company earns healthy profits. This customer orientation must also be balanced with the company's objective of maintaining a profitable volume of sales so the company can continue to do business. Marketing is a creative, ever-changing orchestration of all the activities needed to accomplish both of these objectives. In sum, marketing is based on the principle that all company actions are directed toward satisfying the customer.

MARKETING IN PRACTICE

Real-life marketing relies heavily on common sense. At its core, the spa has an identity and an audience. Using limited financial resources and a variety of media resources, a spa manager works to create and implement a marketing plan.

Marketing decisions are made based on classic marketing strategies, intuition, and experience. Getting a new business off the ground can be gut-wrenching. It is all about selecting the best methods to reach your audience without breaking the bank. Effective marketing develops a line of communication to both current and new customers to help shape and grow the business. Over time, the marketing plan will need to be reevaluated and adjusted to satisfy clients' demands for new and/or innovative services. As the business reshapes itself, the marketing strategy will need to be revisited, adjusted if necessary; sometimes an entirely new plan will emerge. Because of the subjective and emotional nature of clients' experiences, managing a spa requires instinct to be a part of marketing decisions. To best use these principles, a spa should:

▶ Develop a market strategy.
▶ Research and select target markets.

▶ Determine how to satisfy customer needs by identifying a market mix.
▶ Implement the marketing plan.
▶ Evaluate marketing performance.

MARKETING STRATEGY

A **marketing strategy** identifies consumer groups and tailors product offerings, prices, distribution, and promotional efforts toward those groups. Ideally, the strategy should address unmet customer needs that offer optimum potential profitability. A well-developed strategy helps the spa focus on the target markets it can serve best. A marketing strategy allows the organization to concentrate its resources on the greatest opportunities for increasing sales and achieving a sustainable competitive advantage. A marketing strategy should be centered on the key concept that customer satisfaction is the main goal.

A marketing strategy is most effective when it is an integral component of corporate strategy, defining how the organization will successfully engage customers, prospects, and competitors in the market. Because spa customers are the source of the company's revenue, marketing strategy is closely linked to sales. A key goal of marketing strategy is often to keep marketing in line with the company's vision and mission.

A marketing strategy is the foundation of the marketing plan. A *plan* is a set of specific actions; a *strategy* is a series of well-thought-out tactics to make the plan effective. Marketing strategies are the fundamental purpose of marketing plans, designed to answer a need and reach an objective. Plans and their stated objectives need to be tested (evaluated) periodically for measurable results.

A marketing strategy is dynamic and interactive. It is partially planned and partially unplanned. Your marketing strategy should identify what differentiates your spa from its competition. According to Ahmed El-Deen (2010), there are basic strategies that apply well to most spa businesses:

▶ **Strategies based on market dominance.** Spas are classified based on their market share or dominance of an industry. Typically there are three types of market dominance strategies:
  ▶ Leader
  ▶ Challenger
  ▶ Follower
▶ **Innovation strategies.** Thse strategies deal specifically with a spa's new product or treatment development, business model innovation, and industry trends. They ask whether the company is on the cutting edge of technology and business innovation. There are three types:
  ▶ Pioneers
  ▶ Close followers
  ▶ Late followers
▶ **Growth strategies.** In these strategies the focus is, "How should the spa grow?" The four most common answers are
  ▶ Horizontal integration: Acquire existing competitors' customers, or the competing company itself.
  ▶ Vertical integration—Acquire product suppliers as well as other distribution channels.
  ▶ Diversification—Expand into new markets or launch new products.
  ▶ Intensification—Expand existing channels of revenue generation.

Once an owner, manager, and marketing personnel have identified the spa's general market position using the basic strategies described, the more subjective and emotional elements related to the spa's unique environment are incorporated into the overall marketing plan, thereby completing the spa's marketing identity. How you define the business will affect how you will market your spa. Reacquaint yourself with your spa's vision, mission, goals, and concept, and then consider the following:

- ▶ Primary product or service offerings
- ▶ Location—neighborhood, city, regional, national, or international
- ▶ Direct and indirect competition and elements that differentiate your spa from the competition
- ▶ Pricing profile
- ▶ Anticipated or current promotion methods
- ▶ Distribution methods or business location

TARGET MARKETING

Identifying those people most likely to buy a product or service and concentrating marketing efforts on one or a few key market segments is called **target marketing**. Targeting a specific segment of the market allows for more effective use of marketing dollars. Owners of small businesses usually have limited resources to spend on marketing. Target marketing gets the most return from small investments. Whether you are promoting a neighborhood day spa or a large resort spa, the initial approach is the same. Several methods can be used to segment a market:

- ▶ Customer demographic profile—age, gender, income, education level, race, ethnicity, marital status, family makeup, etc. (demographic profile)
- ▶ From where you will attract your customers (geographic profile)
- ▶ How your customers are likely to learn about your product or service (marketing profile)
- ▶ Qualities your customers value most about your product or service—What is their motivation for visiting your spa? (motivational profile)

MARKET RESEARCH

Once the target audience is selected, successful marketing requires timely and relevant market information. Before finalizing your marketing plan, talk to customers, study the marketing strategies of your competition, network with local leaders, and consult with any relevant industry associations to help ensure that marketing money is well spent. An inexpensive research program, using surveys given to current or prospective customers, can often help define the need for new products or services. Market research can also identify trends that affect sales and profitability. Monitoring industry trends and economic changes will enhance your understanding of the market.

THE MARKET MIX

Every marketing program contains four key components:

- ▶ Products and Services
- ▶ Pricing
- ▶ Distribution
- ▶ Promotion

Products and Services

Products and services involve not only the selection of offerings but also how the products and services are presented. This may entail a variety of strategies, such as concentrating on a narrow product line, developing a highly specialized product or service, or providing a product–service package that offers unusually high-quality service. Chapter 3 provides an overview of the most commonly offered spa services, and Chapter 8 provides insight into developing quality spa client presentations.

Pricing

The right price is crucial to maximizing total revenue. Generally, higher prices mean lower volume and vice versa; however, small spas or those that offer high-quality or unique spa experience can often command higher prices. Pricing strategies are detailed in the online resources.

Distribution

Distribution is the act of placing or making available a product or service. When selecting the location for a new spa, small spas should consider cost and traffic flow in site selection, especially because advertising and rent can be reciprocal: A low-cost, low-traffic location means spending more on advertising to build traffic. The nature of the product or service is also important when making distribution decisions. If spa purchases are based largely on impulse, then high-traffic and visibility are critical. On the other hand, location is less of a concern for products or services that customers are willing to go out of their way to find.

Promotion

Every successful company uses some sort of promotion to influence targeted audiences by informing or persuading them. Reasons for promoting a business include increasing visibility, adding credibility to you or your company, enhancing or improving your image, and bringing in new business.

The remainder of this section of the chapter focuses on promoting the spa. Promotion strategies include advertising, public relations, and direct customer interaction. If the spa is already in operation, it is wise to review past practices before changing the current marketing plan. Answering each of the following questions will help you get a clear picture of past marketing efforts:

- ▶ What marketing methods have been used in the past? Of those, which have been most effective?
- ▶ What are promotional costs as compared to sales?
- ▶ What is the cost of promotion per customer?
- ▶ What methods are currently used to measure the results of marketing efforts?

Moving forward, consider the following:

- ▶ What percentage of revenue can be allocated to the marketing campaign? How much money is available for marketing? What types of promotion options are available for this price?
- ▶ What marketing methods are being considered to attract new customers?
- ▶ What methods are available to test new marketing ideas?
- ▶ Which methods will best fit the resources available to the spa?

The final component in a marketing strategy should be the overall promotional objectives: the goals set to communicate your message, create an awareness of your product or service, motivate customers to buy, and increase sales. Objectives make it easier to design an effective campaign and help you keep the campaign on the right track. Once you have defined your objectives, it is easier to choose the method that will be most effective.

FOURTEEN IDEAS FOR PROMOTING YOUR COMPANY

The following are cost-effective, easy-to-execute ideas that have the power to increase sales in a way traditional marketing activities cannot. One of these methods may fit your market and managing style (U.S. SBA, 2010).

1. **Contests.** Develop competitions that encouraging healthy practices. It's a great way to motivate existing clients while reaching new ones.
2. **Newsletters.** Newsletters demonstrate how much you know about your field and do so in a low-key, informative way. These weekly, monthly, or quarterly publications can remind your customers of the benefits of visits to your spa.
3. **Demonstrations.** Demonstrations are an option for attracting people to your place of business. They show participants how best to use your product, provide a sample spa offering, and establish your credibility in the industry. For example, a yoga center might offer a free "community class" each week.
4. **Seminars.** Often more appropriate for business-to-business marketing, seminars are the commercial side of demonstrations. If you hold a seminar, follow these rules for success:
   - Schedule the event at a time convenient to most attendees.
   - Be specific in the invitation about when the event will begin and end.
   - Indicate who will be there and what the agenda is.
   - Follow up the invitations or make personal phone calls.
   - Consider charging for the seminar to give it a higher perceived value.
   - Follow up after the event to get people's reactions and make the sale.
5. **Premiums.** Also called advertising specialties, a premium is a gift of some kind that reminds your customer of your spa. There are thousands from which to choose: candles, water bottles, refrigerator magnets, baskets, pens, bookmarks—just about anything that can be engraved, imprinted, silk-screened, or embroidered with your company name and phone number.
6. **Speeches.** Depending on your topic and market, you can choose to speak before Chambers of Commerce, trade associations, parent groups, senior citizens, or other local organizations.
7. **Articles.** Write an article for a trade journal, reprint it, and mail it off to your friends, customers, and prospects. This positions you as an expert, and is a particularly good way to promote your business.
8. **Bonuses and samples.** Vendors often supply samples of select products that make excellent gifts and allow your customer to try products that are being offered for retail and professional treatment in the spa. Even if you don't have samples to give away, consider offering a small free sample product when customers schedule a service or purchase a complementary retail item.
9. **Coupons.** For best results, the price break should be significant—at least 15 percent. This is an inexpensive way to attract customers and an excellent tool for

evaluating advertising. However, one theory holds that coupons draw people who only buy discount and never become regular customers, so be sure to monitor the results. In some markets, "value-add" options will be more effective—for example, a complimentary gift with purchase.

10. **Donations.** Donating your product or service to a charitable cause often results in positive exposure to community leaders, charity board members, PTAs, and civic groups. Although consumer products are usually most desired, many organizations also look for donations of professional service time. If you have a restaurant or a large meeting facility, consider hosting an event for a charitable organization. This works best if volunteers for that charity are potential customers.

11. **Free services.** If you can't afford to give away products, offering extra services can be a way of generating new business. For example, the spa might offer a free eye-firming treatment or back exfoliation with purchase of a massage.

12. **Special benefits, rates, or notices.** Smart organizations go out of their way to make customers feel important and appreciated. Loyalty programs are the most pervasive example of this kind. Spa reward programs are already taking hold in spas across the country.

13. **Membership.** Allowing customers to "join" the spa is a great way to develop a strong community environment. The program can offer incentives for new members, but the greatest benefit is the recognition the guest receives from the staff.

14. **Say "Thank you."** One of the best ways to let customers know you value their business and encourage their continued patronage is also one of the easiest. Just saying "Thank you" in letters, mailers, statement stuffers, on receipts, invoices, through email, and/or and in person can make all the difference.

Promotion is generally segmented into two areas: advertising and public relations. In general, **advertising** is what the business says about its product; **public relations** is what others say. Table 11.1 provides an overview of the two approaches (U.S. SBA, 2010).

Public Relations

Public relations means working with the media and others to gain free, positive attention or coverage for an organization (Janes, 2006). Because the public generally feels that editorial information is more trustworthy than advertising, there is great value and return on public relation efforts. Examples of public relations include writing a monthly column in a local newspaper, working in partnership for a charitable cause, speaking at a local organization meeting, or informing the media when your spa has a special event, a new offering, or anything newsworthy. The key is to make the effort and get the word out. (See the special section at the end of the chapter for more public relations ideas.)

Advertising

There are limits to what advertising can and cannot do for your business (U.S. SBA, 2010). Advertising can:

▶ Remind customers and prospects about the benefits of your product or service.

▶ Establish and maintain your distinct identity

▶ Enhance your reputation

TABLE 11.1

Advertising versus Public Relations

Advertising	Public Relations
Mass media exposure that must be purchased.	Coverage in mass media that is not purchased.
You determine the message.	Interpretation of the message is in the hands of the media.
You control the timing.	Timing is in the hands of the media.
One-way communication; there is no feedback.	Can allow two-way communication.
Message sponsor is known or identified.	Message sponsor is not overtly identified.
The intention of most advertising messages is to inform, persuade, or remind, usually with the aim of making a sale.	The intention of public relations efforts is often to create goodwill, to keep the company and/or product in front of the public, or to humanize the company so the public relates to its people or reputation, rather than viewing the company as a nonpersonal entity.
The public may view the message negatively, recognizing advertising as an attempt to persuade or manipulate them.	The public often sees public relations messages that have been covered by the media as more neutral or believable.
Very powerful at creating image.	Can also create image, but can sometimes strays from the company's vision.
Writing style is usually persuasive and can be very creative, often taking a conversational tone; it may even be grammatically incorrect.	Writing style relies heavily on journalism talents—any persuasion can be artfully inserted in the fact-based content.

▶ Encourage existing customers to buy more of what you sell
▶ Attract new customers and replace lost ones
▶ Slowly build sales to boost your bottom line
▶ Promote your business to customers, investors, and others.

Advertising cannot:

▶ Create an instant customer base.
▶ Cause an immediate, sharp increase in sales.
▶ Solve cash flow or profit problems.
▶ Substitute for poor or indifferent customer service.
▶ Sell useless or unwanted products or services.

Advertising takes planning, time, and persistence. The effectiveness of advertising improves gradually over time. Because potential customers will not see every one of your ads or all of your efforts, the spa must repeatedly remind prospects and customers about the benefits of doing business with you. Long-term effort triggers recognition and helps special offers or direct marketing pay off. When preparing to advertise, the U.S. Small Business Administration (2010) suggests the following four steps:

1. Design the Framework
   ▶ What is the purpose of your advertising program?
   ▶ Start by defining the spa's long-range goals, then map out how marketing can help attain them

▶ Focus on advertising routes that compliment your marketing efforts.

▶ Set measurable goals so you can evaluate the success of your advertising campaign. How much can you afford to invest? Keep in mind that whatever amount you allocate will never seem like enough. Given your income, expenses, and sales projections, simple addition and subtraction can help you determine how much you can afford to invest. Some companies spend a full 10 percent of their gross income on advertising, others just 1 percent. Research and test to see what will work best for you.

2. Fill in the Details

3. What are the features and benefits of the spa's products or services? When determining features, think of automobile brochures that list engine, body, and performance specifications. Next, determine the benefits those features provide to your customers.

4. How do your products or services actually help customers? Where can you reach your targeted audience? Select advertising (and public relations) strategies to fit those you seek. Knowing your audience will help you choose the media that will deliver your sales message most effectively

5. Revisit your Competition. Knowing your competition will help you find a niche in the marketplace and helps show prospects how your products or services are special and preferred.

6. Build Your Action Plan—Evaluating Media Choices

▶ Your next step is to select the advertising vehicles to carry your message Use as many marketing avenues as are appropriate and affordable. When developing your advertising schedule, be sure to take advantage of any special editorial or promotional coverage planned in the media you select. Newspapers, for example, often run special sections featuring health and wellness, community events, and local business news. Magazines also often focus on specific themes in each issue.

7. Use Other Promotional Avenues

▶ Advertising extends beyond the media described above. Other options include distributing specialties, imprinting the spa name and graphic identity on pens, paper, clocks, calendars, and other giveaway items for your customers. Put your message on billboards, inside buses, airports, and subways, on vehicle and building signs, on point-of-sale displays, and on shopping bags.

▶ Co-sponsor events with nonprofit organizations and advertise your participation, attend or display at consumer or business trade shows, create tie-in promotions with allied businesses, distribute newsletters, conduct seminars, undertake contests or sweepstakes, send advertising flyers along with billing statements, and develop sales kits with brochures, product samples, and application ideas

▶ The number of promotional tools used to deliver your message and repeat your name is limited only by your imagination and your budget.

Online Advertising

E-mail Marketing. E-mail marketing is one of the most effective ways to keep in touch with customers. It is generally cost-effective, has fairly high response rates (5–35 percent), and if done properly, can help build brand awareness and loyalty (U.S. SBA, 2010). One of the benefits of e-mail marketing is the demographic information that customers provide when they sign up for your newsletter. Discovering who your customers are can help you better target products and services.

E-MARKETING NEWSLETTER

If you are considering creating an e-marketing newsletter, consider these points (U.S. SBA, 2010).

- **HTML versus plain text.** Response rates for HTML newsletters are generally far higher than for plain text, and graphics and colors tend to make the publications look more professional. The downside is that HTML e-mail is slower to download, and some e-mail providers may screen out HTML e-mail.
- **Provide an incentive to subscribe to your newsletter.** Boast the benefits of your newsletter and provide to those who sign up helpful tips, informative content, or early notification of special offers or campaigns.
- **Don't just sell.** Many studies suggest that e-mail newsletters are read far more carefully when they offer information that is useful to customers' lives rather than merely selling products and services. Helpful tips, engaging content, and humor are often expected to accompany e-mail newsletters.
- **Limit questions.** Each time you ask a question, you risk reducing customer interest. It is always best to limit the amount of information you solicit, or give customers the option of skipping the questionnaire.

Establishing a Web Presence. e-Commerce has redefined the marketplace and altered business strategies. The term **e-commerce** has evolved from meaning simply electronic shopping to including all aspects of business and market processes that are enabled by the Internet and other digital technologies. Even in an industry as high-touch as spa, these high-tech approaches are changing consumer behavior and expectations. An Internet presence can help any spa, small or large, provide better and faster customer service and communication.

A business website is essential to keeping your customer informed. Including a virtual brochure and menu of spa offerings also allows for updating on demand with little or no cost. Your presence on the Internet can be a useful marketing tool by providing broader presale information or postsale support and services.

The Advertising Campaign

You are ready for action when you are armed with knowledge of your industry and market, have a media plan and schedule, know your product or service's most important benefits, and have measurable goals in terms of sales volume, revenue generated, and other criteria. The first step in developing an advertising campaign is to establish a theme that identifies your product or service and that can be used in all of your advertising. The chosen theme should reflect your spa concept so that all advertising reflects your unique identity and the benefits of your product or service. **Tag lines**, sometimes called marketing statements, are often used in advertising to reinforce the single most important reason for buying your product or service. These brief statements are highly effective in identifying the unique elements of your spa, and they should be used repeatedly in all advertising pursuits. Can you identify these spa tag lines?

1. Celebrating 100 years of beauty
2. The power of possibility
3. Transcend. Transform. Trust the Moment.
4. First we make the world revolve around you. Then we gently slow it down.

MARKETING PERFORMANCE AND EVALUATION

A sound and complete marketing program is essential to the success of your business. After implementing a marketing program, spa managers must evaluate its performance. Every program should have performance standards to compare with actual results. Researching industry norms and past performance will help you to develop appropriate standards.

Managers should audit their company's performance at least quarterly. The key questions are

▶ Has the spa attracted a sufficient number of clients to meet financial goals?
▶ Does the customer profile match that of the targeted audience?
▶ What is the level of customer satisfaction with the product, price, distribution, and promotion?

See Chapter 12 for additional insight into evaluating a spa.

KEY TERMS

Advertising

Distribution

e-Commerce

Marketing

Marketing management

Marketing strategy

Public relations

Tag lines

Target marketing

REVIEW QUESTIONS

1. What aspects of marketing theory are best applied to the spa industry?
2. How do you define a target market?
3. What are five unique marketing ideas for a spa operation, and why do you feel they would be effective?
4. What is the goal of a marketing strategy?

REFERENCES

D'Angelo, Janet M. (2006). *Spa Business Strategies: A Plan for Success.* Clifton Park, NY: Thomson Delmar Learning.

Drucker, Peter (2001). BrainyQuote.com. Retrieved June 22, 2010, from www.brainyquote.com/quotes/quotes/p/peterdruck154444.html.

El-Deen, Ahmed Mohey (2010). Marketing Strategies and Tactics I. Retrieved June 20, 2010, from http://ezinearticles.com/?Marketing-Strategies-and-Tactics-I&id=3895345.

Janes, Patricia C. (2006). *Marketing in Leisure and Tourism: Reaching New Heights.* State College, PA: Venture Publishing.

U.S. SBA (U.S. Small Business Administration) (2010). Market and Price. Retrieved October 18, 2008, from www.sba.gov/smallbusinessplanner/manage/marketandprice/SERV_EMARKETING.html.

100+ MARKETING IDEAS

Marketing, and its related activities, is all about satisfying customer needs. The following represents a comprehensive list of marketing ideas; use it to help better understand customer needs and ways to satisfy those needs (Better Business, 2010).

General Ideas

- Never let a day pass without engaging in at least one marketing activity.
- Set specific marketing goals every year; review and adjust quarterly.
- Maintain a file of ideas for later use.
- Carry business cards/contact information with you (all day, every day).
- Create a personal nametag or pin with your company name and logo on it and wear it at high-visibility meetings.

Target Market

- Stay alert to trends that might affect your target market, product, or promotion strategy.
- Read market research studies about your profession, industry, product, target market groups, etc.
- Collect competitors' ads and literature; study them for information about strategy, product features, benefits, etc.
- Ask clients why they chose you, and solicit suggestions for improvement.
- Ask former clients why they left you.
- Identify a new market.
- Join a list-serve (e-mail list) related to your profession.
- Subscribe to an Internet newsgroup or a list-serve that serves your target market.

Product Development

- Create a new service, technique, or product.
- Offer a simpler/cheaper/shorter version of your existing product or service.
- Offer a fancier/more expensive/faster/bigger version of your existing product or service.
- Update your services.

Education, Resources, and Information

- Establish a marketing and public relations advisory and referral team composed of your colleagues and/or neighboring business owners. Meet quarterly to share ideas and referrals and discuss community issues.
- Create a suggestion box for employees.
- Attend a marketing seminar.
- Read a marketing book.
- Subscribe to a marketing newsletter or other publication.
- Subscribe to a marketing list-serve on the Internet.
- Subscribe to a marketing newsgroup on the Internet.

- Train your staff, clients, and colleagues to promote referrals.
- Hold a monthly marketing meeting with employees or associates to discuss strategy and status and solicit marketing ideas.
- Join an association or organization related to your profession.
- Get a marketing student to take you on as a client; it will give the student experience and you some free marketing help.
- Maintain a consultant card file for finding designers, writers, and other marketing professionals. Hire a marketing consultant and brainstorm.
- Take a creative journey to another progressive city or county to observe and learn from marketing techniques used there.
- Hire a student spa management intern to tap into a fresh new mind.

Pricing and Payment

- Analyze your fee structure; look for areas requiring modifications or adjustments.
- Establish credit card and online payment options for clients.
- Offer gift cards and certificates for sale.
- Give regular clients a free gift.
- Give a discount for the purchase of packages or treatment series.
- Learn to barter; offer discounts to members of certain clubs/professional groups/organizations in exchange for promotions in their publications.
- Give quick-pay or cash discounts.
- Offer financing or installment plans.
- Develop a loyalty program.

Marketing Communications

- Publish a newsletter for customers and prospects. Develop a brochure of services.
- Include a postage-paid survey card with your brochures and other company literature. Include check-off boxes or other items that will involve the reader and provide valuable feedback to you.
- Remember, business cards aren't working for you if they're in the box. Pass them out! Give existing and potential customers two business cards and brochures—one to keep and one to pass along.
- Produce separate business cards/sales literature for each of your target market segments.
- Create a poster, calendar, or other specialty item to give away to customers and prospects.
- Print your slogan (marketing statement) on letterhead, fax cover sheets, and invoices.
- Develop a website.
- Create a signature file to be used for all your e-mail messages. It should contain contact details, including your website address and key information about your company that entices the reader to contact you.
- Include testimonials from customers in your literature.
- Test a new mailing list. If it produces results, add it to your current direct-mail lists or consider replacing a list that's not performing up to expectations.
- Rather than sending direct mail in plain white envelopes, use colored or oversized envelopes to pique recipients' curiosity.
- Announce free or special offers in your direct response pieces. (Direct responses may be direct mail, broadcast faxes, or e-mail messages.) Include

the offer in the beginning of the message as well as on the outside of the envelope for direct mail.

Public/Media Relations

- Update your media list often so that press releases are sent to the right media outlet and person.
- Write a column for the local newspaper, local business journal, or trade publication.
- Publish an article and circulate reprints.
- Send timely and newsworthy press releases as often as needed.
- Publicize your 500th client of the year (or other notable milestone).
- Create an annual award and publicize it.
- Get public relations and media training, or read up on it.
- Appear on a radio, local news, or TV talk show.
- Create your own TV program on your specialty. Market the show to your local cable station or public broadcasting station as a regular program, or see if you can air your show on an open-access cable channel.
- Write a letter to the editor of your local newspaper or trade magazine.
- Take an editor to lunch.
- Get a publicity photo taken and enclose it with press releases.
- Consistently review newspapers and magazines for possible PR opportunities.
- Submit tip articles to newsletters and newspapers.
- Conduct industry research and develop a press release or article to announce an important discovery in your field.
- Create a press kit and keep its contents current.

Customer Service and Customer Relations

- Ask your clients to come back again.
- Return phone calls promptly.
- Set up a fax-on-demand or e-mail system to respond easily to customer inquiries.
- Use voice mail to catch after-hours phone calls. Include basic information in your outgoing messages, such a business hours, location, etc.
- Record a memorable message or tip of the day on your outgoing voice mail message.
- Ask clients what you can do to help them.
- Take clients out to a ball game, show, or another special event—just send them two tickets with a note.
- Hold a seminar at your office for clients and prospects.
- Send handwritten thank you notes.
- Send birthday cards and appropriate seasonal greetings.
- Photocopy interesting articles and send them to clients and prospects with a hand-written FYI note and your business card.
- Send a book of interest or other appropriate business gift to a client with a handwritten note.
- Create an area on your website specifically for your customers/members.

Networking and Word of Mouth

- Join a Chamber of Commerce or other organization.
- Join or organize a breakfast club with other professionals (not in your field) to discuss business and network referrals.

- Mail a brochure to members of organizations to which you belong.
- Serve on a city board or commission.
- Host a holiday party.
- Hold an open house.
- Send letters to attendees after you attend a conference.
- Join a community list-serve (e-mail list) on the Internet.

Advertising

- Advertise during peak seasons for your business.
- Get a memorable phone number, such as 1-800-WIDGETS.
- Obtain a memorable URL and e-mail address and include them on all marketing materials.
- Provide phone stickers or magnets preprinted with your business contact information.
- Promote your business jointly with other professionals via cooperative direct mail.
- Utilize FaceBook, LinkedIn, and other networking sites to link and advertise.
- Write an ad in another language to reach the non–English-speaking market. Place the ad in a publication targeting that market, such as a Hispanic newspaper.
- Distribute advertising specialty products such as pens, mouse pads, or water bottles.
- Mail bumps—photos, samples, and other innovative items—to your prospect list. (A bump is simply anything that makes the mailing envelope bulge and makes the recipient curious about what's in the envelope!).
- Create a direct-mail list of hot prospects.
- Utilize Twitter and "tweet" to keep customers informed.
- Consider nontraditional advertising tactics such as bus backs, billboards, and popular websites.
- Project a message on the sidewalk in front of your place of business using a light directed through words etched in a glass window.
- Consider placing ads in your newspaper's classified section.
- Consider a vanity automobile tag with your company name.
- Create a friendly bumper sticker for your car.
- Code your ads and keep records of results.
- Improve your building signage and directional signs inside and out.
- Invest in a lighted sign to make your office or storefront window visible at night.
- Create a new or improved company logo or recolor the traditional logo.
- Sponsor and promote a contest or sweepstakes.

Special Events and Outreach

- Get a booth at a fair or trade show attended by your target market.
- Sponsor or host a special event or open house at your business location in cooperation with a local nonprofit organization, such as a women's business center. Describe how the organization helped you.
- Give a speech or volunteer for a career day at a high school.
- Teach a class or seminar at a local college or adult education center.
- Sponsor an Adopt-a-Road area in your community to keep roads litter-free.
- Volunteer your time to a charity or nonprofit organization.
- Donate your product or service to a charity auction.
- Appear on a panel at a professional seminar.

- Write a "How to" pamphlet or article for publishing.
- Produce and distribute an educational CD-ROM or audio/video tape.
- Publish a book.

Sales Ideas

- Read newspapers, business journals, and trade publications for new business openings, personnel appointments, and promotion announcements made by companies.
- Give your treatment menu and sales literature to your lawyer, accountant, printer, banker, temp agency, office supply salesperson, advertising agency, etc. (Expand your sales force for free!).
- Put your fax number on order forms for easy submission.
- Set up a fax-on-demand or e-mail system to easily distribute responses to company or product inquiries.
- Follow up on your direct mailings, e-mail messages, and broadcast faxes with a friendly telephone call.
- Try using broadcast fax or e-mail delivery methods instead of direct mail. (Broadcast fax and e-mail allows you to send the same message to many locations at once.)
- Use broadcast faxes or e-mail messages to notify your customers of product service updates.
- Extend your hours of operation.
- Reduce response/turnaround time. Make reordering easy—use reminders. Provide preaddressed envelopes.
- Display product and service samples at your office.
- Remind clients of the products and services you provide that they aren't currently buying.
- Call and/or send mail to former clients to try and reactivate them.
- Take products sales orders over the Internet.

Source: 100+ Marketing Ideas. Retrieved November 12, 2009, from http://betterbusinesscards.blogspot.com/2009/07/100-marketing-ideas.html.

Spa Business Evaluation

→ LEARNING OBJECTIVES

At the end of this chapter, readers will be able to:

- Define and understand key evaluation concepts.
- Appreciate the importance of evaluating a spa business.
- Know how to evaluate various elements of a spa business.
- Identify and implement different evaluation approaches.

The cynic knows the price of everything and the value of nothing.
—Oscar Wilde

To evaluate is "to determine the significance, worth, or condition of, usually by careful appraisal and study" (Merriam-Webster, 2009). **Evaluation** is often described as a systematic examination of something in order to judge its worth or assess its value (Rossman and Schlatter, 2008). To maintain the success of any business, a manager must constantly monitor and adjust the operation. This simple form of evaluation is important, but often it is not enough. There are several important elements to the above definitions of evaluation. First, "careful appraisal" and "systematic examination" imply that evaluation is not just casual consideration, but a thorough and accurate review. Second, evaluation includes not only the study and assessment, but a judgment of value derived from the information that is collected.

There is value in casual, intuitive judgments; however, as the spa industry grows and fluctuations in the economy continue to challenge spa managers, the importance of careful and systematic evaluation has become more and more apparent. This chapter will provide a foundation of knowledge to help the reader understand how to evaluate, and subsequently improve, the spa client experience, spa offerings, and the overall spa operation.

↪ THE EVALUATION PROCESS

Evaluation is not an easy task. It takes forethought, preparation, and attentiveness. Evaluations can provide spa executives with a wide variety of facts and figures to better manage the business. Evaluation helps to generate data, which can be used to provide evidence that the organization's objectives are being met, to help justify future operational changes or purchases, produce comparable benchmarks, provide evidence to funding organizations, or provide evidence of accountability. At the conclusion of a well-executed evaluation project, leaders will emerge with comprehensive, impartial information with which to make decisions and solve problems in the spa operation. Answering the following questions will help focus the project and lead to selection of an appropriate evaluation technique for your purpose.

Why? The Purpose of Evaluation

Before beginning any evaluation project, it is important to understand the purpose of the assessment. Start by asking these questions: What (or who) is motivating you to evaluate? What do you want to know? And how will the information be used? Responding to these questions can help provide focus for the project. Often the answers to these questions will lead a spa manager to understand that the evaluation will help in one of three areas: experience development, organizational management, or operational accountability (Rossman and Schlatter, 2008).

For Whom? Utilizing the Information

Once the evaluation project has a defined purpose, consider who will use the information (and make the judgment) once the project is completed. Owners, managers, and/or direct service providers will gain insight from the data. However, other possibilities include customers, the public, funding agencies, professional associations, or educational institutions. Once the purpose and audience are defined, all other phases of the evaluation process will be easier to complete.

From Whom? Project Completion

Who will conduct the evaluation will likely be determined by the scope and size of the project as well as the financial and human resources available. When making this

Customer Interview

selection, you will typically consider individuals working either inside or outside the spa. There are advantages and disadvantages to using either. The advantages of contracting an outside researcher to complete your evaluation means that the project will be less of a burden on the staff, the researcher will likely have greater training, and there is a better chance of objective judgment at the conclusion of the project. The greatest disadvantage will likely be the cost.

Common practice in the spa industry is to hire trained professionals or spa-savvy outsiders to receive a spa experience and report back to leadership on their experience. These "mystery shoppers" typically receive treatments, mingle with other spa guests, and examine pretreatment and public areas. Although these evaluation experiences may be limited to only a few visits before the employees identify the "shopper," it can be extremely valuable to receive the often illuminating perspective of an outsider.

Advantages of using someone from inside the organization include their familiarity with the spa operation and, therefore, greater insight into the development of the project. The inside researcher may be more accepted by the staff and less obtrusive throughout the project. The greatest disadvantage is the potential for bias in the collection and interpretation of the evaluation data.

When? Timing and Frequency

Evaluations take place at different times, depending on the purpose of the project. Evaluations typically use one of three formats; before and after an experience, once at the conclusion of an experience, or ongoing throughout the experience. If you want to assess a change, evaluation must take place before and after an experience to compare the two measures and identify any change. Consider a common practice at destination spas which specialize in fitness and weight loss. Likely, these organizations will weigh and measure guests at the beginning and end of a stay to determine any changes which can be attributed to the visit.

Performing evaluations at the conclusion of a program is a common technique. Consider common schedules of financial reporting taking place monthly, quarterly, and at the end of the fiscal year. An ongoing evaluation format assesses and collects information during each step of an experience, program, or service. Consider, for example, a fitness trainer monitoring the heart rate of a group of clients throughout a new vigorous workout routine in order to receive feedback to judge the intensity of the workout program. An example of ongoing research is taking website "hit" measurements every hour for the first week after the new launch of a spa's new menu page.

From What? Selecting Evaluation Subjects

The term **subject** is used to describe who or what is to be evaluated. The most common subjects are individuals, such as a spa customer or spa employee; groups, such as spa members, nail technicians, or salon clients; or things, such as fitness equipment, locker room inventory, or treatment rooms. Once again, the purpose of the evaluation will dictate from whom or what you collect your evidence.

Defining a few terms to begin will help in clarifying how to select evaluation subjects. The term **population** is used to describe the entire group of individuals or things from which information is sought. A **sample** is the part of the population that is actually examined to gather information. When there are a small number of accessible subjects to be evaluated or the data are readily available, a project will strive to include the entire population. For example, if evaluating the teaching qualities of a prospective fitness instructor, information can likely be gathered from all participants in a "test" class. Or, if measuring the likelihood of a skin care purchase following a facial during the last month, with an effective retail tracking system, this data will already be available and therefore should be used. When the evaluation sample mirrors the population, the evaluator can be assured that the evidence is complete and free from any unfairness imposed by the improper selection of a sample.

Often, gathering evidence from an entire population is not possible. In this case, the evaluator must select a sample of the population. When using a sample, the evaluator must take measures to ensure that the sample is representative of the full population. If the sample does not reflect the population, the evidence gathered will be biased and may lead to incorrect judgments. The two most common methods used to select a representative sample are simple random sampling and systematic sampling. With either technique, the intention is for every subject to have an equal and independent chance of being selected (Rossman and Schlatter, 2008). These techniques allow the evaluator to make relatively few observations and then generalize from those observations to the wider population (Babbie, 1992).

Both techniques start with a list of the entire population. **Simple random sampling** uses a random number table (found online or in any research text) and assigns a number to each subject or object on the list. Once the size of the sample is determined (e.g., 50), the evaluator simply selects a range of numbers to be included in the sample (e.g., 150–199), and scanning the list, selects the subjects with those numbers as the sample. This method of simple random sampling is thought to imitate picking a number or name out of a hat. The technique can be quite cumbersome, however, if it is used with a population in excess of 100, so in that case it is recommended to use systematic sampling.

Systematic sampling is similar to random sampling, but in this case a structure is interjected for selection. Starting with the population list and after determining the sample size, the evaluator selects the parameters for each subject to be included in the sample. For example, if the population size is 800 and the sample size is set at 200, starting from the top of the list, every fourth subject on the list will be used in the sample.

Although random and systematic sampling techniques are common, sampling using any technique that removes evaluator bias from the selection process can work. Consider, for example, a project in which you want to assess resort guest opinions of your spa. Relying on your own preferences may lead you to sample a disproportionate number of good-looking, happy men. Instead consider selecting a random tile on the floor; if a guest steps on the tile, he or she is selected for the sample. A key idea behind using any sampling technique is to remove individual preferences, or bias, from the selection process.

How Many? Sample Size

If the evaluation project warrants selecting a sample of the population, determining how large a sample to study is a necessary, but often a difficult and complicated step. To make this step as simple as possible, here are a few standards. As the size of the population decreases, the proportion of subjects to be included in the sample must increase. For example, to ensure that there is ample representation from a group of 30 individuals, it is necessary to sample at least 50 percent, or 15, individuals. However, for a group of 3000, 25 percent or 750 would be sufficient.

If your evaluation project includes using your findings for publications or to benchmark against other agencies, it may be beneficial to determine your sample size with help from a qualified statistician. For simple internal evaluation projects, sample sizes can be less robust. According to Rossman and Schlatter (2008), a general rule of thumb is that, for populations under 500, a sample of 50 percent should be drawn; from 500 to 1500, approximately 30 percent; from 1500 to 2500, approximately 25 percent; and over 2500, 400 individuals should be sufficient.

What? Components of Evaluation

Probably the most difficult decision during the development of an evaluation project is what elements the evaluation will address and how will those elements be measured. The purpose of the project will drive what will be included in the evaluation. Common categories and evaluation elements are given in Table 12.1, using a modified version of Henderson and Bialeschki's (1995) "Five Ps of Evaluation."

Selection of the elements that relate directly to the overall purpose of the evaluation is essential. Selecting too many elements to evaluate will likely dilute your research and overwhelm your subjects and researchers. Endeavor to cover only one or two categories in a single evaluation, making certain that the evidence collected presents a balanced and comprehensive view of what you are evaluating.

When measuring any evaluation element, the aim must be **accuracy**. This is a simple task for most measurements. Measuring things such as total purchase amount, number of class participants, or the length of a treatment are likely accurate. Even individual inquiries such as gender, state of residence, employment status, or other similar concepts are understandable, definite, and not of a sensitive nature, so accuracy is likely present. Conversely, when measuring concepts that are less precise, vague, or of a sensitive nature, careful attention must be given to accuracy. The development of measurements for concepts such as customer attitudes, motivations, or value perceptions would need greater attention.

For a measure to be accurate, it must be both valid and reliable. **Validity** refers to the extent to which a measurement adequately reflects the real meaning of the concept under consideration. **Reliability** tests whether, if a particular measurement is applied repeatedly to the same subject, it would yield the same result each time. If it would, this consistency confirms that the measure is reliable (Babbie, 1992). If a measure is found to be either not reliable or not valid, the result is bias, and therefore, inaccuracy in the measure.

How? Evaluation Techniques

Once the categories and elements are defined, the next task is to identify how best to measure them. A variety of common techniques are used in evaluation research projects in the spa industry. One of the most common is the use of surveys.

TABLE 12.1

Five Ps of Evaluation

Participants:
- Motivations
- Satisfaction
- Changes in attitudes, knowledge, skills, and/or abilities
- Interactions with guests
- Onsite actions
- Carryover actions
- Price/value perceptions
- Characteristics
- Privacy and protection
- Number of participants

Programs and Offerings:
- Characteristics of service provision
- Scheduling and timing
- Promotion techniques
- Safety and security
- Ample and adequate offerings
- Number of programs

Place:
- Interior characteristics
- Exterior characteristics
- Safety, security, and privacy
- Ample and adequate facilities
- Cleanliness and sanitation

Paperwork:
- Financial accountability
- Inventory management
- Operational efficiencies

Personnel:
- Training and development
- Goal achievement
- Characteristics
- Service and sales performance
- Guest interactions
- Safety, security, and privacy

Source: Modified from Henderson, K. A., and Bialeschki, D. (1995). *Evaluating Leisure Services: Making Enlightened Decisions,* p. 31. State College, PA: Venture Publishing.

Survey Evaluation

Surveys come in many shapes and sizes, but they are typically applied in one of three ways: self-administered, interview, or observation checklist. **Self-administered surveys** are provided to subjects in paper or electronic form in the hope that the individual will complete and return the survey. Self-administered surveys can be mailed, e-mailed, handed to, or strategically placed for subjects to pick up. The primary advantages include that subjects are allowed to complete the survey at their leisure, allowing for a longer length in some cases, and that this technique is comparatively inexpensive. The primary disadvantages are the absence of support personnel to help clarify survey content and motivate the subjects toward completion; hence, when they are optional, self-administered surveys tend to have a low response rate. Even with the noted disadvantages, spa guest comment cards or employee written performance evaluations are common practice in a spa operation.

Interviews, whether face to face or on the phone, eliminate the primary disadvantages associated with self-administered surveys. Also, in an interview the evaluator has the opportunity to establish rapport with the subject and, if necessary, integrate further probing questions to help clarify an answer. Because interviewers are employed, this format tends to be more costly, more prone to interviewer bias, and, in some cases, content must be condensed to accommodate a subject's limited available time.

The third survey method, a survey **checklist**, is used primarily when evaluating "things" or using observation to evaluate. In this case a checklist is used by the evaluator to record either observed characteristics of individuals, groups, or things, or actions of individuals or groups. Consider testing the preferred temperature of a treatment room for the service provider, the fitness instructor's perceived exertion ratings recorded throughout a 60–minute spinning class, or noting the customer's "first stop" in the retail boutique.

Focus Groups

A **focus group** is a specific style of structured interview, which is typically used to investigate far-reaching aspects of an issue or idea. If you are evaluating elements that are difficult to measure, such as customer motivations, or employee attitudes, or are considering the introduction of a new product or service, this technique may produce a greater depth of information. Focus groups typically bring together twelve to fifteen individuals (selected on the basis of relevancy) to discuss and evaluate a topic. Trained moderators pose questions and provide guidance to group discussions to reveal the sought-for evidence. Using focus groups to evaluate can be useful, but, because of the unstructured format and small sample size, focus group evaluation is not generally seen as a bias-free form of evaluation. Typically, more than one focus group meets during a given project, to help provide a wider range of opinions to consider. However, even when using more than one focus group, the data gathered are not seen as being as compelling as when they come from a project with greater structure.

Experiments

Although experiments are not as common as surveys in the spa industry, they can be a very valuable evaluation methodology. The word *experiment* often congers up a vision of researchers in a controlled laboratory testing, retesting, and then testing again. This is necessary for some forms of research;, in spa evaluation, however natural experiments will likely be the experimental technique used. A **natural experiment** is not carried out in a controlled laboratory environment, but rather during the regular course of events. As humans, we are experimenting all the time. Imagine you are on a mission to lose weight. One week you may elect to change one element of your routine, such as increasing your water intake, exercising longer, or decreasing the number of sweets you eat. At the end of the week you judge the results and adjust your routine accordingly. Simple as that, experiments typically involve changing a circumstance and observing and recording the consequences. To help lessen interference, experiments aim to make only one change, to help ensure that any outcomes are associated with the element of interest. The evaluator's responsibility in natural experiments is to observe, record, analyze, and judge. If the change influenced the end result, you have gained new knowledge, which can assist in the evaluation and improvement of the spa. Experiments can be helpful when changing the front desk check-in routine to enhance efficiency, testing a new treatment protocol to enhance customer relaxation, or considering a product-line change.

No matter what technique is used, managers must be aware that clients visit spas for the experience, not to evaluate the operation. Managers need to be concerned with how the evaluation project may interfere with the experience and work to lessen this interference. Receiving permission, keeping surveys clear and concise, and offering incentives for guest or employee participation are all techniques that can help diminish any imposition.

Analysis and Reporting

After the evaluation data have been collected, the analysis begins. An evaluation project will generate words or numbers, qualitative or quantitative data, respectively. Whichever the case, this evidence can be condensed into tallies or percentages of responses in each category, and through this, a category ranking can be constructed. If the evidence is ordinal, such as ratings from 1 to 5 or from "strongly agree" to "strongly disagree," a range and a midpoint can be identified. If the data are actual numbers, such as age, frequency of visits, or number of absences from work in a given time period, an average or mean score can be generated. There are more sophisticated forms of data analysis available. If you are interested, seek a trained evaluator or researcher for greater detail.

Reporting the results of the analysis can take many formats. Oral or written reports are standard and can be used effectively. The type of reporting will depend on for whom the project and report are intended. Standard content in any report includes a brief description of each of the stages of the evaluation project; the why, from whom, when, from what, how many, what, and how, before the final analysis and judgment are revealed. Final reports also include an explanation of any concerns observed during the project that may affect or limit the outcome and judgment.

⟶ EVALUATION PROJECTS COMMON TO THE SPA INDUSTRY

A successful spa manager is always striving for excellence in three key areas: the spa client experience, spa offerings, and the overall spa operation. It is not surprising, therefore, to find that these areas are typically the focus of evaluation projects in a spa setting. This section provides a brief overview of each of the areas and a sample technique that is used to assess each area.

Spa Client Experience

Customers are the lifeblood of any business. Essentially, if clients are not happy with their spa experiences, your business will suffer. Client assessment can provide the spa manager with the necessary information to improve services and operational systems, evaluate staff and guest satisfaction, initiate test marketing, evaluate safety efforts, identify current and potential clients, and keep the spa competitive. Client evaluation should not be a once-in-a-while thing, but an ongoing process used to check the overall efficiency and effectiveness of the spa operation.

Evaluation that includes collecting information directly from customers can help the customers feel a connection with the organization. Evaluation provides a mechanism for customers to provide feedback directly to spa managers, while allowing customers a feeling of control over their experiences. Many client evaluations allow for feedback on

Spa Client Written Evaluation

experience satisfaction and/or goal achievement, but they can also include operational elements.

COMMON FEATURES OF SPA CLIENT EVALUATIONS

- Customer satisfaction. Information collected from customers can give spa leadership an accurate reading on whether customers are having satisfying experiences. Satisfaction can come from a variety of sources, including the spa facility, offerings, interaction with spa personnel, and what benefits the client was seeking in the experience.
- Goal achievement. All customers, whether they are motivated toward stress release, education, wellness, beauty, or some other benefit, enter a spa seeking something. Evaluation can provide feedback to help assess whether customers achieved their goals.

Customer Satisfaction Evaluation

In assessing satisfaction, customers are typically surveyed after or toward the end of their experience. They are asked a series of questions reflecting various elements of the experience that relate to overall satisfaction. Wisnom and Janes (2008) identified five possible satisfaction areas for a spa: physical environment, offerings, interactions, customer motivations, and service recovery. Service recovery was used to feature the way in which any service "breakdown" was resolved. The areas and corresponding survey items are given in Figure 12.1.

Spa managers can select items, such as those identified in Figure 12.1; pair each item with a rating scale, such as a 5-point scale from "Extremely Satisfied" to "Not at All Satisfied"; add an overall experience satisfaction item for comparison; and use this as the starting point for a satisfaction survey for their customers. An alternative satisfaction technique, called importance–performance analysis, is described later in the chapter.

Spa Offering Evaluation

Offerings are often the catalyst that entices customers to visit a spa. If customers have a quality experience, they will likely return. Many things that happen throughout a spa experience can affect the happiness of the customer and staff. Evaluation can help spa leaders better understand the spa experience and identify ways to make improvements. Evaluation helps spa managers understand how customers make service selections. Evaluation enables the spa to get to know customer likes and dislikes regarding select spa offerings. Evaluation provides feedback to treatment providers, who in turn can work toward enhancement of spa offerings. Evaluation can provide managers with evidence on the efficiency, consistency, and cost of services. Evaluation helps the spa marketing team understand what it is about a menu item that entices a customer purchase. Evaluation can uncover which spa services are most popular, which offerings lead to retail purchases, which treatment rooms are preferred by staff, which providers are most successful at booking repeat appointments, all of which help improve the managers' understanding of the operation. In short, evaluation allows for better understanding of the entire spa experience, so that all spa personnel can make informed judgments to improve its offerings.

Figure 12.1   Satisfaction Areas
and Sample Customer Items

PHYSICAL ENVIRONMENT
  Ample signage
  Cleanliness
  Ambiance
  Layout/accessibility
  Safety
  Overall spa exterior
  Overall spa interior

OFFERINGS
  Treatment quality
  Price/value
  Treatment availability
  Adequate equipment and supplies
  Spa brochure quality
  Staff identifiable
  Staff appearance

MOTIVATION FOR VISIT
  Body Maintenance
  Socialize/Enrich a Relationship
  Improve Appearance
  Relax/Stress Release
  Pampering
  Experience Something New
  Seek Solitude
  To Feel Physically Energized
  Stimulate Your Mind
  Improve Overall Health/Wellness
  Temporary Escape from Daily Routine

INTERACTION
  Reception/Spa Attendant/Treatment
  Provider:
  Greeting
  Friendliness
  Appreciation
  Honesty
  Knowledge
  Efficiency
  Closing

SERVICE RECOVERY
  Positive response
  Empathy
  Listening
  Offers for resolution
  Satisfactory resolution
  Response time

Source: Wisnom, Mary & Janes Patricia L. (2008). Expectations and their Role in the Service Industry. Presentation at Resort and Commercial Recreation Association National Conference, New Paltz, NY.

Provider Summary Checklist

Few would argue that spa service providers have the greatest influence on guests' experience. A common technique used by spas and service providers to gather information to help improve spa offerings is a written guest survey. Before receiving a treatment, the guest is asked to complete a form, recording information such as contact information, how the guest heard about the spa, and the reason for the visit. To assist providers, especially massage therapists, hair stylists, and estheticians, with the development of treatments, a health history, treatment preferences, and level of familiarity with spa services may be assessed.

These surveys are stored and reviewed prior to a guest's return. It is good practice for service providers to document additional guest preferences in the guest file after each treatment, and to interview guests prior to each service and record any updates in the guest file. Samples of customer surveys are available in the online resources for this book.

Spa Operation Evaluation

Spas, like all businesses, contain a mix of human, financial, informational, and technical resources. They operate within a complicated legal environment and institute policies and procedures to help the business run effectively. Systems and programs are developed to enhance the enterprise, and checks and balances are instituted to prevent carelessness. There are many ways that managers monitor all the workings of a spa. Most integrate some form of evaluation.

Because evaluation provides information about the costs and benefits of spa programs and services, such information is useful in the overall decision making of the business. Evaluation aids in the development, monitoring, and control of business and employee performance standards. Evaluation can help appropriately link the various operational areas of the spa to financial allocations. Evaluation can help managers test the success of marketing efforts.

Financial and operational benchmarks have been established in the spa industry. Benchmarking helps a business compare its operation against an industry standard. Evaluating the spa's financial information and producing comparative data can help management gain a better understanding of how their operation differs from others in the industry. Chapter 10 details several common formulas, which can be used for financially evaluating any spa business or for industry benchmarking.

Goal and Objective Evaluation

As described in Chapter 2, spas are founded on a vision, a mission, goals, and objectives, all of which guide the business toward success. Objectives are generated to bring focus to the overarching vision, mission, and agency goals and are developed to measure spa inputs, processes, programs, or outcomes. Objectives should be specific, measurable, challenging, yet attainable, and provide usable insight to the organization. Another useful element of a well-designed objective is the integration of a time dimension, such as "Participant enrollment will reach capacity in *two weeks* from announcement." This helps monitor and track the evaluation to completion.

Objectives, however, are only useful if you evaluate how well they are being met. One of the most common ways to evaluate a business is to start with the established operating objectives. Certainly, the first step to this type of evaluation is to ensure that you have well-defined and insightful objectives. Objectives for a spa operation can pertain to any resource of the business and to any aspect of the spa's planning or performance. However, the evaluator must monitor the process, test the established criteria, and report on the result.

Imagine you have built your spa on an educational foundation, and one of the central ambitions of your spa is to have the most knowledgeable service provider staff in the area. This goal can be translated into several specific objectives. The following might be objectives developed to focus your evaluation:

▶ All new service provider hires to the spa will have the required licensure and as a minimum, five years of full-time experience in the service for which they are hired.
▶ Over the next year, the spa will institute no less than ten in-house training sessions for each category of service providers.
▶ By December 31, the spa will have 80 percent of all service providers licensed in more than one specialty.
▶ Customer surveys will reflect a rating of no less than 4.5 (on a scale of 1 to 5, 1 being less and 5 being more knowledgeable) when asked to rate the knowledge of the service provider compared to that of others in the tri-county area.

As you can see, when objectives are developed appropriately, the evaluator's job is simple: Measure the accomplishment, report on any discrepancy, and indicate whether the objective has been met.

⟶ AN EVALUATION TECHNIQUE FOR TODAY'S SPA CUSTOMER: IMPORTANCE–PERFORMANCE ANALYSIS

It's a great time to be a spa customer! Spa patrons not only have more offerings than ever before, they also have more establishments providing the services they desire. With so many opportunities, spa customers can be more selective. They can demand more from spas—and they are. If spas want to remain competitive and successful, they must find ways to discover and cater to the particular needs of the spa customer.

The needs of a spa customer come in many forms. The customer's needs may reflect a certain spa service, the attributes of that service, or the benefits the customer seeks from the experience. For example, a customer may desire a service that will allow for social interaction, exercise, and a chance to learn something new. The customer may desire a yoga class, but may need a convenient location and reasonable cost. Being aware of varying needs will not only allow spa managers to better understand the needs of the customer, but also to have the information necessary to alter products and services to fit those needs. If the needs of customers are fulfilled, they are more likely to be satisfied with the spa experience.

In this chapter, a number of ideas have been shared on how to assess the satisfaction of a spa customer. Each is useful, but none takes a comprehensive approach to evaluation. It is believed by many that customer satisfaction is a function of both expectations related to certain elements of an experience and judgments related to the execution of those elements. Consider a common definition of **quality service**, meeting or exceeding customer expectations, implying that one must have knowledge of a customer's expectations to produce a quality product. Because the needs of customers differ, providing quality service must include both an assessment of the *importance* of each of the elements and an assessment of each element's *performance* in order for an evaluation to be comprehensive.

Importance–performance analysis (I-P) was developed by J. A. Martilla and J. C. James (1977) to assess customer satisfaction with a product or service. This technique accesses importance and performance information related to a customer's experience and translates this information into easy-to-understand management suggestions. As our society becomes more diverse and spa customers more demanding, spa managers need a comprehensive evaluation technique that can help lead them into a successful future. I-P involves three simple steps: (1) identify elements describing the service, (2) measure importance and performance for each element, and (3) average measures across customers and map on a two-dimensional action grid.

Step 1: Identify Elements Describing the Service

Elements describing the service can be identified in a variety of ways. The best way to develop a list is by soliciting information from current customers, potential future customers, and/or customers of a similar business. This can be done using focus groups, unstructured interviews, and/or surveys. Determining what elements to measure is critical. If factors important to the customer are overlooked, the usefulness of I-P will be severely limited. In a recent spa "mystery shopper" study, each of the elements listed in Figure 12.2 was used (Wisnom and Janes, 2008).

Figure 12.2 Sample Importance and Performance Questions

Please circle your response to the following criteria based on your expectations prior to arriving at the spa.

	Importance				
MOTIVATION FOR VISIT	Low				High
Body Maintenance	1	2	3	4	5
Socialize/Enrich a Relationship	1	2	3	4	5
Improve Appearance	1	2	3	4	5
Relax/Stress Release	1	2	3	4	5
Pampering	1	2	3	4	5
Experience Something New	1	2	3	4	5
Seek Solitude	1	2	3	4	5
To Feel Physically Energized	1	2	3	4	5
Stimulate Your Mind	1	2	3	4	5
Improve Overall Health/Wellness	1	2	3	4	5
Temporary Escape from Daily Routine	1	2	3	4	5

Please circle your response to the following criteria based on your perceptions of the spa's performance.

	Performance				
MOTIVATION FOR VISIT	Low				High
Body Maintenance	1	2	3	4	5
Socialize/Enrich a Relationship	1	2	3	4	5
Improve Appearance	1	2	3	4	5
Relax/Stress Release	1	2	3	4	5
Pampering	1	2	3	4	5
Experience Something New	1	2	3	4	5
Seek Solitude	1	2	3	4	5
To Feel Physically Energized	1	2	3	4	5
Stimulate Your Mind	1	2	3	4	5
Improve Overall Health/Wellness	1	2	3	4	5
Temporary Escape from Daily Routine	1	2	3	4	5

Source: Wisnom, Mary, and Janes, Patricia L. (2008). Expectations and Their Role in the Service Industry. Presentation at Resort and Commercial Recreation Association National Conference, New Paltz, NY.

Step 2: Measure Importance and Performance for Each Element

Once a list of selected elements is established, customers are asked how important each attribute is to them and how well the spa performed with regard to that element. Using a five- or seven-point rating scale has been suggested for measuring each element (Martilla and James, 1977; Guadagnolo, 1985). Numbered scales with descriptive end points can be used; or a descriptive scales, such as an importance scale of Extremely Important, Very Important, Important, Somewhat Important, and Not at all Important; or a performance scale of Excellent, Very Good, Good, Fair, and Poor. See Figure 12.2 for a sample of the survey questions asked in the mystery shopper study using a numbered scale (Wisnom and Janes, 2008).

It is always best for customer importance ratings to be assessed prior to the spa visit and performance after the experience. However, when this is not feasible, placing items at different locations on a survey (the importance question appearing before the performance), will suffice.

TABLE 12.2

Spa Importance and Performance Sample Mean Ratings for Customer Motivations

Performance MOTIVATION FOR VISIT	Importance	
	(Mean)	(Mean)
Body Maintenance	4.55	3.84
Socialize/Enrich a Relationship	2.25	2
Improve Appearance	3.2	2.90
Relax/Stress Release	4.8	4.47
Pampering	4	4.32
Experience Something New	4	4.68
Seek Solitude	3.25	3.11
To Feel Physically Energized	3.55	3.05
Stimulate Your Mind	3.55	2.89
Improve Overall Health/Wellness	4.55	3.37
Temporary Escape from Daily Routine	4.4	3.89
Grand Mean	**3.83**	**3.5**

Step 3: Average Measures Across Customers and Map on a Two-Dimensional Action Grid

Customer responses are coded for each measure, as, for example, as shown in Table 12.2, then all the element codes are totaled and average (mean) or midpoint (median) scores are established for the sample of customers. Mean scores were used for the mystery shopper study and are shown in Table 12.2.

The importance and performance mean (or median) scores are then plotted on a two-dimensional, four-quadrant grid, as shown in Figure 12.3. Positioning the vertical and horizontal axes on the grid is a matter of judgment. Some use a mean of the mean scores (grand mean), whereas others base placement on the values and goals of the spa. The horizontal axes represent the separation of the importance scores, the vertical axes the separation of the performance scores. When creating the grid for reviewing the customer motivations for the visit in the mystery shopper study, a grand mean was selected to plot the axes.

The location of each attribute on the grid provides information to help managers allocate resources, make changes, and establish priorities in the operation to better meet customer preferences. The four quadrants are interpreted as follows:

▶ *Concentrate Here.* The upper left quadrant includes elements that are important to the customer but for which performance is low. These attributes require the most attention.

▶ *Keep up the Good Work.* The upper right quadrant includes elements that customers view as important and for which the business receives high performance marks. The spa is doing well with respect to these elements. It is important that these attributes remain in this quadrant.

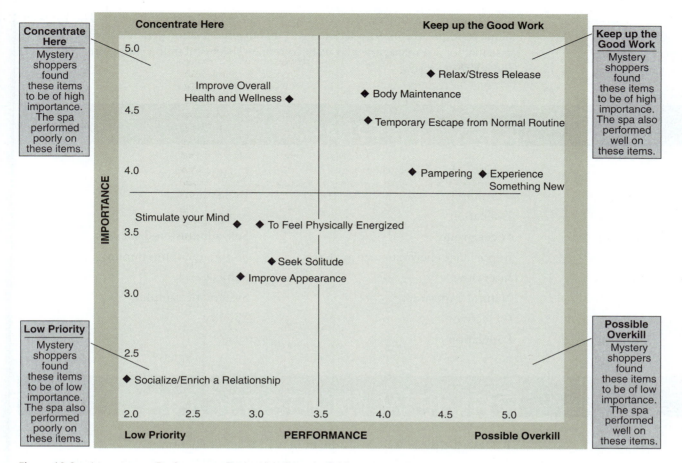

Figure 12.3 Importance–Performance Evaluation Sample Grid

Source: Wisnom, Mary, & Janes, Patricia L. (2008). Expectations and their Role in the Service Industry. Presentation at Resort and Commercial Recreation Association National Conference, New Paltz, NY.

▶ *Low Priority.* The lower left quadrant includes elements that receive low marks on both the importance and performance scales. Elements in this quadrant require little attention, however, because customers view these areas as lower in importance.

▶ *Possible Overkill.* The lower right quadrant contains elements that received low importance ratings and high performance ratings. It is suggested that some attention could be diverted from these elements to those in the *Concentrate Here* quadrant.

Based on the I-P evaluation example provided in Figure 12.3, the spa attribute in need of the most attention is providing opportunities for guests to improve their overall health and wellness. One of the key motivations, in which the spa has been successful, is allowing customers the opportunity to relax and relieve stress. The motivation rated as lowest in performance was the opportunity to socialize. If this evaluation project had been completed without assessing importance data from the customers, a spa might wrongly focus efforts on enhancing this area. However, in this study the importance data for socializing was also low, and therefore, interpreted as a low priority. With this sample, no motivations fell into the *Overkill* quadrant.

The findings from an importance–performance evaluation study can be used in a variety of ways, including marketing, planning, training, and customer assessment. Most important, I-P can be used to improve spa facilities and services to better fit the needs of its customers. The example provided is one of customer assessment, and although this technique is used mainly with external customers, it can also be very effective with a spa's internal customers, such as employees, vendors, and contractors. The I-P technique is simple, the interpretations clear, and the information generated from I-P can be essential for spa managers who want to remain successful in the competitive climate of today's spa industry.

KEY TERMS

Accuracy	Quality service
Checklist	Reliability
Evaluation	Sample
Focus group	Self-administered surveys
Importance–performance analysis	Simple random sampling
Interview	Subject
Natural experiment	Systematic sampling
Objectives	Validity
Population	

REVIEW QUESTIONS

1. Describe three ways a spa might benefit from evaluation.
2. What is sampling, and why is sampling important in an evaluation project?
3. List five common categories or elements in spa evaluation?
4. What two elements are required for an accurate measure?
5. Develop a survey question that can be used to measure spa client satisfaction.
6. When using importance–performance evaluation, in which quadrant of the action grid would a spa manager want to find the majority of his or her researched operational elements? Why?

REFERENCES

Babbie, Earl (1992). *Practicing Social Research,* 6th ed. Belmont, CA: Wadsworth.

Guadagnolo, F. (1985). The Importance-Performance Analysis: An Evaluation and Marketing Tool. *Journal of Park and Recreation Administration,* 3(2), pp. 13–22.

Henderson, K. A., and Bialeschki, D. (1995). *Evaluating Leisure Services: Making Enlightened Decisions.* State College, PA: Venture Publishing, p. 31.

Martilla, J. A., and James, J. C. (1977). Importance-Performance Analysis. *Journal of Marketing,* 41(1), pp. 77–79.

Merriam-Webster (2009). Evaluate. Retrieved December 29, 2009, from www.merriam-webster.com/dictionary/evaluate.

Rossman, J. Robert, and Schlatter, Barbara Elwood (2008). *Recreation Programming: Designing Leisure Experiences,* 5th ed. Champaign, IL: Sagamore.

Wilde, Oscar (1892). *Lady Windemere's Fan.* New York: Collier.

Wisnom, Mary, and Janes, Patricia L. (2008). Expectations and Their Role in the Service Industry. Presentation at Resort and Commercial Recreation Association National Conference, New Paltz, NY.

The Spa Management Professional

13

→ **LEARNING OBJECTIVES**

At the end of this chapter, readers will be able to:

- Define skills necessary for a spa professional.
- Employ assessment tools for self-evaluation.
- Utilize industry tools for professional development.

Management is efficiency in climbing the ladder of success; leadership determines whether the ladder is leaning against the right wall.

—Stephen Covey

For a leader in the spa industry, the opportunities for a dynamic and fulfilling career are endless. The skills necessary to be successful, however, are still evolving as the industry matures and the demands increase. As professional degree programs expand and the resources developed by the industry pioneers become widely available, the challenges are sharply defining the skill set of spa owners, directors, and managers. Skills have evolved to move the business of wellness to the next level. According to Bankoski and Register (2010), the following responsibilities provide a framework for success for the spa professional:

1. *Strategy:* Defining what is important to the spa's success and creating a system to turn intentions into reality. Examples include characterizing the culture, setting the spa's vision, mission and goals, and strategic planning such as the spa's treatment menu and required facilities, equipment, and supplies (see Chapter 2).

2. *Leadership:* Building leadership and management skills. Spa leadership motivates people and manages the system of processes as a cohesive whole. Spa leadership communicates roles and responsibilities and evaluates the spa's effectiveness and efficiency. Examples include establishing the culture; ensuring that the spa's vision, mission, and goals are integrated into spa operations; analyzing training needs; hiring and training staff; allocating resources; deploying the strategy; and evaluating key business performance indicators (see Chapter 6).

3. *Customer experiences:* Planning and managing the delivery of guest services and identifying ways to improve the guest experience. Examples include booking appointments, welcoming guests warmly, treatment delivery (standard operating procedures/protocols), and offering retail products (see Chapter 8).

4. *Operations support:* Mastering back-of-the-house processes to ensure that the spa delivers safe and consistent treatments and that the spa meets all legal and regulatory requirements to optimize the spa business operations. Examples include cleaning and sanitizing the spa facility and equipment, purchasing and receiving, product storage, and maintaining equipment and facilities (see Chapter 7).

5. *Improvement:* Identifying opportunities for the spa to minimize risks and continually improve all aspects of the spa business as well as guest satisfaction. Examples include analyzing guest feedback; root-cause analysis (finding and correcting problems at their source); self-examination and assessments; using audits, testing systems, and personnel to identify what needs improvement; and identifying and eliminating sources of waste (see Chapter 12).

Within the five areas, there are four activities that describe the cycle needed for a comprehensive spa quality-assurance system: plan, document, manage, and evaluate (Bankowski and Register, 2010):

▶ *Plan* long and short-term preparation activities.
▶ *Document* and process key documents and records.
▶ *Manage* activities needed for control.
▶ *Evaluate* information collection and analysis to demonstrate how well the spa planned, documented, and managed.

Ongoing professional development and growth should focus on maximizing your existing strengths and finding opportunities to develop areas that may need improvement. Professional development will assist with self-examination and help you find the balance between vision and operations.

→ CHANGE MANAGEMENT

Businesses are environments in a constant state of change and movement. Whether driving that change or along for the ride, **change management** skills include leadership development to encourage people to believe in you, marketing and sales abilities to promote your case for change, and communication skills to help build support for the decision to change.

The first focus in a changing environment is leadership development. It is common to focus too much on business processes and not enough on good, strong examples of leadership. As the leader in your spa, others look to you for direction not only in terms of business needs, but also in terms of behavior, ethics, and standards. If you are seeking, or driving, change and desire others to do so, you must set the example. Consider these practices outlined by the U.S. Small Business Administration (2009):

▶ *Eliminate perks.* Perks suggest division and hierarchical thought processes. By eliminating or reducing your own perks, you show your desire to level the playing field.

▶ *Be visible.* Successful leaders interact with their employees; they "manage while walking around," getting to know their employees and learning about the problems employees face on a day-to-day basis.

▶ *Be genuine.* Let others get to know you. By interacting with employees on a one-on-one basis, you will build rapport and trust.

▶ *Have passion.* To be an effective leader, you must have passion for your vision. Without it, you will soon find yourself facing burnout. Leadership can be tiring and drain energy at a very high rate, so find the passion in what you do.

Once employees trust what you are doing, you can begin to introduce the reasons for change. Your employees will want to know how they will be affected personally by the changes you are proposing. Your approach should be to address the different groups in the spa and provide reasons why change is necessary for each.

Although good, honest communication can help transition a change, all changes come with some resistance. To reduce frustration as a leader, it helps to know the six stages people go through when they experience change, whether personal or professional, as described in the Small Business Administration Leadership Resource Guide (U.S. SBA, 2009):

▶ *Stage 1: Anticipation.* This is the waiting phase. Individuals don't know what to expect, so they wait, anticipating what the future holds.

▶ *Stage 2: Confrontation.* At some point, individuals will begin to realize that change is happening.

▶ *Stage 3: Realization.* Once the change has happened, people realize that nothing is ever going to be as it once was. Often, this realization will plunge them into Stage 4.

▶ *Stage 4: Depression.* A necessary step in the change process, this is the stage at which people mourn the past. Not only have they realized the change intellectually, now they are beginning to comprehend it emotionally as well.

▶ *Stage 5: Acceptance.* Marking the point at which people begin to accept the change emotionally, in Stage 5, individuals are beginning to see some of the benefits even if they are not completely convinced. They may still have reservations, but they are no longer fighting the change.

▶ *Stage 6: Enlightenment.* Accepting the new change, in this stage, many wonder how they ever managed the "old" way. Overall, they feel good about the change and accept it as the status quo from here forward.

Spa employees will proceed through the different phases at different rates and may possibly approach some stages out of sequence. Some will require only a few months to go through the stages; others may take upwards to a year. There is no easy way to determine how long a change will take to implement; however, using the skills outlined will increase the chance of managing change more effectively.

THE FOUNDATION OF EFFECTIVE LEADERSHIP

Ethics is the discipline that considers good and bad, and the moral obligations and principles of conduct governing an individual or a group. Business ethics are a hot topic these days; with everything you hear in the news media, it is no surprise that businesses are focusing more on ethical leadership. However, a number of unknowns come with this new focus. Many factors can weigh on a manager making an ethical decision. While this topic is found at the center of many heated debates, it is important to be able to define appropriate behaviors and construct the necessary boundaries that will allow the spa to be a place of well-being. Developing an ethics policy can be a revealing exercise, but it is the actualization of the conduct described in the policy that will ultimately define the business.

REALITY CHECK

As a spa director, I am consistently challenged by two requests: to allow children (under age 18) into the spa to receive massage and body treatments, and to allow our pregnant customers to receive massage during the first trimester. Both represent customers seeking the services we offer. My questions are always: Does our policy go far enough to protect both my employees and my customer? Does the underage guest need to be in a room alone with a therapist? Is the child at risk? Is my therapist at risk? If there is difficulty after the massage with the customer's pregnancy, am I exposing my employee to a potentially harmful legal claim? There are extensive arguments and concessions to be made for both of these customers, and an equal number of risks. What is my ethical responsibility to both parties?

Developing an Ethics Policy

A well-defined ethics policy, along with an outline of related standards of conduct, provides the framework for ethical and moral behavior within the company. There are definite advantages to owning the business when establishing an ethics policy. Ethical standards come from the top. Setting the example at the top is crucial to convincing employees that they, too, should be ethical in their business dealings. The benefits of developing such a policy include higher employee morale and commitment, which, in most cases, leads to higher profits.

An ethics policy looks at how the organization relates to society as a whole. The responsibility of the spa manager is to the greater good. However, it is important to note that most of the opponents of good ethics are focusing on short-term versus long-term results. Many organizations that have recently chosen to downsize, or deviated from their business model, are beginning to realize that they have traded long-term employee morale and productivity for short-term profit margins. The bottom line is always: "What goes around, comes around." If employees are treated in an ethical manner, chances are they will show greater respect for the company, the customers, vendors, and their fellow employees.

When developing an ethics policy, it is important to decide what the spa stands for, put it in writing, and then enforce it. According to Blanchard and Peale (1988), an ethics policy can be based on five fundamental principles:

▶ *Purpose.* A purpose combines both your business vision and values. It comes from the top and outlines specifically what is considered acceptable and unacceptable in the conduct in your business.

▶ *Pride.* Pride builds dignity and self-respect. If employees are proud of where they work and what they are doing, they are much more apt to act in an ethical manner.

▶ *Patience.* All businesses must focus on long-term versus short-term results. In a spa setting you must develop a certain degree of patience. Without it, you will become frustrated and will be more tempted to choose unethical alternatives.

▶ *Persistence.* Persistence means standing by your word. It means being committed. If you are not committed to the ethics you have outlined, then they become worthless.

▶ *Perspective.* In a world in which there is never enough time to do everything we need and want to do, it is often difficult to maintain perspective. Stopping and reflecting on where your business is headed and why you are headed that way can help you make the best decisions in both the short and long term.

A company policy is a reflection of the values deemed important to the business. As you develop your policy for ethical conduct, focus on what you would like the world to be like and not on the vision of others.

Staying Connected

Networking is meeting people. It is an invaluable tool that anyone in the business world can utilize. Effective networking can be your best form of marketing, as well as being extremely affordable. Networking occurs when there is a planned event or gathering with the primary goal of connecting with others. Sometimes the best networking happens spontaneously! The primary focus is to meet people, and to have people meet you. This is an opportunity to market yourself and your business in a relaxed, social environment.

There are many opportunities to network in every community and industry. As a spa manager, the most productive starting point may be to join a local chamber of commerce, travel bureau, or professional association. Generally, in member organizations, members pay dues to receive the benefits. To make sure that the organization is right for you before you join, it is usually acceptable to request to visit the group first as a guest at little to no cost. This will enable you to get to know the group and make sure it is right for you before incurring any expense.

You may want to visit, and possibly join, several chambers or organizations, but whatever you choose to do, it will only be effective if you use it. Regular attendance at the meetings is extremely important for effective networking. People will get to know you and your company, and thus refer clients to your business. You will do the same for them to reciprocate. Personal referrals and word-of-mouth advertising are invaluable and highly effective.

To make the most of your networking time, here are a few guidelines you should follow (U.S. SBA, 2009):

▶ Arrive early. You will be assured the maximum opportunity to meet everyone.
▶ Arrive with a goal. Example: Meet and speak with five new people.
▶ Bring writing materials, business cards, and marketing materials.
▶ Shake hands when introduced, or when you introduce yourself.
▶ Be approachable. You will meet more people if you don't appear to be busy with idle conversation.
▶ Take the initiative to approach people you don't know and introduce yourself.
▶ Wear a name tag that includes the name of your spa.
▶ Make friends. Networking meetings are to be social and relaxed, not a time for "hard selling."
▶ Develop a system to remember names of those you have met.

Your appearance is the first thing people will notice. Consider these tips:

▶ Be well groomed—good haircut, clean nails, etc.
▶ Wear clothes that are setting-appropriate and fit properly.
▶ Pay attention to detail in jewelry and accessories. Less is more is a good rule.
▶ Be yourself. Remain comfortable and confident.

After the gathering, it is important that you follow up with the people you have met in a timely manner. If someone was interested in your company, don't wait two or three weeks to make contact. Your attention to detail provides information about the way you do business. Networking can be costly in fees, dues, luncheons, and so on, but if it is done effectively, it can be an invaluable investment in the success of the business.

Roundtables

Roundtables are informal group discussions among professional people (typically from the same or complementary industries) who serve voluntarily as information and support resources for each other. Participants meet regularly and learn from each other's experiences. Over time, professional relationships develop and participants become familiar with each other's businesses.

Practical support and guidance from individuals with varied backgrounds who understand the ups and downs of being a business owner, and who know you and your business, are extremely powerful. Roundtables provide an excellent, cost-effective way to gain fresh ideas, new perspectives, and detailed answers to even your most specific business questions. Online versions of roundtables, called forums, are also available and can be extremely valuable.

Newsgroups

Newsgroups are similar to online bulletin boards where discussions can occur and be reviewed at the participants' convenience. Newsgroups are similar in that they can be ongoing like physical roundtables, but are unlike physical roundtables in that they aren't live. Many new forums are emerging, such as blogs, podcasts, live webcasts, Facebook, Linked-In, Twitter, and online meetings. There are no quantitative data yet on the use of these forums for networking success; however, any communication that can support learning, inspiration, and communication can only be beneficial in the long run.

There are a number of resources available to keep a spa manager in touch with industry happenings. See the Appendix for detailed lists of available spa resources. According to the U.S. SBA (2009), some techniques to stay informed include the following:

▶ Subscribe to industry or trade publications that focus on your business or the business of your clients and customers.

▶ Join a professional association, chamber of commerce, or network with other entrepreneurs in similar industries.

▶ Use the Internet to research the spa industry. Watch for opportunities to interact with business or industry experts in chatroom interviews. Subscribe to Internet newsgroups that focus on your industry.

▶ Read newspapers—local and national—to track business trends.

▶ Talk to your customers, guests, and clients. What is on their minds? What is their mission? How does it align with yours? Ask yourself, "How might this affect my business?"

▶ Invest in training: Attend International Spa Association (ISPA) or other spa association knowledge networks. Visit or call your city library or check out the library at a nearby college. Find out what resources—periodicals, newspapers, reference materials—they offer for someone interested in a spa business

▶ Enroll in a local or online spa management course.

▶ Recognize that at some point you may not be able to know everything about your business. Learn to use consultants or hire employees who can compensate for the gaps in your knowledge.

▶ Review a spa management textbook.

▶ Cultivate your curiosity. Don't be afraid to try new things. The most important skill you can develop is not the ability to remember information, but the ability to seek out and find the information you need, when you need it, and then use it for the benefit of your business.

▶ Offer to speak about "relaxation" at a chamber of commerce luncheon. Members of Rotary, Kiwanis, Elks, Moose, and other organizations are all local residents of your community who just need an invitation to become your clients.

⟶ WALKING THE WALK

Be patient with yourself. Self-growth is tender; it's holy ground. There's no greater investment.
—Stephen Covey

There is nothing more powerful than receiving advice from someone who has achieved what you desire. As a spa professional you are surrounded by and focused on sharing the techniques to maintain balance, health, and overall well-being. Could the message be better received if you were able to model these conditions? You are your best marketing, the most effective teacher and ultimate role model for your employees and customers.

REALITY CHECK

I was asked to be a guest instructor at a local massage school. It was the first month, so the students were not yet performing massage. As the students took turns to introduce themselves and tell me why they wanted a spa career, I was shocked to hear that more than half of them had never even received a professional massage. Almost every one of them wanted to help others! I hoped I made the point that they will never have a career truly helping others if they are not able to take care of themselves. A few weeks later I received a thank-you note from one of the students with the quote, "Be the change you want to see in the world . . ." and her sincere appreciation for my advice. She wrote, "Thank you for the reality check! I hope to inspire my clients by living what I teach . . ." I posted her note in my office to remind myself that my best self is still in development!

KEY TERMS

Change management

Ethics

Networking

Newsgroups

Roundtables

REVIEW QUESTIONS

1. What do you see as your strengths as a leader? What are your weaknesses?
2. Describe an experience when you were faced with an ethical dilemma. What did you do? Would you make the same decision if the situation occurred again?
3. What are the things you do that enable you to be at your best?

REFERENCES

Bankoski, Linda, and Register, Julie (2010). The International Standards of SpaExcellence(SM)2010. Retrieved June 23, 2010, from www.spaquality.org/pages/pressrelease2010standards.htm.

Blanchard, K., and Peale, N. V. (1988). *The Power of Ethical Management.* New York: William Morrow, 1988.

Covey, Stephen (n.d.). BrainyQuote.com. Retrieved June 22, 2010, www.brainyquote.com/quotes/quotes/s/stephencov130675.html http://thinkexist.com/quotes/stephen_r._covey/3.html.

U.S. SBA (Small Business Administration) (2009) Lead. Retrieved May 7, 2009, from www.sba.gov/smallbusinessplanner/manage/lead/SERV_CHANGE.html.

Trends and the Future of the Spa Industry

14

→ LEARNING OBJECTIVES

At the end of this chapter, readers will be able to:

- Identify and explain various trends affecting the spa industry.
- Differentiate economic, social, environmental, and spa treatment trends.
- Understand what select spa leaders identify as the future direction of the industry.

Remember! Things in life will not always run smoothly. Sometimes we will be rising toward the heights—then all will seem to reverse itself and start downward. The great fact to remember is that the trend of civilization itself is forever upward, that a line drawn through the middle of the peaks and the valleys of the centuries always has an upward trend.

—Endicott Peabody, U.S. educator (1857–1944)

A *trend* is a general direction in which something tends to move or to veer in a specified direction. In its dramatic growth over the last decade, the spa industry has veered in many different directions, and trend watchers are predicting a number of new paths in the future. The industry has seen new types of spas emerging, changes in the makeup of the spa customer, new spa offerings, and expanding facilities. The economy has influenced the spa industry, and the spa industry has influenced the economy. As the world works its way toward being more planet-friendly, so do spas. This chapter will provide an overview of some of the most common trends in the industry, a select number of emerging trends, and some predictions for the future of the industry. In addition, spa leaders with varied backgrounds provide their comments and predictions of upcoming significant industry changes.

⤳ ECONOMIC/INDUSTRY TRENDS

Particular trends have their roots in finance and the wealth of the nation. Economic trends have driven the spa industry toward both scarcity and abundance, while industry trends are changing the face of spas.

Globalization

Globalization is the process by which something becomes international. In today's high-tech society, economies and cultures have become integrated through a globe-spanning network of communication and exchange. Certainly this phenomenon affects all industries. For spa businesses, adapting cross-cultural spa traditions and services is common. For consumers, seeking international spa vacations is increasing (SpaFinder, 2007). As revealed in a 2006 study of affluent international travelers, 48 percent visited a spa at a luxury hotel or resort at least once in the previous year, and 43 percent cited visiting a spa as a "recreation activity of interest" while on vacation, followed by 33% citing golf and 31% citing gambling (Yesawich, 2007).

Travelers tend to select familiar brands in their lodging selections. Brand selection is a potential progression for spas as well. Global branding of spas by major hotel chains is affecting the way spa travelers select their destinations and accommodations. For spa managers working in or with lodging establishments, the importance of developing a spa that can draw and maintain an international audience is increasing.

Thanks to globalization, other forms of spa travel are also on the rise. **Health tourism** or **medical tourism** combines many elements of a relaxing spa visit with medical procedures. This blending of spas and hospitals has created a unique opportunity for travelers. Medical tourism services typically that are sought include elective procedures as well as complex specialized surgeries such as joint replacement, cardiac surgery, and cosmetic surgeries. Whatever the procedure, health travelers are selecting medical tourism for a reduction in overall cost, physician expertise, or the unique rehabilitation offerings.

> In Europe, countries such as Poland, Switzerland and Germany have cultivated international medical tourism. In other parts of the world such as China, India, and New Zealand, doctors who have been trained in different techniques are available to treat international patients. Countries such as Mexico, Costa Rica and Panama are also developing highly efficient medical facilities to cater to advances in the medical field.
>
> —Hugh Jones, HUW Enterprises, Plantation, Florida, 2010

REALITY CHECK

As reported at the 2010 Global Spa Summit by SRO International (2010), three mega-trends will ensure continued growth in wellness: (1) an aging world population; (2) failing conventional medical systems, with consumers, health-care providers, and governments seeking more cost-effective, prevention-focused alternatives to a Western medical/sickness model focused on solving health problems rather than preventing them; (3) increased globalization, with consumers more aware of alternative health approaches via the Internet and the powerful reach of celebrity wellness advocates such as Oprah Winfrey, Deepak Chopra, and Jamie Oliver.

North American Spa Growth

Day spas have outnumbered all other types of spas for quite some time in the modern world. However, several new types of spas have begun to emerge, and it is anticipated that some of these spas will continue their growth. Medical spas have shown tremendous growth in the last several years. Medical spas are presently the fastest-growing type of spa in the industry. This trend is predicted to continue based on several changes, most notably the aging "baby boomers" and rapid growth in medical spa technology. Based on these same societal changes, and with the growing recognition of the therapeutic effects of spa services, it is anticipated that spa services and facilities will continue to grow in medical operations.

Economic Environment

A dramatically fluctuating economic environment will not only challenge a business, it will also lead to new creative directions. Some trends that emerged during the recent global recession include a decrease in the number of employees and the number of guests visiting individual spas. Although the industry overall has continued on a path of growth, the amount of revenue per spa decreased slightly each year from 2005 through 2009 (ISPA, 2009a). This trend has forced spa managers to develop more efficient operations.

According to the ISPA (2009a), the number of spas in the United States has seen a five-year average growth rate of 17 percent. With this remarkable growth, industry leaders have indicated difficulty finding qualified individuals to fill almost all provider and management positions in their spas (ISPA, 2009b). To counter this trend, "spa schools" across the globe are now offering a wide variety of educational offerings for treatment providers and managers. Although licensing and certification programs have been available for many years, in North America there are now associate's and bachelor's degrees programs in spa management available to help develop a greater pool of qualified candidates to manage spas (See the Appendix for a list of North American educational programs in spa management).

Increased opportunities for educational training and degree programs at national universities [are likely, and along with this trend comes] higher expectations of more qualified and highly skilled professionals working [in spa businesses].

—Kathie Pedit, Colonial Country Club, Ft. Myers, Florida, 2010

As students begin to graduate from accredited schools with spa management degrees and more focused education in the spa industry, we will begin to see a more sophisticated business model develop in the industry. The "build it and they will come" mentally which made so many spas incredibly successful over the past few years will not sustain the same financial success in this tougher economic climate. Companies will begin to look for managers with stronger financial and operational experience to streamline the business and maintain profitability as the industry stabilizes.

—Ginger McLean, The Spa at The Hotel Hershey, Hershey, Pennsylvania, 2009

In a recent study, 79 percent of active spa goers noted price as the most significant issue preventing them from spa visits (Coyle Hospitality Group & WTS International, 2009). Driven by a combination of economic change and consumer demand, several new types of "discount spas" have emerged. For those seeking lower-priced options, single-service or niche spas are becoming more readily available. A **niche spa** focuses on a specific modality and provides excellence through the provision of one or a few wellness or beauty services. Because of the nature of this type of business, select-service spas have the ability to offer their services at very competitive prices. This helps to make spa services available to a larger number of individuals. Some "big box" stores also offer convenience and discounted spa services, such as SmartStyle Family Hair Salons located in select Walmart stores.

I can see the spa industry in the next 1–5 years "polarizing." In other words, very affordable; back to basics "smart" spas and selections vs. high-end "experiential" spas. Mediocrity hasn't really ever fit the spa model.

—Leslie Lyon, Spas2b, Waterloo, Ontario, 2010

The spa world has and will continue to flex its creative arms as it seeks creativity in meeting the needs of all types of clientele and income brackets. Spa Envy can be accredited for introducing spa to medium and lower income brackets and for taking the "luxury" persona out of spa. While currently having the monopoly on this market segment, this is surely not going to remain as such as eager entrepreneurs will surely find ways to tap into this "cash cow" as they create a similar yet slightly variant concept to keep ahead of the game.

—Vanessa Carter, Golden Door Spa at the Naples Grande Resort, Naples, Florida, 2010

During tough economic times, state governments often look for ways to increase state revenues to help balance their budgets. Over the last few years, legislation was considered in Illinois, Washington, New York, New Jersey, Tennessee, Texas, and Arkansas to impose a tax on cosmetic procedures (ASPS, 2005). To date, no state has elected to impose such a **cosmetic tax**. However, management will need to look to this possibility as a future trend.

→ SOCIAL TRENDS

Social trends map behaviors and attitudes of individuals in various realms of their lives, including family, community, health, work, leisure, and lifestyle. Some social trends affecting the spa industry are chronicled in this section.

Less Free Time

Although not always supported by data, those in modern society have an ever-increasing perception that they are experiencing less and less free time in their daily lives. More time is being consumed by work and other obligations, and less time is available for leisure. Less free time means that individuals must be more selective about their daily activities. Although some perceive spa treatments as an obligation or a necessity, for the vast majority of individuals, visiting a spa is a leisure-time and elective pursuit. To combat this perception, management must make spa services more time-efficient or continue to develop creative new ways to draw customers into the spa and ensure that customers understand and experience the benefits of a spa visit. If customers are experiencing increased health and well-being through their spa experiences, spa visits are more likely to become a priority.

> . . . treatments that require [less] "down time" are no doubt going to be a big part of future technology developments in the industry. People want to look younger faster, and without any interruption in their day-to-day activities.
>
> —Sharon Boes, Murad, Inc., El Segundo, California, 2010

Spa-going has become more convenient for those looking for "spas on the go." The emergence of mobile spas—providers who come to your home or guest room—has helped make spa treatments easier to enjoy. Smaller niche spas, such as those in the Massage Envy franchise, are more readily available. Receiving a spa treatment while in transit has become a possibility for some. Select airport terminals now have drop-in spas, and trains and airplanes have opened treatment rooms for travelers.

More Stress

Everyone experiences stress. Experts say some levels of stress are healthy; however, an overabundance of stress can be harmful. Nearly half of all Americans report that stress has a negative impact on both their personal and professional lives (APA, 2008). What is the primary reason that individuals cite for visiting a spa? Of course, the answer is stress release. As a matter of fact, each of the fifteen countries included in the 2008 Global Consumer Study cited relaxing and stress release as the primary motivation for visiting spas (ISPA, 2008a). Not surprisingly, we have seen an increase in spa visits over the past decade.

Health Concerns and Health Care

In addition to the negative effects of stress, adult obesity rates in 2009 increased in twenty-three states and did not decrease in a single state. Furthermore, the percentage of obese children is at or above 30 percent in thirty of the United States (TFAH, 2009).

Physical and mental illness is plaguing many societies, and the spa industry is taking action. Spas are wellness sanctuaries, aimed at increasing the health of all those who enter. It has been said that hospitals treat people, spas heal them. By providing spa services focused on enhancing the customer's mind, body, and spirit, spas can be part of the solution to our health crisis.

Recent trends include more spas taking a holistic approach to offerings, and expanding the traditional massage and skin-care offering to provide services in nutrition, behavioral counseling, physical fitness, meditation and yoga, and creative therapies. Some spas are partnering with health-care facilities to provide rehabilitative offerings to patients. Seeing the benefits for all individuals in the hospital, some of the more progressive institutions are offering massage, acupuncture, energy work, and fitness services to both patients and employees.

> I envision that more and more hospitals, clinics and wellness centers will implement spa treatments to expedite overall healing processes. Also, that follow-up treatment in the health care industry will more and more include massage and body treatments, as well as education on healthier lifestyles and preventative approach in public healthcare.
>
> —Stella Sigfusdottir, formerly of Ponte Vedre Inn & Club, Ponte Vedre Beach, Florida 2010

Over the next few years, it is anticipated that the spa industry will take a long-awaited turn that will be especially notable in the U.S. market. Though it is expensive, the Western medical system provides substantial and effective "disease care," while leaving a cavernous vacancy in the area of actual "health care." The spa industry has cultural and social acceptance as a place for wellness, and it would be a natural move to fill the void in true and sustaining health-care education and practices. This will surely require the standardization of practitioner and management education and the expansion of therapeutic staff to include naturopathic physicians, Ayurvedic physicians, nutritionists, counselors, and acupuncturists. Although these types of health providers have typically been marginalized in Western culture, it is due to the simple fact that their power lies in the prevention of disease—they have not been utilized for the maintenance of health, but rather discounted as not being able to abate extensive illness. As the opportunity presents itself for spas, especially community-focused local establishments, to expand treatment and service proficiencies, we will see these well-positioned businesses begin to accommodate the customer's need for reasonably priced health education and partnership.

> . . . industry analysts are turning their attention to how the spa world can assist the masses. Key emphasis is being preventative in one's healthcare and so instead of placing a band aid on the issue, focusing on ways that the industry can help to alleviate the problem in the first place. With industry statistics stating that 86% of illnesses are stress related, the demand for affordable alternatives has become the driving force behind the shift in public perception of spas and wellness.
>
> —Vanessa Carter, Golden Door Spa at the Naples Grande Resort, Naples, Florida, 2010

In five years we will see a greater synergy with traditional spa services and CAM [complementary and alternative medicine] treatments in spas, wellness centers, hospitals and senior living communities. As spa consumers continue to strive for effective ways and affordable ways to reduce stress and increase well being, treatments such as energy therapies, chiropractic, acupuncture, art and music therapy, deep breathing exercises, yoga and meditation will offer solutions. Fitness, nutrition, and stress management will blend into traditional and CAM spa services. The result is a holistic model that addresses overall lifestyle for all ages at a variety of price points.

—Christi Cano, Innovative Spa Productions, Las Vegas, Nevada, 2010

Family Togetherness

Family time is important for the well-being of the family unit and for individual family members. With evidence that new threats to family time are emerging, it is now more important than ever for businesses offering leisure time pursuits to consider expanding offerings to include services that can encompass a larger portion of the family. Although recent research indicates that only a small percent of active spa goers (17 percent) are interested in this option, this market is growing (Coyle Hospitality Group & WTS International, 2009). Certainly the spa industry has historically targeted adults, but there is evidence that with the right program choices, children and teens can also benefit from visiting a spa. Mother/daughter and sister/guest combinations are already the norm at the spa, and father/son time in a fitness facility. A possible option for spas in the future could include other family combinations.

Gyms and spas mergers will probably accelerate and family spas, like family restaurants, will emerge soon.

—Philippe Therene, SpaEquip, Calistoga, California, 2009

Social Spa Going

Social spa going has been a regular occurrence for those visiting their favorite spa for salon-type treatments, and visits to the spa for massage or skin-care treatments have been a time for quiet, peace, and personal reflection. Today, visitors are looking for a variety of experiences when visiting all areas of the spa. With people in modern society drawn to multitasking, combining regular spa treatments with a time for socializing with friends and family members seems natural. Although it is cited as a primary motivation by less than 10 percent of those surveyed in a 2006 spa-goers study (ISPA, 2006), many industry leaders are predicting social interaction as a growing trend (Bain, 2009; Brown, 2008; ISPA, 2007, 2008b; Minton, 2007; Osborn, 2008; Sarfati, 2006).

People do like to use the spa for networking and business meetings . . . so having spa areas available for this purpose is a must.

—Luane McWhorter, Grand Spa, Dallas, Texas, 2009

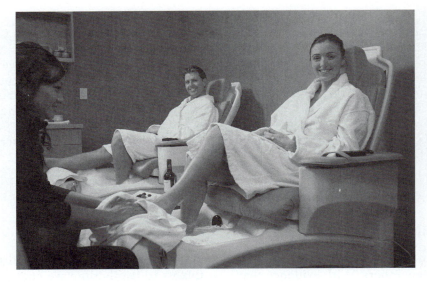

Couples Pedicure Treatment

Innovation and Technology Trends

Some may think it challenging to create a high-touch experience in a high-tech world, but in many ways, high-tech changes have helped spas become more effective operations. Technology and innovation have changed the way all of us get information and make purchases. In a 2009 study, active spa-goers indicated that their first two methods for finding spa offers are through online sources (71 percent) and e-mail (59 percent) (Coyle Hospitality Group & WTS International, 2009). With the vast expansion of the Internet, it is now easier for spa customers to review spa menus, find directions, check spa reviews and ratings, or seek out and book the perfect spa vacation. Spas can now enhance experiences with light therapy, biofeedback, programmed aromatherapy, infusion or hydrotherapy experiences, and provide an Internet connection to those who desire it.

> . . . spas will participate more and more in the prevention aspect of health care. One example . . . is the introduction of body scans and health monitoring systems.
>
> —Philippe Therene, SpaEquip, Inc., Calistoga, California, 2009

Spa managers can change, edit, and publish new offerings at literally the touch of a button. E-mail, Twitter, Facebook, and other forms of network communication have allowed spa managers to spread spa news or fill afternoon treatment times by "blasting" special offerings to potential customers. Staff training can be completed online. Upgraded equipment is now more sanitary and easier to operate. So although high tech and high touch may seem mismatched, if they are used effectively, these opposites can lead to spa management success.

Protecting the Environment

Being good to the planet is just good business. It is good for the company image and has potential to be good for the spa's bottom line. It is clear that environmental sustainability has gained momentum over the past several years. For an industry that focuses on health and wellness, environmental consciousness is fitting. For spa managers, spa development and operational practices have become more earth-friendly. Concepts related to environmentally friendly spa design have been discussed in Chapter 4, and eco-friendly operations have been covered in Chapter 7.

When spa guests were recently asked which spa trends they found of most interest, "organic" and "green" spas made the "top 5," being cited as most appealing by 49 percent and 40 percent of respondents, respectively (Coyle Hospitality Group & WTS International, 2009). Society as a whole has increased its focus on the environment, but spa-savvy guests are demanding more change. Spa customers are seeking spas that protect the environment and offer services that are naturally healthy for the consumer as well.

> The desire to provide powerful antioxidants and ingredients found in nature into skin care formulations will continue to be a big trend. Ingredients found in nature will be shown to work even more impressively when formulated through advanced scientific technology over the next five years.
>
> —Sharon Boes, Murad, Inc., El Segundo, California, 2010

With so many companies jumping on the eco-bandwagon, the disturbing concept of **greenwashing** has emerged, with companies claiming environmentally conscious practices without implementing them. The sensible spa manager will recognize the power of being "green" and make suitable changes in the spa to adapt to this growing trend.

MARKET TRENDS

As the customer changes, so does the business. Market changes can occur with a change in demography, actions, expectations, and lifestyle. Several market trends are directly affecting how spas do business today.

Men in Spas

In countries with rich histories in spa, the spa customer demographic reflects the general makeup of that country. For those in an emerging market, there are select groups that often are more likely to participate than others. For the spa industry in North America, it is women who are the primary spa customers. Industry data fluctuate, but in general, male spa visitors in North America typically represent from 10 to 40 percent of the total clientele, with day spas on the lower end and resort spas on the higher end. One trend the industry is seeing is a gradual increase in men visiting spas. While other countries are seeing men-only spas opening, those in North America are tapping into the male market by offering products and services designed specifically for men and increasing the number of results-oriented skin and body treatments, a principal motivator for men (Ellis, 2006; Whitman, 2007). Popular men's spa offerings include barbering, facials, massages, and pedicures, with 48 percent of spas offering packages designed specifically for men (ISPA, 2007). Top medical nonsurgical spa treatments for men include injectables (including

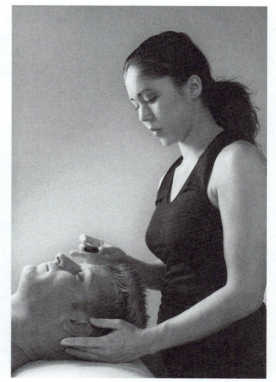

Gentleman's Facial

Botox and hyaluronic acid), microdermabrasion, laser hair removal, chemical peels, and laser skin resurfacing (ASAPS, 2008).

> The male market is the one that is growing the quickest for the spa industry. Over the years, spas have refocused offerings to be more purpose-driven. As men tend to be driven by results in their treatments, this change has helped really draw men into the spa.
>
> —Robert Vance, Sanctuary on Camelback Mountain, Scottsdale, AZ, 2010

Kids and Teens

In an attempt to expose a greater number of individuals to the benefits of a spa visit and to widen the customer base, family-friendly and kids-only spas are making their way into the market. Family-friendly spas offer select services to a variety of age groups. Some offer activities for children and sitting services for parents visiting the spa. Kids-only spas are popping up in resorts or as day spas, specializing in beauty and wellness treatments for the younger generation. For most spa managers this is not an easy offering. Typically, it includes the development of a new, separate spa space and retraining providers on the nuances of working with nonadults. For some spa managers, this may be a niche to pursue.

Pampered Populations

There are three groups of individuals for whom visiting a spa is nearly a necessity: brides, honeymooners, and moms-to-be. Each of these groups is natural to pamper. The aches and pains that come from being pre- and postnatal will subside with appropriate spa offerings. Spas have recognized this need and often offer massage and body treatments designed specifically for this population. Nearly half of all spas were identified as having specific packages designed for pregnant women (ISPA, 2007). Brides, bridal parties, and honeymooners are also natural spa visitors. Whether the goal is to relax, recuperate, or beautify, spas have the perfect combination of offerings and ambiance to cater to this population. A recent trend at resort, destination, and some day

Children's Pedicure Party

spas is the creation of separate private spa area, called a suite or villa, for group spa events such as bridal spa parties, couples spa experiences, or even children's parties.

> Travel agents report the #1 emerging spa travel trend is people increasingly hitting stay spas for special occasions like the big "Os,", anniversaries, weddings, and retirement parties. This concept was born at the day spa (with its long tradition of bachelorette, graduation and "girlfriend" parties), and it's migrating into the travel arena.
>
> —Michelle Kelthy, The Ritz-Carlton, Naples, Florida, 2009

Some spas have begun a practice of selecting populations to pamper. What started out as a means to generate public awareness has become a regular practice, as select spas provide services to worthy groups. Teachers, military, hospice workers, and other deserving groups have all been on the receiving end of this image-enhancement technique (ISPA, 2009c). Spa managers report that the benefits of this technique are fourfold: It can increase spa traffic during slow times, reward a deserving population, provide a way to give back to the community, and be recognized for the effort.

Customization

Ever since the 1980s, when the Japanese were surpassing all others in the area of quality production, many have worked to increase quality to compete. Unlike the early days of the Industrial Revolution, when mass production was the norm, quality today is all about personalizing products and services to fit individual customer needs. Because of the nature of most spa services, which are offered by one provider to one customer, spa offerings can easily be tailored to the distinct needs of the customer—and customers are demanding it.

Recent research indicates that one-third of all active spa-goers are interested in custom treatments (Coyle Hospitality Group & WTS International, 2009). In the current economy, when people are closely watching their spending, spas have begun converting traditional spa services to one-of-a-kind experiences. Instead of a fifty-minute Swedish massage, you may desire an invigorating thirty-minute chair massage during your lunch break, or an in-room postflight back-relief massage. In today's world of customization, you can get it. Presently, spa managers are integrating into their practices personalized health screenings and wellness programs. Along with the typical offering of customized fitness programs, customers can now get personalized spa treatments and nutritional supplements (Chambers, 2009).

> We're finding more and more people walking in the door having been to a spa previously. Most of these guests enter the spa thinking they know what they want. Often they will make an appropriate selection. However, if the guest is basing his/her decision on preconceived notions or past bad experiences, this guest may not be making the best choice. It is now our responsibility as spa employees to take a more active role in educating the guest. Although it may be more difficult with the spa savvy guest, interviews must take place to collect ample information, such as benefits sought, past experiences, treatment goals, etc., to help ensure the treatment selection is the best possible option, based on the guest needs and preferences.
>
> —Robert Vance, Sanctuary on Camelback Mountain, Scottsdale, AZ, 2010

Companies can analyze your DNA and provide nutritional supplements that are personalized to your needs rather than taking a supplement from a health food store that may not be appropriate for your age or physical condition.

—Hugh Jones, HUW Enterprises, Plantation, Florida, 2010

For those looking to extend their spa experience beyond a one-hour treatment, a weekend resort stay, or even a week-long destination spa visit, residential spa communities are offering customized spa lifestyles for all residents. Although there were only a handful of residential spa communities in early 2000, SpaFinder noted 250 such communities in 2008. The population's increasing desire for healthier, longer lives is sure to continue to drive the growth of these communities. Spa communities currently include fitness, hydrotherapy, spa, and salon facilities. Along with the lodging, and food and beverage management staff, these communities also often include medical, nutritional, fitness, sports, and treatment providers all working to create a healthy living environment for each individual resident.

Residential spas are still in their infancy in North America, but several current trends could lead to growth in this sector. First, there has been an increase in the number of individuals seeking a healthier lifestyle. As well, private residential communities are always seeking new ways to meet the needs of their residents. Third, although private residential communities and country clubs have traditionally been built around golf amenities, many are now seeking lower-cost alternatives for their residents. In addition, golf participation has declined in recent years (CB Richard Ellis, 2008), and spa participation is on the rise. Finally, home purchases in the past were generally made by the man in the family. Times have changed, and with more women getting involved in home purchase decisions, home purchases in wellness lifestyle communities may increase.

Gated communities or private clubs will realize the importance of spa programming and vital benefits it offers the membership. . . . [I predict] expansion of square footage in clubs for spa amenities [to enhance] the club lifestyle experience.

—Kathie Pedit, Colonial Country Club, Ft. Myers, Florida, 2010

→ TREATMENT TRENDS

There seems to be a never-ending supply of new spa treatments in the industry. Some could be described as truly new innovations; others may use new products, techniques, or just a clever name to change a common offering; still others are fusions of two or more spa experiences; and others adopt techniques that have been used by other cultures for centuries and call them their own.

Over the last several years, industry experts have predicted many treatment trends. Increasing pre- and postnatal treatments, cryotherapy, gemstone skin products, vinotherapy, hammams, and even cyber treatments have been forecasted (Burkholder, 2007; Osborn, 2008; Sarfati, 2006; Gelula, 2009; Spavelous, 2008). (See Chapter 3, Spa Offerings Glossary, for definitions.) Some new treatments are temporary fads; others seem to be here to stay. Spa managers have the dubious job of sifting through the recent crazes and finding those that can have a positive long-term impact on their business. The foundation of "tried and true" treatments is legitimacy. **Legitimacy** means being sincere and having a strong foundation. Although this characteristic seems to be common sense for most managers, some offerings seem to be more gimmicky than genuine. Legitimacy can come from a variety of sources. Those most commonly found in spa treatments are historic or indigenous foundations, quality, and, of course, verified results.

> The gimmick treatments will be replaced with more of the traditional treatments and spas will focus on delivering *exceptional traditional, focus services* rather than listing dozens of treatments and services that is difficult to deliver consistently.
>
> —Dr. Carl A. Boger, Conrad N. Hilton College, University of Houston, Texas, 2009

Historic and Indigenous Foundations

Spa visitors are generally drawn to treatments that are rich with history or that carry the culture and flavor of the local area. Historic treatments have withstood the test of time. Ancient sweat houses have generated modern-day steam and sauna rooms. Early prehistoric shaman techniques used to chase demons from the body have evolved into present-day massage therapy. The use of these services over the years and the numerous accounts of improved wellness lend legitimacy to treatments with historic foundations.

> The spa industry will continue to grow and develop in the next five years and I believe that it will move much closer to its original European concept here in the U.S.
>
> —Stella Sigfusdottir, formerly of Ponte Vedre Inn & Club, Ponte Vedre Beach, Florida, 2010

Indigenous treatments have the ability to give you an experience you could not have elsewhere. Consider performing a hot stone massage at a beach-front community using smoothed shells harvested there, or using local maple syrup for an exfoliating treatment in northern states or provinces. Using indigenous aromas, tools,

Native American Temazcal

sounds, ceremonies, and products allows the customer to connect with local traditions while experiencing a treatment. Instituting services and treatments with historic and indigenous foundations will provide legitimacy to spa treatments and therefore is a certain long-term trend for the spa industry.

Quality

All customers seek quality experiences. Quality has many definitions. One that has been accepted by many in the spa industry is that a quality experience meets or exceeds the customer's expectations. Customers have expectations in all areas of the business: timeliness, cleanliness, efficiency, friendliness, safety, and staff knowledge are only a few. If spa managers have a clear understanding of their customer's expectations, then execution is easy. A key step to ensure quality is to take the necessary actions to know your customers. Observe, ask, and listen to better identify what your spa customers are seeking.

Results-Based

Whether your customers' goals are to increase their quality of sleep, detox, look younger, or just relax, you want to provide a treatment that will accomplish the task. With the increasing number of spa-savvy customers and more individuals searching for a quality experience, spa visitors are seeking proven results. For years, managers have used industry research to improve their spa's operations. With the increase and availability of treatment research, managers are making their treatment selections the same way.

REALITY CHECK

The amount of spa industry research is increasing quickly. To illustrate, when seeking the number of research articles published in 1999 on the topic of massage, the popular medical journal search engine, PubMed.gov, generated approximately 200 articles. When completing the same search for 2009 articles, just ten years later, the number surpassed 500!

The data are out there. Spa managers will be ill-advised to jump on what seems like the "new, hot idea." A successful manager will make research-based decisions. Patrons are demanding evidence-based treatments and will not stand for less. So, if your spa is electing to place relaxing snake massages on your spa menu or using a new product for your facials that claims to completely rejuvenate your skin, make sure you have the research and results to support the claims you are making. Selecting services and treatments with proven results will ensure your customers get what they pay for and ultimately lead to long-term success of the spa.

The fallout from heavily publicized spa horror stories and consumer insistence on no-gimmick treatments with real, measurable benefits will quicken a rising industry spa trend. Expect increasing demand for evidence-based therapies, stricter industry standards, and greater transparency/resources to help spa-goers separate the wheat from the chaff.

—Michelle Kelthy, The Ritz-Carlton, Naples, Florida, 2009

With the influence of the health care and medical communities it is imperative that Inclusive Health Spas [will] operate on a philosophy that is rooted in science and can show the progress of a client with measurable results. The expectations of visiting a spa for relaxation, pampering, and self indulgence will be a by product, with the consumers focus clearly shifting to measurable wellness results.

—Tracey Sameyah, Murad Inclusive Health, El Segundo, California, 2010

THE FUTURE OF THE SPA INDUSTRY

In addition to the spa industry leader commentary included in this chapter, several industry leaders have provided additional thoughts on what they foresee as the future direction of the industry. Each was asked to provide their five-year vision of the industry. Here are some additional predictions.

FUTURE VISION

Growth of Spa Membership Programs

Spas are being creatively re-imagined as places of "belonging," not just places where you "go" for the occasional treatment. This is happening through the big rise in membership programs, and in the diverse ways spas are being recast as social or communal hubs, which contributes to emotional health.

—Michelle Kelthy, The Ritz-Carlton, Naples, Florida, 2009

Quieting the Spa Environment

The spa environment will trend towards "silence" in the spa. Blackberry's, iPods and even reading material will be banned in common areas and the relaxation rooms. White noise will replace the background noise, to help drown out the technology overload.

—Terri Beckham, The Stoneleigh Hotel, Dallas, Texas, 2009

Smaller Spas

Many [full-service] spas that were built in the last 20 years were very big, from 30,000 square feet to more than 50,000 square feet. The new buildings are likely to be smaller, in the 10,000 square feet to 20,000 square feet range. This will be less expensive to build and get into the spa business and owners and investors should see a quicker return on their investment.

—Hugh Jones, HUW Enterprises, Plantation, Florida, 2010

(continued)

Daily Spa Visits

Spas will also evolve into communal/bathing health retreats, sometimes becoming a daily routine, especially for the baby boomer generation.

—Philippe Therene, SpaEquip, Calistoga, California, 2009

Influences from Enhanced Technology

Consumers are already online searching for spas, booking treatments, joining online weight loss and coaching groups, and embracing social networking sites, such as Facebook and Twitter. Get ready for gaming while you exercise, for having health information (like your blood pressure and heart rate) automatically uploaded for access online by your spa or doctor, and for spas to use yield management software that— much like the airlines—enables price variation, so spas can offer a less expensive massage on weekday mornings, compared to Saturday afternoons.

—Michelle Kelthy, The Ritz-Carlton, Naples, Florida, 2009

Increased Spa Leader Networking

The mere nature of the spa industry provides a level of care in which touch and personal interaction are a requirement. No surprise—skills highly refined by many of our finest industry leaders. Gathering together as an industry is critical for our growth and the foundation of strong relationships. The camaraderie developed when we meet up with each other creates many benefits, both tangible and intangible. By coming together we foster a sense of understanding, inspiration, the chance to figure out best practices, as well as the potential to build on other's knowledge and experience. I fully anticipate in the years to come that spa professionals will place an emphasis on building powerful regional groups, spending time together and networking more often as one of the best tools to grow the industry.

—Kristi Konieczny, The Spa Buzz, Denver, Colorado, 2009

An Inclusive Health Model

Historically Beauty, Wellness, Prevention and Health have been seen as parallel industries whereas under an Inclusive Health model all will work together to create the ultimate destination for clients. An Inclusive Health Spa could be housed in a hospital, urban setting, resort/destination, corporate structure, etc., and will become part of everyday living offering affordable and manageable lifestyle programs for all with a focus on topical skin health, internal cellular health, and sense of self.

—Tracey Sameyah, Murad Inclusive Health, El Segundo, California, 2010

KEY TERMS

Cosmetic tax

Greenwashing

Health tourism

Legitimacy

Medical tourism

Niche spa

REVIEW QUESTIONS

1. Name an economic or industry trend that is presently influencing the spa industry and provide an example of how spas and spa managers are responding to the trend.
2. Name a social trend that is presently influencing the spa industry and provide an example of how spas and spa managers are responding to the trend.
3. Name a market trend that is presently influencing the spa industry and provide an example of how spas and spa managers are responding to the trend.
4. What is driving new treatment trends?
5. Which spa leader quote about the future do you find most significant and why?

REFERENCES

APA (American Psychological Association) (2008) Stress a Major Health Problem in the U.S., Warns APA. Retrieved November 1, 2009, from www.apa.org/releases/stressproblem.html.

ASAPS (American Society of Aesthetic Plastic Surgeons) (2008). 2008 Gender Distribution for Cosmetic Procedures. Retrieved November 4, 2009, from www.surgery.org/sites/default/files/2008stats.pdf

ASPS (American Society of Plastic Surgeons) (2005). 2005: The Year in Plastic Surgery; Top 10 Plastic Surgery Hot Topics. Retrieved December 20, 2010, from www.redorbit.com/news/science/340859/2005_the_year_in_plastic_surgery_top_10_plastic_surgery/index.html.

Bain, Geri (2009). Five Trends to Tap. *Resort + Recreation,* 2009, pp. 48–49.

Beckham, Terri (2009). Personal e-mail communication, December 31.

Boes, Sharon (2010). Personal e-mail communication, January 7.

Boger, Carl A. (2009). Personal e-mail communication, December 18.

Brown, Anitra (2008). Top Spa Trends. Retrieved June 17, 2008, from http://spas.about.com/od/stressmanagement/a/trends2007.htm.

Burkholder, Preethi (2007). *Start Your Own Day Spa and More.* Irvine, CA: Entrepreneur Press.

Cano, Christi (2010). Personal e-mail communication, January 1.

Carter, Vanessa (2010). Personal e-mail communication, March 19.

CB Richard Ellis (2008). Golf Market Analysis. Retrieved January 15, 2010, from www.dailybusinessreview.com/images/news_photos/50046/2008%20Golf%20Market%20Analysi.pdf.

Chambers, Doug (2009). Spas Get Personal. *Resort + Recreation,* received online September 7, 2009.

Coyle Hospitality Group & WTS International (2009). Spa Sentiment Research Report 2009. Retrieved November 3, 2009, from www.coylehospitality.com/Press/latest-spa-consumer-trends.asp.

Ellis, Susie (2006). Top 10 European Spa Trends. Retrieved August 28, 2006, from www.spafinder.com/spalifestyle/insider/newsletter/trendseuropean.jsp.

Gelula, Melisse (2009). Top Ten Spa Beauty Trends to Look for in 2009. Retrieved January 8, 2009, from www.spafinder.com/lifestyle/beauty/top-beauty-trends-for 2009_422.htm.ISPA (International Spa Association) (2006). *ISPA 2006 Spa-Goer Study.* Lexington, KY: International Spa Association.

ISPA (International Spa Association) (2007). *2007 Spa Industry Study.* Lexington, KY: International Spa Association.

ISPA (International Spa Association) (2008a). *2008 ISPA Global Consumer Study.* Lexington, KY: International Spa Association.

ISPA (International Spa Association) (2008b). *Taking Care of Business: Thoughts from Leading Spa Industry Professionals.* Lexington, KY: International Spa Association.

ISPA (International Spa Association) (2009a). *2009 ISPA United States Industry Update.* Lexington, KY: International Spa Association.

ISPA (International Spa Association (2009b). Snapshot Survey August 2009. *Pulse,* October, p. 94.

ISPA (International Spa Association) (2009c). 2010 ISPA Association Trend Watch. Retrieved November 23, 2009, from http://experienceispa.com/articles/index.cfm?action=view&articleID=249.

Jones, Hugh (2010). Personal e-mail communication, January 4.

Kelthy, Michelle (2009). Personal e-mail communication, December 28.

Konieczny, Kristi (2009). Personal e-mail communication, December 29.

Lyon, Leslie (2010). Personal e-mail communication, January 1.

McLean, Ginger (2010). Personal e-mail communication, December 28.

McWhorter, Luane (2009). Personal e-mail communication, December 29.

Minton, Melinda (2007). Spa Trends for 2007-08, *Spa Management Journal,* 17(4), pp. 50–56.

Osborn, Kerrie (2008). Trends in the Profession: Insight and Opportunity. *Massage and Bodywork,* January/February, pp. 43–50.

Peabody, Endicott (n.d.) Randomquotes.com. Retrieved June 20, 2010, from www.randomquotes.org/quote/21085-remember-things-in-life-will-not-always-run-smooth.html.

Pedit, Kathie (2010). Personal e-mail communication, January 6.

Pubmed.gov (2010) Retrieved June 18, 2010, from pubmed.gov.

Sameyah, Tracey (2010). Personal e-mail communication, January 27.

Sarfati, Lydia (2006). Spa Trend Report: 3 Trends Lydia Likes, *Spa Management Journal,* October, pp. 64 and 65.

Sigfusdottir, Stella (2010). Personal e-mail communication, January 1.

SpaFinder (2007). SpaFinder's 2007 State of Spa Travel Survey. Retrieved November 2, 2009, from www.spafinder.com/about/press_release.jsp?relId=25.

SpaFinder (2008). 10 Spa Trends to Watch in 2008. Retrieved November 5, 2009, from www.spafinder.com/spalifestyle/insider/newsletter/trends2008.jsp.

Spavelous (2008). Being Cold Is Very Hot Indeed. Retrieved November 23, 2009, from www.spavelous.com/EB/N080808/ColdSpaTreatments05.html.

SRO International (2010). Wellness is no Passing Fad. Retrieved December 20, 2010, from www.globalspasummit.org/images/stories/pdf/gss_wellness2010.pdf.

TFAH (Trust for America's Health) (2009). F as in Fat 2009. Retrieved November 11, 2009, from http://healthyamericans.org/reports/obesity2009.

Therene, Philippe (2009). Personal e-mail communication, December 23.

Vance, Robert (2010). Personal e-mail communication, June 17.

Whitman, Cheryl (2007). Ten Amazing New Medical Spa Trends. *Spa Management Journal—Medical Spas,* February, pp. 17–19.

Yesawich, Peter (2007). Popularity of Spas Continue to Increase, *Hotel & Motel Management,* 222(78), April 14.

APPENDIX

Spa Industry Resources

Knowledge is of two kinds. We know a subject ourselves, or we know where we can find information upon it.

—Samuel Johnson

Spa Management Education Programs in North America

Spa Management Bachelor's Degree Programs

Endicott College
376 Hale Street
Beverly, MA 01915, USA
978-927-0585 or 800-325-1114
www.endicott.edu
Bachelor of Science in Hospitality and Tourism
Administration
Concentration in Spa & Resort Management

Florida Gulf Coast University
Sugden Hall
10501 FGCU Blvd. South
Fort Myers, Fl 33965, USA
239-590-7742
cps.fgcu.edu/resort
Bachelor of Science in Resort and Hospitality Management
Concentration in Spa Management

University of Minnesota, Crookston
2900 University Avenue
Crookston, MN 56716-5001, USA
800-UMC-MINN (862-6466)
www.umcrookston.edu
Bachelor of Science in Hotel, Restaurant, and Institutional
Management
Emphasis in Resort/Spa Management

Spa Management Associate's Degree Programs

Asheville-Buncombe Technical Community College
340 Victoria Road
Asheville, North Carolina 28801, USA
828-254-1921
www.abtech.edu
Associate in Applied Science Degree in Resort
and Spa Management

Hocking College
3301 Hocking Parkway
Nelsonville, Ohio 45764, USA
877-462-5464
www.hocking.edu
Associate of Technical Study in
Spa Management

Sandhills Community College
3395 Airport Road
Pinehurst, NC 28374, USA
910-692-6185 or 800-338-3944
www.sandhills.edu
Associate of Applied Science Degree in Resort and
Spa Management

Scottsdale Community College
9000 East Chaparral Road
Scottsdale, AZ 85256-2626, USA
480-423-6000
www.scottsdalecc.edu
Associate in Applied Science in Spa and
Wellness Center Management

Spa Management Diploma and Certificate Programs

Academy Canada
Corner Brook Campus
2 University Drive
Corner Brook, NL A2H 5G4, Canada
709-637-2100
www.academycanada.com
Faculty of Esthetics: Esthetics and Spa Management Certificate

Arizona State University
Exercise and Wellness Program
7350 E. Unity Avenue
Mesa, AZ 85212, USA
480-727-1945
www.nursing.asu.edu/saas/wellness/spa
Spa Management Certificate

Canadian Tourism College
Vancouver Campus
#501-1755 West Broadway
Vancouver, BC V6J 4S5, Canada
604-736-8000
www.tourismcollege.com
Resort and Hotel Spa Management Diploma

Elmcrest College of Applied Health Sciences & Spa Management
North York Campus
1200 Lawrence Ave. West
North York, ON M6A 1E3, Canada
416-630-6300 or 888-641-6300
www.elmcrestcollege.com/spa_management
Spa Manager/Director Diploma Program and Spa Leadership
Certificate Program

Humber College
Humber North Campus
205 Humber College Blvd.
Toronto, ON M9W 5L7, Canada
416-675-5000, x4089
www.humber.ca
Esthetician/Spa Management Diploma

International SPA Association
2365 Harrodsburg Road, Suite A325
Lexington, KY 40504, USA
888-651-4772 or 859-226-4326
www.experienceispa.com
Spa Supervisor Certification

Orange Coast College
2701 Fairview Road
Costa Mesa, CA 92628-5005, USA
714-432-0202
www.orangecoastcollege.edu
Spa Management Certification

Seneca College of Applied Arts & Technology
1750 Finch Ave. East
Toronto, ON M2J 2X5, Canada
416-491-5050, x2800
http://www.senecac.on.ca/fulltime/SPA.html
Spa Management Certification

SpaQuality
1024 Oriente Avenue
Greenville, DE 19807, USA
302-426-0274
www.spaquality.com
Spa and Hospitality Management Certificate

University of California, Irvine
P.O. Box 6050
Irvine, CA 92616-6050, USA
949-824-9304
www.extension.uci.edu/spa
Spa and Hospitality Management Certification

Spa Trade and Consumer Magazines

Alternative Medicine
Publisher: InnerDoorway Health Media
www.alternativemedicine.com

Alternative Therapies in Health and Medicine
Publisher: InnoVision Communications
www.alternative-therapies.com

American Salon
Publisher: Advanstar Communications
www.americansalonmag.com

American Spa
Publisher: Questex Media
www.americanspamag.com

Beauty Launchpad
Publisher: Creative Edge Publications
www.beautylaunchpad.com

Body Sense
Publisher: Association of Skin Care Professionals
www.bodysensemagazine.com

Body + Soul
Publisher: Body & Soul Omnimedia
www.wholeliving.com

Cosmetics & Toiletries
Publisher: Allured Business Media
www.cosmeticsandtoiletries.com/magazine

CosmeticWorld
Publisher: The Ledes Group
www.cosmeticworld.com

The Colorist
Publisher: Creative Age Publishing
www.coloristmag.com

DaySpa
Publisher: Creative Age Publishing
www.dayspamagazine.com

Dermascope
Publisher: Aestheticians International Association
www.dermascope.com

Destination Spa Vacation
Publisher: Destination Spa Group
www.destinationspavacations.com

Fitness Magazine
Publisher: Meredith
www.fitnessmagazine.com

Healing Arts Guide
Publisher: Healing Arts Stores
www.healingartsguide.com

Healing Lifestyle & Spas
Publisher: JLD Publications
www.healinglifestyles.com

Les Nouvelles Esthetiques & Spa (American Edition)
Publisher: Les Nouvelles Esthetiques
www.lneonline.com

LiveSpa Magazine
Published: International Spa Association
www.livespamagazine.com

Lifestyles of Health & Sustainability Journal
Publisher: Conscience Wave Inc.
www.lohas.com

Massage and Bodywork
Publisher: Associated Bodywork and Massage Professionals
www.massageandbodywork.com

Massage Magazine
Publisher: Massage Magazine
www.massagemag.com

MedEsthetics Magazine
Publisher: Creative Age Publications
www.medestheticsmagazine.com

Men's Health Magazine
Publisher: Rodale
www.menshealth.com

Modern Salon
Publisher: Vance Publishing
www.modernsalon.com

Nailpro
Publisher: Creative Age Publishing
www.nailpro.com

Natural Health
Publisher: Weider Publications
www.naturalhealthmag.com

Nails Magazine
Publisher: Bobit Publishing
www.nailsmag.com

New Beauty
Publisher: Sandow Media
www.newbeauty.com

Organic SPA
Publisher: Oceans Publishing
www.organicspamagazine.com

Oxygen Magazine
Publisher: Canusa
www.oxygenmag.com

Pulse
Publisher: ISPA and HOST Communications
www.experienceispa.com

Renew
Publisher: Vance Publishing
www.renewprofessional.com

Resort & Recreation
Publisher: Tandem Publishing
www.resort-recreation.com

Skin Deep
Publisher: Association of Skin Care
Professionals
www.skindeepworld.com

Skin Inc.
Publisher: Allured Business Media
www.skininc.com

Spa
Publisher: Bonnier Publishing
www.spamagazine.com

Spa Asia
Publisher: TWG Media
www.spaasia.com

Spa Business
Publisher: The Leisure Media Company
www.spabusiness.com

Spa Finder
Publisher: SpaFinder
www.spafinder.com

Spa Fresh
Online Magazine: Body Systems Nature
Sourced Skincare
www.spafreshmag.com

Spa Life
Publisher: Harworth Publishing
www.spalifemagazine.com

Spa Management
Publisher: Publicom
www.spamanagement.com

Spa Opportunities (Sister Publication of Spa Business)
Publisher: The Leisure Media Company
www.spaopportunities.com

Spa Textbooks

Spa Management and Operations

101 Salon Promotions
1999
Oppenheim, Robert
Publisher: Delmar Cengage Learning

Become a Spa Owner
2006
McCarthy, Jeremy, and Jennifer James
Publisher: Fabjob, Inc.

Big Bang Marketing for Spas: See Your Profits Explode with These Easy and Effective Advertising and Publicity Ideas (3rd ed.)
2004
Colbert, Judy, and Saul Fruchthendler
Publisher: Tuff Turtle Publishing

Building Your Medispa Business
2009
Hill, Pamela, RN
Publisher: Cengage Delmar Learning

Cosmetology, Learning the Art of Doing Business: Federal Taxation Curriculum for Cosmetology Students
2003
Publisher: Internal Revenue Service

Fast Forward Salon and Spa Business Resource: The Salon Industry's Definite Business Management Reference Guide for Owners, Managers, and Key Staff
2000
Ducoff, Neil
Publisher: Strategies Publishing Group

Financial Management for Spas
2011
Schmidgall, Raymond S. & Korpi, John R.
Publisher: American Hotel and Lodging Association and International Spa Association

Fitness, Racquet Sports, and Spa Projects: A Guide to Appraisal, Market Analysis, Development, and Financing
1989
Gimmy, Arthur
Publisher: American Institute of Real Estate Appraisers

Health and Wellness Tourism
2008
Smith, Melanie, and Laszlo Puczko
Publisher: Butterworth-Heinemann

How to Start & Manage a Health Spa Business: A Practical Way to Start Your Own Business
2007
Lewis, Jerre G., and Leslie D. Renn
Publisher: Lewis & Renn Associates

The International Standards of Spa Excellence, 2007: A Quality Management & Certification Framework for Spas
2006
Spa Quality LLC
Publisher: SpaQuality

ISPA Foundation's Compensation Workbook
2004
Compensation Consulting Consortium
Publisher: ISPA Foundation

ISPA Spa Operations Manual
2005
International Spa Association
Publisher: ISPA Foundation

One Year to a Successful Massage Therapy Practice
2009
Allen, Laura, NCTMB
Publisher: Wolters Kluwer Health/Lippincott Williams & Wilkins

Opening a Spa
2002
Minton, Melinda
Publisher: Minton Business Solutions

Retail Management for Spas
2005
ISPA Foundation
Publisher: American Hotel & Motel Association

The Reluctant Spa Director and the Mission Dream
2003
Williams, Skip
Publisher: Infinity Publishing

Salon & Spa Management Tools
2007
Milady and Salon Training International
Publisher: Salon Training International

Salon & Spa Skill Certification Manual and CD Tools
2001
Manuel, Eric
Publisher: Strategies Publishing Group

Salon Ovations Day Spa Operations
1996
Miller, Erica
Publisher: Delmar Cengage Learning

Salon Client Care: How to Maximize Your Potential for Success
1999
Spear, J. Elaine
Publisher: Delmar Cengage Learning

Spa: A Comprehensive Introduction
2008
Johnson, Elizabeth, and Bridgette Redman
Publisher: American Hotel and Lodging Association and International Spa Association

Spa Basics: A Consumer's Guide to Day Spa Services
2003
Kelleher, Robin
Publisher: Trafford

Spa Bodywork: A Guide for Massage Therapists
2006
Williams, Anne
Publisher: Lippincott Williams & Wilkins

Spa Business Strategies: A Plan for Success
2006
D'Angelo, Janet
Publisher: Delmar Cengage Learning

Spa Management Best Practices
2004
Melinda M. Minton
Publisher: Minton Business Solutions

Spa & Salon Alchemy: The Ultimate Guide to Spa & Salon Ownership
2005
Moren, Sandra Alexcae
Publisher: Delmar Cengage Learning

Spa Secrets of Success: Unlocking the Secret Behind Successful Spas
2007
Shannon, Burson Smith
Publisher: AuthorHouse

Spa Survival
2009
Melinda Minton
Publisher: Minton Business Solutions

Start Your Own Hair Salon and Day Spa: Your Step-by-Step Guide to Success
2005
Sandlin, Eileen Figure
Publisher: Entrepreneur Press

Start Your Own Day Spa and More
2007
Calmes, Jere L.
Publisher: Entrepreneur Press

Successful Salon Management for Cosmetology Students (5th ed.)
2002
Tezak, Edward J.
Publisher: Delmar Cengage Learning

Understanding the Global Spa Industry
2008
Cohen, Marc, and Gerard Bodeker
Publisher: Butterworth-Heinemann

Uniform System of Financial Reporting for Spas
2005
Publisher: Educational Institute of the American Hotel &
Lodging Association

Spa Services and Treatments

Aromatherapy for Bodyworkers
2008
Shutes, Jade & Weaver, Christina
Publisher: Pearson/Prentice Hall

Advanced Face and Body Treatments for the Spa
Hill, Pamela
2008
Publisher: Delmar Cengage Learning

*Anatomy Trains: Myofascial Meridians for Manual and
Movement Therapists*
2001
Myers, Thomas W., LMT
Publisher: Churchill Livingstone

Aquatic Exercise Therapy
1996
Bates, Andrea
Publisher: Saunders

*Ayurvedic Massage: Traditional Indian Techniques for Balancing
Body and Mind*
1996
Johari, Harish
Publisher: Healing Arts Press

Ayurvedic Spa
2008
Sachs, Melanie, and Robert Sachs
Publisher: Lotus Press

Beard's Massage (4th ed.)
1997
De Domenico, Giovanni, and Elizabeth C. Wood
Publisher: Saunders

The Balanced Body: A Guide to Deep Tissue and Neuromuscular Therapy
2002
Scheumann, Donald W.
Publisher: Lippincott Williams & Wilkins

Balancing Senses: The Six Senses Spa Book
2007
O'Brian, Kate
Publisher: Editions Didier Millet

Clinical Reflexology: A Guide for Health Professionals
2002
Mackereth, Peter A., and Denise Tiran (eds.)
Publisher: Churchill Livingstone

The Complete Book of Essential Oils and Aromatherapy
1991
Worwood, Valarie Ann
Publisher: New World Library

Dictionary of Alternative Medicine
1998
Segen, J. C.
Publisher: Appleton & Lange

*Direct Release Myofascial Technique: An Illustrated Guide
for Practitioners*
2004
Stanborough, Michael
Publisher: Churchill Livingstone

Encyclopedia of Thai Massage
2004
Salquero, C. Pierce
Publisher: Findhorn Press

*Handbook of Massage Therapy: A Complete Guide for the Student and
Professional Massage Therapist*
1999
Cassar, Mario Paul
Publisher: Butterworth-Heinemann

*Hands Heal: Communication, Documentation, and Insurance Billing
for Manual Therapists*
2002
Thompson, Diana L.
Publisher: Lippincott Williams & Wilkins

Hawaii's Spa Experience
2004
Strausfogel, Sherrie
Publisher: Mutual Publishing

The Healing Touch of Massage
1995
De Paoli, Carlo
Publisher: Sterling Publishing Co.

Healing with Nature
2003
Scott, Susan S.
Publisher: Helios Press

*The History of Massage: An Illustrated Survey from
Around the World*
2002
Calvert, Robert Noah
Publisher: Healing Arts Press

Hydrotherapy for Health and Wellness
2008
Richard Eidson
Publisher: Milady

*The Japanese Spa: A Guide to Japan's Finest Ryokan
and Onsen*
2006
Seki, Akihiko
Publisher: Charles A. Tuttle

Massage and the Original Swedish Movements
1997
Ostrom, Kurre W.
Publisher: University of Virginia Library

Massage for Therapists
1998
Hollis, Margaret
Publisher: Blackwell Science

A Massage Therapist's Guide to Pathology
1998
Werner, Ruth A., and Ben E. Benjamin (eds.)
Publisher: Lippincott Williams & Wilkins

Massage Therapy: The Evidence for Practice
2002
Rich, Grant Jewell (ed.)
Publisher: Mosby

Massage Therapy: Theory and Practice
1999
Loving, Jean
Publisher: Appleton & Lange

Massage Therapy a Medical Dictionary, Bibliography, and Annotated Research Guide to Internet References
2004
James N. Parker and Philip M. Parker (eds.)
Publisher: ICON Health Publications

Milady's Standard Fundamentals for Estheticians (9th ed.)
2003
Gerson, Joel
Publisher: Delmar Cengage Learning

Milady's Theory and Practice of Therapeutic Massage
1994
Beck, Mark
Publisher: Delmar Cengage Learning

Mosby's Fundamentals of Therapeutic Massage
1995
Fritz, Sandy
Publisher: Mosby Lifeline

Mosby's Visual Guide to Massage Essentials
1996
Fritz, Sandy
Publisher: Mosby

The Myofascial Release Manual
2001
Manheim, Carol J.
Publisher: SLACK

Muscle Energy Techniques
2006
Chaitow, Leon
Publisher: Elsevier Churchill Livingstone

Natural Spa and Hydrotherapy: Theory and Practice
2009
Mihina, Ann, and Sandra Anderson
Publisher: Prentice Hall

Nutrition & Diet Therapy (9th ed.)
2007
Roth, Ruth
Publisher: Delmar Cengage Learning

Organic Body Recipes
2007
Tourles, Stephanie
Publisher: Storey Publishing

Prevention Magazine's Hands-on Healing: Massage Remedies for Hundreds of Health Problems
1995
Feltman, John (ed.)
Publisher: Wings Books

Procedures in Cosmetic Dermatology Series: Chemical Peels
2005
Rubin, Mark G., M.D.
Publisher: Elsevier Churchill Livingstone

Qigong: Essence of the Healing Dance
1999
Garripoli, Garri
Publisher: Health Communications

Recovery Yoga: A Practical Guide for Chronically Ill, Injured and Postoperative People
1997
Dworkis, Sam
Publisher: Three Rivers Press

Reflexology: The Definitive Practitioner's Manual
1997
Crane, Beryl
Publisher: Element

Salon Ovations Advanced Skin Care Handbook
1994
Schorr, Lia
Publisher: Delmar Cengage Learning

Skincare: Beyond the Basic Workbook
2006
Lees, Mark
Publisher: Delmar Cengage Learning

The Spa Book: The Official Guide to Spa Therapy
2005
Crebbin-Bailey, Jane, John Harcup, and John Harrington
Publisher: Delmar Cengage Learning

Spa Bodywork: A Guide for Massage Therapists
2006
Williams, Anne
Publisher: Lippincott Williams & Wilkins

The Spa Encyclopedia: A Guide to Treatments & Their Benefits for Health & Healing
2003
Leavy, Hannelore R., and Reinhard R. Bergel, Ph.D.
Publisher: Delmar Cengage Learning

Spa: The Official Guide to Spa Therapy at Level 2 & 3
2006
Scott, John, and Andrea Hauison
Publisher: Delmar Cengage Learning

Spa: Refreshing Rituals for Body and Soul
2003
Wolski, Leslie
Publisher: Atria Books

Spa & Salon Alchemy: Step by Step Spa Procedures
2006
Moren, Sandra Alexcae
Publisher: Delmar Cengage Learning

Spice Spa
2003
Marriot, Susannah
Publisher: Carroll and Brown Publisher

Tappan's Handbook of Healing Massage Techniques: Classic, Holistic, and Emerging Methods
1998
Tappan, Frances M.
Publisher: Appleton & Lange

Thai Spa Book: The Natural Asian Way to Health and Beauty
2003
Jotisalikorn, Chamsai
Publisher: Periplus Publishing

Therapeutic Massage & Bodywork: 750 Questions & Answers
1997
Garofano, Jane Schultz
Publisher: Appleton & Lange

Therapeutic Massage in Athletics
2007
Archer, Patricia A.
Publisher: Lippincott Williams & Wilkins

Touch Therapy
2000
Field, Tiffany
Publisher: Churchill Livingstone

Touch for Health
2005
Thie, John, and Matthew Thie
Publisher: DeVorss Publications

The Tropical Spa: Asian Secrets of Health, Beauty, and Relaxation
2004
Benge, Sophie
Publisher: Periplus Publishing

Ultimate Spa: Asia's Best Spas and Spa Treatments
2006
Chapman, Judy
Publisher: Hong Kong: Periplus Publishing

Understanding Sports Massage
1996
Benjamin, Patricia J.
Publisher: Human Kinetics

Walking Medicine: The Lifetime Guide to Preventive and Rehabilitative Exercise Walking Programs
1990
Yanker, Gary
Publisher: McGraw-Hill

Spa Design and Photography

Best Designed Wellness Hotels: North & South Africa, Indian Ocean, Middle East
2004
Kunz, Martin Nicholas
Publisher: Avedition; Fusion Publishing

Best Designed Wellness Hotels: North and South America, Caribbean, Mexico
2002
Kunz, Martin Nicholas
Publisher: Birkhauser

Cool Hotels: Spa & Wellness
2008
Kunz, Martin Nicholas.
Publisher: teNeues

Onsen: Design for Japanese Style Spas
2007
Ebiswa, Hiroshi
Publisher: Azur Corporation

Relax: Best of Spa Design
2008
Publisher: Verlaghaus-Braun

Relax: Interior for Human Wellness
2007
Frame Publishers, Karim Rashid, Anneke Bokern, and Joeri Bruyninckx
Publisher: Frame Publishers

Salons and Spas: The Architecture of Beauty
2005
Eakin, Julie Sinclair
Publisher: Rockport Publisher

SPA
2008
Arieff, Allison, and Bryan Burichart
Publisher: Taschen

Spa Design
2006
Daab
Publisher: Daab

Spa & Health Club Design
2005
Castillo, Encarna, and Ana G. Canizares (eds.)
Publisher: teNeues Publishing Group

Spa & Wellness Hotels
2005
Paco Asensio (ed.)
Publisher: teNeues Publishing Group

Spas (Archidesign)
2006
Katya Pellegrino
Publisher: Fitway Publishing

Spas (Architectural Interiors)
2007
Editors of Rotovision
Publisher: Rotovision

Spas: Beauty, Health, and Design
2007
Quartino, Daniella
Publisher: Loft Publishing

Spa Locator Books

100 Best Spas of the World (2nd ed.)
2003
Burt, Bernard, & Pamela Price
Publisher: The Globe Pequot Press

101 Vacations to Change Your Life: A Guide to Wellness Centers, Spiritual Retreats, and Spas
1999
Holms, Karin Baji
Publisher: Carol Pub. Group

Affordable Spas and Fitness Resorts: The Insider's Guide to Health-Oriented Vacations & Weekends
1988
Vollmer, Ryan
Publisher: Ventana Press

The Best Spas
1988
Van Itallie, Theodore B., and Leila Hadley
Publisher: Harper & Row

Best Spas USA: The Guidebook to Luxury Resort and Destinations Spas of the U.S.
2007
Barish, Eileen
Publisher: Bestspausa

The Complete Idiot's Guide to Self-Healing with Spas and Retreats
1999
Short, Linda
Publisher: Alpha Books

Fodor's Healthy Escapes
2003
Swiac, Christine
Publisher: Fodor's Travel Publications

Great Spa Escapes
2003
Foley, Jo
Publisher: Dakini

Health and Wellness Tourism: Spas and Hot Springs
2009
Cooper, Malcolm
Publisher: Channel View Publications

New Spas and Resorts
2007
Quartino, Daniela Santos
Publisher: Harper Collins

Spa Guide
2003
Segesta, John, and Anne Stein
Publisher: Open Road Pub.

Spa Journeys: For Body, Mind, and Soul
2004
Troeller, Linda, and Annette Foglino
Publisher: PowerHouse Books

The Spa Sourcebook
2000
Lazarus, Judith
Publisher: Roxbury Park/Lowell House

Thailand's Luxury Spas: Pampering Yourself in Paradise
2006
Jotisalikorn, Chamsai
Publisher: Periplus Publishing

Spa Treatment/Alternative Medicine Research Journals

Alternative Health Practitioner—The Journal of Complementary and Natural Care
1995–1999
Publisher: Springer Publication Company

Alternative Medicine Alert
1997–
Publisher: American Health Consultants

Alternative Medicine Review
1996–
Publisher: Thorne Research, Inc.

Alternative Therapies in Health and Medicine
1995–
Publisher: InnoVision Communications

American Salon
1984–
Publisher: Service Publications—National Hairdressers and Cosmetologists Association

BMC Complementary and Alternative Medicine
2001–
Publisher: BioMed Central

CAM at the NIH: Focus on Complementary and Alternative Medicine
2005–
Publisher: National Institutes of Health, Office of Alternative Medicine

Complementary and Alternative Medicine at the NIH
1999–2004
Publisher: National Institutes of Health, Office of Alternative Medicine

Complementary Health Practice Review
2000–
Publisher: Sage Productions

Complementary Therapies in Medicine
1993–
Publisher: Harcourt

Evidence-Based Complementary and Alternative Medicine
2004–
Publisher: Oxford University Press

HealthWorld
1986–
Publisher: Health World Co.

Healthy and Natural Journal
1994–
Publisher: Measurements & Data Corp.

The Internet Journal of Alternative Medicine
2002–
Publisher: Internet Scientific Publications

Japanese Journal of Complementary and Alternative Medicine JCAM (English Version)
2004–
Publisher: Japanese Society for Complementary and Alternative Medicine

Journal of Alternative and Complementary Medicine
1995–
Publisher: Mary Ann Liebert

Journal of Bodywork and Movement Therapies
2009–
Published: Elsevier Churchill Livingstone

Journal of Complementary and Integrative Medicine
2004–
Publisher: Berkeley Electric Press

Journal of Holistic Healthcare
2004–
Publisher: British Holistic Medicine Association

Journal of Integrated Care Pathways
2001–
Publisher: Royal Society of Medicine Press

Lifestyles of Health & Sustainability Journal
2000–
Publisher: Conscience Wave Inc.

Massage Therapy Journal
1987–
Publisher: American Massage Therapy Association

The Original Internist: A Scientific Publication on Natural Health Care
1999–
Publisher: Clint Publications

Scientific Review of Alternative Medicine
1997–
Publisher: Prometheus Books

Online Resources

Spa Locators

www.spa-addicts.com

www.spa-booker.com

www.spafinder.com

www.spagoer.com

www.spaindex.com

www.spasofamerica.com

www.spavelous.com

www.spaweek.com

www.thespasdirectory.com

General Spa Information and Spa Job Postings*

www.bestspajobs.com

www.discoverspas.com

www.intelligentspas.com

www.metspasolutions.com

www.salonchannel.com

www.salonemployment.com

www.spa.about.com

www.spacast.com

www.spaclique.com

www.spaelegance.com

www.spaexec.net

www.spajobs.com

www.spa-jobs.com

www.spalook.com

---

*For additional spa job posting sites, visit professional associations online.

www.spaopportunities.com

www.spatherapy.com

www.spatrade.com

www.spawire.com

www.thespabuzz.com

www.virtualspa.com

www.wayspa.com

Spa Human Resources

www.ascpskincare.com (Sample Service Contracts & Employment Applications)

www.eeoc.gov (U.S. Equal Employment Opportunity Commission)

www.osha.gov (U.S. Department of Labor, Occupational Safety and Health Administration)

State Licensure Information

Spa Technicians
www.ascpskincare.com
www.beautyschoolsdirectory.com/faq/state_req.php

Massage Therapists
www.massageregister.com/StateRequirements.asp
www.amtamassage.org/government/state_laws.html

Chiropractors
www.life.edu/StateChiropracticLicensure

Electrolysis
www.electrolysisreferral.com/rules.htm

Spa Professional Associations

General Industry

American Association of Oriental Medicine
PO Box 162340
Sacramento, CA 95816, USA
916-443-5570
www.aaaomonline.org

American Chiropractic Association
1701 Clarendon Boulevard
Alrington, VA 22209, USA
703-276-8800
www.acatoday.org

American Holistic Medical Association
23366 Commerce Park, Suite 101B
Beachwood, Ohio 44122, USA
216-292-6644
www.holisticmedicine.org

The Club Spa and Fitness Association
4521 PGA Blvd #279
Palm Beach Gardens, FL 33418, USA
561-667-0156

www.csfassociation.com

The Day Spa Association
310 17th Street
Union City, NJ 07087, USA
201-865-2065
www.dayspaassociation.com

Destination Spa Group
888-772-4363
www.destinationspas.com

Green Spa Network
P.O. Box 2437
Sebastopol, CA 95473, USA
800-275-3045
www.greenspanetwork.org

International Health, Racquet & Sportsclub Association
Seaport Center
70 Fargo Street
Boston, MA 02210, USA
800-228-4772
www.ihrsa.org

International Medical Spa Association
520 23rd St.
Union City, NJ 07087, USA
201-865-2065
www.medicalspaassociation.org

The International Spa Association (ISPA)
2365 Harrodsburg Rd., Ste. A325
Lexington, KY 40504, USA
859-226-4326
www.experienceispa.com

Leading Spas of Canada
P.O. Box 157
Sooke, BC V9Z 0P7, Canada
800-704-6393
www.leadingspasofcanada.com/web

Medical Spa Society
60 East 56th Street
New York, NY 10022, USA
866-MEDISPA
www.medicalspasociety.com

National Independent Health Club Association
400 10th St. NW, Suite #229
New Brighton, MN 55112, USA
866-484-9173
www.nihca.org

General Health and Wellness

Aerobics and Fitness Association of American
15250 Ventura Blvd., Suite 200
Sherman Oaks, CA 91403, USA
877-968-7263
www.afaa.org

Allied Health Association
9233 Park Meadows Drive
Lone Tree, CO 80124, USA
800-444-7546
www.alliedhealth.net

American Association of Naturopathic Physicians
2366 Eastlake Ave E, #322
Seattle, WA 98102, USA
206-323-7610
www.naturopathic.org

American Alliance for Health, Physical Education,
Recreation & Dance
1900 Association Dr.
Reston, VA 20191-1598, USA
800-213-7193
www.aahperd.org

American College of Sports Medicine
401 West Michigan Street
Indianapolis, IN 46202-3233, USA
317-637-9200
www.acsm.org

American Council on Exercise
4851 Paramount Drive
San Diego, CA 92123, USA
888-823-3636
www.acefitness.org

American Health Source
2040 Raybrook SE, Ste. 103
Grand Rapids, MI 49546, USA
888-375-7245
www.americanhealthsource.com

American Holistic Medical Association
23366 Commerce Park, Ste 101B
Beachwood, OH 44122, USA
216-292-6644
www.holisticmedicine.org

American Medical Association
515 N. State Street
Chicago, IL 60654, USA
800-621-8335
www.ama-assn.org

American Naturopathic Medical Association
P.O. Box 96273
Las Vegas, NV 89193, USA
702-897-7053
www.anma.com

Ancient Healing Arts Society
P.O. Box 1785
Bensalem, PA 19020, USA
1-866-843-2422
www.ancienthealingarts.org

Ayurvedic Institute
P.O. Box 23445
Albuquerque, NM 87192, USA
505-291-9698
www.ayurveda.com

Herb Research Foundation
4140 15th St.
Boulder, CO 80304, USA
303-449-2265
www.herbs.org

IDEA Health & Fitness Association
10455 Pacific Center Court
San Diego, CA 92121, USA
800-999-4332, x7
www.ideafit.com

International Association of Yoga Therapists
115 S. McCormick St., Ste. 3
Prescott, AZ 86303, USA
928-541-0004
www.iayt.org

National Center for Complementary and Alternative Medicine (NIH)
9000 Rockville Pike, Bldg. 31
Bethesda, MD 20892, USA
888-644-6226
www.nccam.nih.gov

National Health Practitioners of Canada Association
600-10339 124 St.
Edmonton, AB T5N 3W1, Canada
888-711-7701
www.nhpcanada.org

National Strength and Conditioning Association
1885 Bob Johnson Drive
Colorado Springs, CO 80906, USA
800-815-6826
www.nsca-lift.org

National Wellness Institute, Inc.
1300 College Court
PO Box 827
Stevens Point, WI 54481, USA
715-342-2969
www.nationalwellness.org

President's Council of Physical Fitness and Sports
Department W
200 Independence Ave., SW, Room 738-H
Washington, DC 20201-0004, USA
202-690-9000
www.fitness.gov

The Wellness Council of America
9802 Nicholas St., Suite 315
Omaha, NE 68114, USA
402-827-3590
www.welcoa.org

Cosmetology and Esthetics

Aestheticians International Association (AIA)
4402 Broadway Blvd. Ste. 14
Garland, Texas 75043, USA
469-429-9300
www.aiaprofessional.com

Allied Beauty Association (ABA)
145 Traders Blvd. Stes. 26 & 27
Mississauga, ON L4Z 3L3, Canada
905-568-0158
www.abacanada.com

American Academy of Dermatology
P.O. Box 4014
Schaumberg, IL 60168, USA
847-330-0230
www.aad.org

American Academy of Medical Aesthetics
303 National Road
Exton, PA 19341, USA
610-363-0225
www.aaoma.org

American Association of Cosmetology Schools (AACS)
15825 N. 71st St., Ste. 100
Scottsdale, AZ 85254, USA
800-831-1086 or 480-281-0431
www.beautyschools.org

American Association for Esthetics Education (AAEE)
401 N. Michigan Ave.
Chicago, IL 60611, USA
800-648-2505 or 312-245-1570
www.americasbeautyshow.com

American Board of Certified Hair Colorists (ABCH)
28132 Western Ave.
San Pedro, CA 90732, USA
310-547-0814
www.haircolorist.com

American Electrology Association
106 Oak Ridge Road
Trumbull, CT 06611, USA
www.electrology.com

American Health & Beauty Aids Institute (AHBAI)
P.O. Box 19510
Chicago, IL 60619-0510, USA
708-633-6328
www.ahbai.org

American Society for Aesthetics
c/o Armstrong Atlantic State University
11935 Abercorn Street
Savannah, GA 31419, USA
912-961-1395
www.aesthetics-online.org

Associated Skin Care Professionals
25188 Genesee Trail Road, Suite 200
Golden, CO 80401, USA
800-789-0411
www.ascpskincare.com

Comite International D'esthetique et de Cosmetologie (CIDESCO)
Witikonerstrasse 4a
8037 Zurich, Switzerland
+41 44 448 22 00
www.cidesco.com

Cosmetology Advancement Foundation (CAF)
E. 51st Street
New York, NY 10022, USA
212-750-2412
www.cosmetology.org

Nails, Skin and Hair of America
118 Park Ave. SW, Suite 600
Aiken, SC 29802, USA
803-270-2106
www.nailsskinhair.org

National Accrediting Commission of Cosmetology Arts & Sciences
4401 Ford Ave., Ste. 1300
Alexandria, VA 22302, USA
703-600-7600
www.naccas.org

National Beauty Culturists' League (NBCL)
25 Logan Cir. NW
Washington, DC 20005, USA
202-332-2695
www.nbcl.org

National Coalition of Estheticians, Manufacturers/ Distributors & Associations
484 Spring Ave.
Ridgewood, NJ 07450, USA
201-670-4100
www.ncea.tv

National Cosmetology Association (NCA)
401 N. Michigan Ave., 22nd Flr.
Chicago, IL 60611, USA
866-871-0656
www.ncacares.org

National-Interstate Council of State Boards of Cosmetology, Inc.
7622 Briarwood Circle
Little Rock, AR 72205, USA
501-227-8262
www.nictesting.org

National Psoriasis Foundation
6600 S.W. 92nd Ave., Ste. 300
Portland, OR 97223, USA
800-723-9166 or 503-244-7404
www.psoriasis.org

National Rosacea Society
800 S. Northwest Hwy., Ste. 200
Barrington, IL 60010, USA
888-662-5874
www.rosacea.org

Personal Care Products Council
1101 17th St. NW, Ste. 300
Washington, DC 20036, USA
202-331-1770
www.personalcarecouncil.org

Professional Beauty Association (PBA)
15825 N. 71st St., Ste. 100
Scottsdale, AZ 85254, USA
800-468-2274 or 480-281-0424
www.probeauty.org

Professional Beauty Federation (PBF)
15825 N. 71st St., Ste. 100
Scottsdale, AZ 85254, USA
800-468-2274 or 480-281-0424
www.probeautyfederation.org

Society of Dermatology and Skincare Specialists (SDSS)
484 Spring Ave.
Ridgewood, NJ 07450, USA
201-670-4100
www.sdss.tv

Society of Permanent Cosmetic Professionals
69 North Broadway
Des Plaines, IL 60016, USA
847-635-1330
www.spcp.org

Massage and Bodywork

American CranioSacral Therapy Association
The Upledger Institute
11211 Prosperity Farms Road, Suite D-325
Palm Beach Gardens, FL 33410, USA
561-622-4334
www.acsta.com

American Massage Therapy Association
500 Davis Street, Suite 900
Evanston, IL 60201-4695, USA
877-905-2700
www.amtamassage.org

American Massage Council
1851 East First Street, 1160
Santa Ana, CA 92705, USA
800-500-3930
www.massagecouncil.com

American Medical Massage Association
1845 Lakeshore Drive, #7
Muskegon, MI 49441, USA
1-888-375-7245
www.americanmedicalmassage.com

American Polarity Therapy Association
122 North Elm Street, #512
Greensboro, NC 27401, USA
336-574-1121
www.polaritytherapy.org

Associated Bodywork & Massage Professionals
25188 Genesee Trail Road
Golden, CO 80401, USA
800-458-2267 or 303-674-8478
www.abmp.com

Commission on Massage Training Accreditation (COMTA)
5335 Wisconsin Avenue, NW, Suite 440
Washington, DC 20015, USA
202-895-1518
www.comta.org

Craniosacral Therapy Association of North America
150 Cross Creek Court
Chapel Hill, NC 27517, USA
734-904-0546
www.carniosacraltherapy.org

Federation of State Massage Therapy Boards
7111 W 151st Street, #356
Overland Park, KS 66223, USA
913-681-0380
www.fsmtb.org

Guild for Structural Integration
3107 28th Street
Boulder, CO 80301, USA
303-447-0122
www.rolfguild.org

International Institute of Reflexology
P.O. Box 12642
5650 First Ave. N.
St. Petersburg, FL 33733, USA
727-343-4811
www.reflexology-usa.net

International Massage Association, Inc.
P.O. Box 421
Warrenton, VA 20188, USA
540-351-0800
www.imagroup.com

International Thai Therapies Association
P.O. Box 1048
Palm Springs, CA 92263, USA
760-641-0756
www.thaimassage.com

National Certification Board for Therapeutic Massage and Bodywork
8201 Greensboro Drive, #300
McLean, VA 22102, USA
800-296-0664
www.ncbtmb.com

National Association for Holistic Aromatherapy
3327 W. Indian Trail Rd.
PMB 144
Spokane, WA 99208, USA
509-325-3479
www.naha.org

Reflexology Association of America
P.O. Box 714
Chepachet, RI 02814, USA
980-234-0159
www.reflexology-usa.org

United States Medical Massage Association
P.O. Box 2394
Surf City, NC 28445, USA
888-322-5520
www.usmedicalmassage.org

Nail Professionals

Council for Nail Disorders
2323 North State Street
Bunnel, FL 32110, USA
386-437-4405
www.nailcouncil.org

Excellence Nail Association of Canada
9093 Mari Victorin
Contecoeur, QC JOL 1CO, Canada
514-893-2799
www.excellencenail.com

International Nail Technicians Association
2035 Paysphere Circle
Chicago, IL 60674, USA
312-321-5161
www.internationalnailtechassociation.com

International Pedicure Association
1755 Maryland Ave.
Niagara Falls, NY 14305, USA
866-326-7573
www.pedicureassociation.com

Spa Equipment and Supplies Companies

Belvedere Company
800-435-5491
www.belvedereco.com

CCI Beauty
800-708-0789
www.ccibeauty.com

Equipment for Salons
800-362-6245
www.equipmentforsalons.com

International Beauty and Barber Equipment
800-824-7007
www.ibbe.net

New Life Systems
800-852-3082
www.newlifesystems.com

Skin for Life
866-312-7546
www.skinforlife.com

Spa Development International
888-474-4SDI (4734)
www.spadev.com

Spa Elegance
877-200-SPAS (7727)
www.spaelegance.com

SpaEquip
877-778-1685
www.spaequip.com

Takara Belmont
732-469-5000
www.takarabelmont.com

Touch America
800-678-6824
www.touchamerica.com

Universal Companies, Inc.
800-558-5571
www.universalcompanies.com

REFERENCE

Johnson, Samuel (n.d.). BrainyQuote.com. Retrieved June 16, 2010, from www.brainyquote.com/quotes/quotes/s/q101039.html.

Page references followed by *f* and *t* indicate figures and tables respectively.